D0996566

THE ZEN OF NAKA

To Mum and Dad – thanks for everything

THE ZEN OF
NAKA

The Journey of a Japanese Genius

MARTIN GREIG

Foreword by
GORDON STRACHAN

MAINSTREAM
PUBLISHING

EDINBURGH AND LONDON

First published in Great Britain in 2008 by
MAINSTREAM PUBLISHING COMPANY
(EDINBURGH) LTD
7 Albany Street
Edinburgh EH1 3UG

ISBN 9781845963576

A catalogue record for this book is available
from the British Library

Typeset in Caslon and Helvetica

Printed in Great Britain by
Clays Ltd, St Ives plc

Acknowledgements

I AM GRATEFUL FOR THE COOPERATION AND SUPPORT OF Celtic Football Club, in particular Peter Lawwell, the chief executive, and commercial director David Thomson. Thanks also to manager Gordon Strachan, who was fascinating on the subject of Nakamura. Many players and coaches, past and present, also agreed to be interviewed and offered absorbing insights.

In Scotland, many thanks to Eleanor Cowie for encouraging me to write a book and to all my colleagues at *The Herald*, in particular Hugh 'The Mamba' MacDonald, the chief sports writer, and deputy sports editor James Porteous for offering essential feedback. Graham Spiers of *The Times* offered great help in getting the project off the ground, as did my agent Mark 'Stan' Stanton. Thanks to all the staff at Mainstream Publishing. David Friel at *Celtic View* was a tremendous source of information, and Steven Tweed also helped me greatly.

In Italy, thanks to everyone in Reggio Calabria for welcoming us so warmly, including Pasquale Foti, Massimo Bandiera and Takashi Yuge. Special thanks to Mark Palmer of the *Sunday Times*, who interpreted from English to Italian during our trip.

In Japan, special thanks to Hiyushi Kanbayashi, who facilitated, interpreted and even organised us a game of football (a rousing Scottish victory). Thanks to Sebastian Moffett, whose exceptional book on the J. League, *Japanese Rules: Why the Japanese Needed Football and How They Got It*, provided an invaluable resource. Thanks also to Jason Cranwell, my unofficial agent and official photographer, and The Seiyo Ginza Hotel, Ginza, Tokyo (www. seiyo-ginza.com), whose hospitality and kindness went above and beyond the call of duty.

Finally, thanks to Nakamura's dedicated band of journalists – Shin Toyofuku, Daisuke Nakajima, Makoto Sassaki, James Morrison – and Makoto Kaneko, Nakamura's interpreter and trusty sidekick.

Martin Greig
August 2008

Contents

'Our greatest glory is not in never falling,
but in rising every time we fall.'

Confucius

Foreword

FOR PURE ABILITY, SHUNSUKE NAKAMURA IS THE BEST footballer I have worked with, in both my playing and management careers. I played alongside guys such as Bryan Robson and Kenny Dalglish, who were better all-round footballers, and Gary McAllister was another tremendous player, but in terms of pure ability Nakamura comes out on top. I was captain of Leeds United when Eric Cantona was there. Eric was a very dedicated professional in his technical approach to the game, and Nakamura is in exactly the same mould. Eric was a giant of a man and brought a physicality to the game that Nakamura doesn't, but in terms of pure ability Nakamura can do anything that the big Frenchman could.

When I talk about 'pure' ability, I mean ball control, vision, touch and change of direction. What he has on top of that is a great work ethic. Nakamura and Scott Brown cover more ground than anybody else in our team. Then there is the bravery aspect to his game. He takes so many kicks and just gets up and gets on with it. When you put all of that together, you have the complete package and someone who is a fantastic ambassador for his country and his family.

Nakamura is not at the same level as guys such as Kaká and Ronaldinho, because they have physical attributes that he hasn't. However, I think he has enough quality to play for any of the top teams in the world, including Barcelona or Real Madrid. If he went to the Premiership, he might find it a bit crash, bang, wallop at times, so I think Spain would be the best environment for his talent to shine.

The first time I saw him was at the Confederations Cup in 2005. I got DVDs of the tournament, and I asked Tommy Burns, the Celtic first-team coach, and Garry Pendrey, the assistant manager, to watch them. They both came back and said, 'Let's try and get this lad.' His vision and touch – it was all there. I hadn't realised before that point how good he was.

He came in at a difficult time – after we had lost to Artmedia Bratislava in the 2005 Champions League qualifiers and had drawn with Motherwell in the first league game of the season – but turned in a fantastic debut against Dundee United and continued to go from strength to strength.

Nakamura is third on the list of people he wants to please. Number one are the coaches, number two are his teammates and then it is himself. There are other players whose mentality is 'Number one is me, number two is me and number three is me', but Nakamura always puts others first. He never says anything against his teammates or opponents and is an absolute role model in how the game should be played. He goes to the gym after games and does everything he can to make himself the best player he can be. His balance and technique come from constant practise and stretching. If I was a youth coach, I would go to Japan and see how they are training their kids, because it is obviously working.

On a personal level, no one could ever say a bad word about Naka – it's impossible. He's different from his countryman Koki Mizuno, who is more open with people. There is a language barrier, but Nakamura understands what I'm saying. We get on well together.

I would like to get closer to him, but that is the way he likes it. If you intruded on his private time, he would probably feel a bit uncomfortable.

He's such a great footballer to watch. I love standing on the sidelines watching him play, but all the players at Celtic feel the same. I've seen his teammates stop and clap at some of the stuff he does in training. He's given me as much pleasure as anyone I've ever signed.

Gordon Strachan
August 2008

Introduction

I WROTE AN ARTICLE ON SHUNSUKE NAKAMURA FOR *The Herald* the day after he had scored his famous goal against Manchester United in November 2006, which took Celtic into the last 16 of the Champions League for the first time in their history. The piece focused on Nakamura's lengthy post-match fitness routine. While his teammates were celebrating their achievement, the man of the moment had slipped away to the gym to run through his extensive warm-down session – running, stretching and a cold bath followed by a hot one. Not even the drama of a victorious Champions League evening could detract him from his purpose. The article produced an unusually large response from readers, more women than men, all expressing their admiration of the focus and dedication that Nakamura brought to his profession.

In the course of researching this book, it soon became clear that context, both historical and social, were central to the story of Japanese sporting success. The values of their top sportsmen and women are an extension of the values of Japanese society as a whole. Humility, respect and, most of all, unparalleled dedication have been the cornerstones of the country's rapid economic development since the Second World War and, in a football context, their incredible progress since the J. League started in 1993. Nakamura's huge popularity is as much because of his embodiment of these values as it is his achievements on the pitch.

It is a matter for debate how great a player he is in a global context. However, few professional footballers have worked harder to maximise their natural talent. Nothing has come easily for Nakamura. The richness of his story lies in the constant battle to prove his doubters wrong. At every stage of his career, he has faced some form of rejection. Even now, sceptics still remain, but they are finally outnumbered by the converts. His is a universal tale of triumph over adversity.

Not that his natural talent should be underplayed. On his day, Nakamura is a glorious footballer, a player with a velvet first touch and the vision to see things most others do not. And neither should his achievements be underplayed. He is a mainstay of the Japan national team, has played at the World Cup finals, become a regular in the Champions League and has established himself as one of the best players in Scotland. Like Henrik Larsson before him, he has found his spiritual home at Celtic Park. Three years with Serie A strugglers Reggina provided enough evidence that *catenaccio* still lurked in the nation's football psyche, but Celtic, and the attack-minded philosophy of manager Gordon Strachan, offered a broader canvas for his artistic skills. He has not disappointed.

His dead-ball abilities, in particular free-kicks against Manchester United in November 2006 and Kilmarnock in March 2007, have established him as a cult hero whose name is sung from Tollcross to Tokyo. He has shaped Celtic's history in a way only a few players achieve, but the club has also shaped him. Neither will ever be the same again.

ONE

The Shot Heard
Around the World

'It was the best goal of my life. Edwin van der Sar is one of
the best goalkeepers in the world, and now I have beaten him
twice. The free-kick at Old Trafford was good, but this was
better. There are a lot of young players outside Japan now, and
hopefully this has proved that they can be at this level.'

Shunsuke Nakamura

GREAT OCCASIONS PLUS GREAT PLAYERS EQUALS GREAT
moments. A simple equation, but what makes a 'great' moment
truly resonate? It is one you remember vividly, one that becomes
uniquely personal. You remember where you were, who you were
with, how you reacted, what you did afterwards. It becomes seared
in your memory for ever, part of your frame of reference, a small
bookmark in the narrative of your life. What are your great football
moments?

A by-product of a west-of-Scotland upbringing is a ritual immersion in the mythology of Hampden Park. It seems every Glaswegian under the age of 40 has a father, grandfather or uncle who witnessed the great Real Madrid side, inspired by Ferenc Puskás and Alfredo di Stéfano, destroy Eintracht Frankfurt 7–3 in the 1960 European Cup final. It still ranks as one of the greatest moments in Hampden's history and one of world football's most famous games.

For Scots of a younger generation, Zinedine Zidane is the modern memory-maker. In the 2002 Champions League final against Bayer Leverkusen at Hampden, the Real Madrid player produced a moment to cherish with one majestic sweep of his left boot, sending a crashing volley into the roof of the net – a moment to bore sons, daughters and grandkids with for the next 50 years. (Why should they get off lightly?) A recent vote decreed it the best Champions League goal ever. And it happened on the south side of Glasgow. This century.

There are other moments in Scottish football folklore, from James McFadden's wonder goal against France in September 2007 to Joe Jordan's diving header against Czechoslovakia in 1973, which took Scotland to the World Cup finals the following year, and Stevie Chalmers steering the ball into the net to win Celtic the European Cup in 1967.

In a wider context, there was Ryan Giggs's amazing solo strike against Arsenal in the semi-final of the FA Cup in 1999, Marco van Basten's incredible volley against the USSR in the 1988 European Championships and Diego Maradona slaloming through England defenders like a downhill skier on a gold medal run in the 1986 World Cup quarter-final . . . all moments of universal sporting significance with a personal resonance for many.

CELTIC V. MANCHESTER UNITED, CHAMPIONS LEAGUE MATCH DAY FIVE

LOCATION: CELTIC PARK, GLASGOW, SCOTLAND

DATE: 21/11/06

TIME: 9.22 P.M.

Eighty-one minutes of a featureless tie have passed when Nakamura picks the ball up on the right flank and threads a neat pass to Jiří Jarošík, thirty yards from goal. The Czech midfielder turns his marker, Nemanja Vidić, who lunges in and makes a challenge from behind. The contact on Jarošík is minimal, but he goes to ground, and the referee awards a free-kick. Vidić is incensed. With his hands clasped to his cheeks in horror, his pleas fall on deaf ears. The clumsiness of his challenge had left the referee with little option. It is almost as if Vidić knew what was coming next, as if he sensed that his transgression would have a severe penance. He would have had an inkling. Nakamura had served notice of his threat at Old Trafford three months previously with an exquisite curling free-kick over the United wall and into the net.

Jarošík retrieves the ball and throws it to Nakamura. He places it carefully, takes six paces back, two to the right. He flicks his fringe away from his eyes and glances up at the big screen behind the goal. Nine minutes to go. The Celtic fans hold their breath. The midfielder steps up and strikes the ball. His body is at a 45 degree angle, twisted like a corkscrew to achieve the necessary curl. The ball starts its flight ten feet over the bar. The trajectory is breathtaking, the power of the shot deceptive. It clears the wall and then starts to dip viciously. Edwin van der Sar throws himself full length, frantically clawing at the air, straining every sinew of his six feet six inches frame. He is close to it and at the same time nowhere near it. It is unsaveable. Postage stamp. First class. Celtic Park erupts in the way only Celtic Park can on European nights.

LOCATION: TORONTO, CANADA

DATE: 21/11/06

TIME: 4.22 P.M.

James McAvoy's determined search for a football-friendly pub had led him to a small establishment in downtown Toronto. The Glaswegian movie star was in town to promote his latest film, *The Last King of Scotland*, which was showing at the city's film festival, but there were more important matters on his mind. The glitz and the glamour, the champagne and the red carpets would have to wait. Tonight, his team were playing Manchester United in the Champions League, and he simply couldn't miss it, so he made his excuses and slipped away.

He hurriedly entered the pub just in time for kick-off and looked around. 'Great, they've got a big screen,' he thought. He took another look around and his heart sank. Red strips as far as the eye could see. 'Shit, they're showing the Arsenal game.' He looked around a third time and spotted a tiny screen mounted in the corner. 'Bingo.' He pulled up a chair and craned his neck to watch the tiny ten-inch television showing the Celtic game and took a long sip from his pint. Sorted.

'But then I realised there was no commentary,' he says, laughing. 'In the States and Canada, the ESPN commentator is a guy called Tommy Smyth, who is utterly depressing to listen to, but he is still better than listening to the game in silence. Then, a big Canadian guy came and sat down beside me and just wanted to talk. He kept calling Celtic 'Keltic', which made me even more annoyed.

'But then Nakamura scored, and I just went mental. I was jumping about and managed to spill my pint down the front of my English mate, who was sitting watching the game with me. The place was full of ex-pat Arsenal fans, and they were wondering what all the noise was about. What a scene it was. There was me, in this wee bar in Toronto, surrounded by Arsenal fans, forced to watch Celtic on a tiny screen in the corner. *The Last King of Scotland* is a story set in Uganda about the African dictator Idi Amin who empowers a young Scottish doctor – and I thought that here was Nakamura doing it for this Scotsman in Canada.'

And so, in a pokey bar in downtown Toronto, the 'Last King of Scotland' stood on his chair and raised his pint to toast the new football king of Scotland. Cheers.

LOCATION: SICILY, ITALY

DATE: 21/11/06

TIME: 10.22 P.M.

Jim Kerr laughs at the memory, the emotion and drama of the night rushing back to him in an instant as his mind is transported back to that unforgettable moment in time. How could he possibly forget *that* night? The Simple Minds lead singer was on the island of Sicily, where he owns a hotel and bases himself for part of the year. The indoctrination of the locals in the 'Celtic Way' had been long since completed. Over the years, he had taken some of them to Celtic Park, even brought a few along to Seville with him for that unforgettable pilgrimage to the UEFA Cup final in 2003. One of them had installed a plasma screen in his house for such nights. So there they sat, half a dozen football-mad Sicilians and one famous Glaswegian with an unsinkable passion for his team – beers in hand, volume at an obscene level and Shunsuke Nakamura standing over a free-kick against one of the best teams in the world.

'The thing about that night was that you really couldn't see where a Celtic goal was going to come from,' recalls Kerr. 'Manchester United were one of the best teams in the world, and Celtic never looked like scoring. So, against that backdrop, the whole thing became even more exaggerated. It was a killer free-kick. The place just erupted. I said to myself when the ball hit the net, "There is a God!" I have spent a lot of time in Japan, and I knew that it would be a goal that would be shown on all the big screens on the streets in Tokyo. I knew how much it would mean to them. Then you hear about how much work he puts into it, and you appreciate that it is no fluke. You can see that it has been honed.

'Just imagine what it is like – the seconds in your head before you hit it, the expectation on you. It must take incredible concentration, particularly amongst bedlam like that. We have seen him do it against teams such as Kilmarnock and Motherwell, but to do it in that situation, against a team of that quality, was incredible. It was always going to take something otherworldly to beat Manchester United that night.'

LOCATION: LONDON, ENGLAND

DATE: 21/11/06

TIME: 9.22 P.M.

'De Dera De Dera De De Dera Dera De'

'Chelsea Dagger', The Fratellis

Every great movie has a killer soundtrack. The score for *Nakamura: The Return* was written by The Fratellis. As his second free-kick against Manchester United in three months hit the net, and the midfielder wheeled away in ecstasy, a chorus of 'Chelsea Dagger' blasted over the Tannoy at Celtic Park. In a hotel room somewhere in London, the band members were too busy bouncing around in celebration to realise that their greatest hit had formed the backdrop to the best Celtic goal of the modern era.

'Chelsea Dagger' has since become a permanent fixture at Celtic Park. Every time the net bulges, Parkhead pogos to the strains of The Fratellis, but it still had novelty value when used in the Manchester United game. 'It was only the second time they had played "Chelsea Dagger" at Celtic Park,' recalls Barry 'Fratelli' Wallace, the band's bassist, with no little pride. 'The first time it happened was the week before the Manchester United game, and everybody had told me about it. But the thing was, I didn't actually hear it at the

Manchester United game, because I was too busy jumping around the hotel room.

'I was trapped in London of all places. A lot of our crew were Man United fans, which made it interesting. We were watching the game in our hotel room. There was me and John [the band's lead singer] and a couple of crew members who were United fans. It was good *craic* . . . then the goal went in, and we went mad.

'John and I went on *Soccer AM*, and they played the goal back. That was the first time I got to hear our song being played in the background. That was just an added bonus, because it was such an amazing night anyway. It was the first time we had reached the last 16, and no Celtic fan worth their salt will ever forget that goal. Nakamura nailed his place in Celtic history that night.'

Wallace's Celtic connections run deep. He has supported them all his life, fondly recalls the Double-winning centenary year of 1988, watched the UEFA Cup final in a chip shop in Seville while suffering from heatstroke and cites Danny McGrain as his favourite player of all time: 'He looked cool as fuck with that big beard.' The band's unofficial Celtic anthem has also allowed him greater access to the club where he has held a season ticket since the age of 16.

'I did an interview with David Friel at *Celtic View* and got to know a few people around the club,' says Wallace, who used to work as a charge hand in McChuills, the well-known Irish bar in Glasgow's city centre. 'Then they phoned me up and asked me to come and draw the Paradise Windfall at half-time during the Spartak Moscow game. It was a surreal experience walking out at half-time to do the draw with everybody singing our song. Then Billy Connolly gave me a wee wave.'

Nakamura and Japan are also close to Wallace's heart. He fell in love with the country while touring with the band and has spent a lot of time there recently. 'I love Nakamura, and Japan is my favourite country at the moment. I met my future wife in Japan. She was over there working. Whenever I have had any time off recently, I have gone to Japan. I'm an honorary member of the Tokyo Celtic Supporters Club. Celtic are massive in Japan now. When the Japanese go for something, they go for it big style.'

LOCATION: NASHVILLE, TENNESSEE, USA

DATE: 21/11/06

TIME: 3.22 P.M.

Dario Franchitti is the reigning Indianapolis 500 and IndyCar Series champion. He is a genuine racing-car superstar. He collects Ferraris. He is good-looking. He is a millionaire. He is married to Hollywood actress Ashley Judd. He lives in a beautiful house in Nashville, Tennessee. But there is something missing. Or rather there is something he misses: Celtic Park; the match-day atmosphere; 60,000 fans singing 'You'll Never Walk Alone'. But Franchitti is resourceful. The ever-present laptop has Channel 67 (Celtic's online subscription service, which provides live match coverage) top of his favourites list, and satellite TV is piped into his bus at the racetrack. Naturally, he also has a room in his home in Nashville set aside for his viewing pleasure.

On 21 November, he was relaxing at home. No dodgy Internet connection, no screeching racing car engines to disrupt his viewing pleasure. Domestic bliss.

'I get the big European games on Setanta, and that one was on live, which was great.' A night in front of the TV, Hoops strip on, feet up, Celtic v. Manchester United in the Champions League and Nakamura lining up a free-kick with a glint in his eye . . .

'Whenever I think about Nakamura, it's those big, curling free-kicks,' he says. 'Against Manchester United, I remember the moment when the ball hit the net and thinking, "Oh my God!" It was one of those momentous occasions that, as a fan, takes a few seconds to sink in. And yet whenever he gets into that position, you think, "He can do this."

'I have a real soft spot for Henrik Larsson, and some of his goals over the years were incredible. But Nakamura's goal was just so special, because of what it meant. It was 0–0, against a team such as Manchester United, and then he steps up. Physically, he is not the biggest player on the pitch, but he's got such a great touch, and he is just magic with set-pieces.'

Franchitti, originally from Bathgate, cemented his reputation as one of the best racing-car drivers on the planet when he won the 91st Indianapolis 500 in 2007. In doing so, he became only the second Scottish-born driver to win it, the first being Jim Clark in 1965.

He drew inspiration from watching clips of the Lisbon Lions defeat Inter Milan in the 1967 European Cup final. 'I watched it before the Indy 500. Those guys were some players. We talk about Larsson being one of the legends of the modern era, but those guys were all legends. When you watch something like that, a team of underdogs going abroad and winning against the best in Europe, it can't help but inspire you.'

A couple of days after his famous victory in the Indy 500, Franchitti found himself in New York on a tour of interviews. He was asked to name a venue to fulfil his media commitments. After barely a moment's thought, he led a scrum of print journalists and film crews to The Parlour Bar, home of the New York Celtic Supporters Club. They filmed him as he recreated the famous podium celebration of all Indy500 winners by glugging from a jug of milk on the front steps of the bar. 'I had watched a few Old Firm games in there, and it seemed like a good place to go.'

Work commitments have prevented him from attending many Celtic matches in the Gordon Strachan era. However, Franchitti did form a close relationship with his predecessor, Martin O'Neill. 'After games, we used to go and talk with Martin for two or three hours. It would be Martin, Robbo [John Robertson, O'Neill's assistant], Geraldine [O'Neill's wife], the girls [O'Neill's daughters], my friend Tony and Ashley. I was always really interested to hear his thoughts on the game. One thing I noticed is that he would never criticise any of his players in conversation. We would talk about all sorts of things. He is just a great guy. He is as determined a character as anyone I've ever met. I haven't had the chance to go back to games much since Gordon Strachan has been the manager, but he always reminds me of my good friend and fellow racing driver Allan McNish. Every time I see Gordon shouting on the touchline, I think of Allan. They look almost identical.'

Franchitti has even indoctrinated his American actress wife in the Celtic way. 'Ashley came to three or four of the European games. I remember the first time I took her. We walked from the lounge up the steps and came out to all the Celtic fans standing with their scarves up, singing "You'll Never Walk Alone". She just stopped dead and said, "This is amazing." I defy anyone to experience that and not be moved.'

LOCATION: LAS VEGAS, NEVADA, USA

DATE: 21/11/06

TIME: 1.22 P.M.

Outside, the dry desert heat was rising, the afternoon sun shimmering over the neon capital of the world. Las Vegas was shaking off the excesses of another night of high-rolling. Inside The Crown and Anchor pub on Tropicana Avenue, however, the stakes had never been higher. This was Champions League day at the Las Vegas Celtic Supporters Club. The pub was awash with holidaymakers, mostly clad in green-and-white hoops, but there was a sprinkling of Manchester United tops as well. Tom Strain, the club's president, stood at the front of the throng. Five years before, he had saved the ailing CSC, breathing fresh life into it by offering holidaying Hoops the chance to watch their team. But he had done it for selfish reasons, too. He had supported Celtic since he was a young boy growing up in the Gorbals. He had been raised with the Lisbon Lions and the 'Quality Street Kids'. He was, and is, a Celtic man through and through, and he was damned if a 5,000-mile gulf was going to prevent him from following his team.

This was the sort of moment he had dreamed of when he revived the club – standing there with a drink in his hand and hope in his heart, 30 yards between Celtic and the last 16 of the Champions League. 'I thought, "This is it." I had a real belief that he could do it,' says Strain. 'I had seen free-kicks from that range go in before. When we were awarded the free-kick, my thoughts went straight back to the Old Trafford game when he scored. I really believed Nakamura could do it. When he hit it into the top corner, the roar that went up in the pub was amazing. The Arsenal game was on at the other end of the pub, and all the guys who were watching that came rushing over to see the replay. Then came the penalty. I can't remember going from such a high to such a low in my life, even against Porto [in the UEFA Cup final of 2003, which Celtic lost in extra time]. Artur Boruc's save was like scoring another goal. Then there were seven minutes to go, and it was such a nail-biting time.

'At the end, not a lot of people knew we had qualified. There were mini-debates everywhere. People were reaching for pens and napkins. That was another buzz, but I knew we were through, because we had beaten Manchester United in the head-to-head. When everyone had taken it all in, it was amazing – the realisation that we had achieved something great in our history. The whole night was just full of highs.

'There were about seven or eight Manchester United fans in that night. Even after their team was beaten, there were plenty of handshakes and congratulations. There's never any tension. If you are 5,000 miles away and are coming to watch your team, you're more likely to be a genuine fan.'

Then came the celebrations. So was it straight to The Bellagio or Caesars Palace for a night of high-rolling? Not likely. 'After the game, we all went to a pub called Nine Fine Irishmen in the New York, New York hotel,' says Strain, who now runs a painting contractors business in Las Vegas after leaving Scotland for the States 25 years ago. 'They play live music, and by night-time everyone was singing along. They played a lot of U2, and there was a bit of "Fields of Athenry" in there, but nothing political, just good music. Of course, we had a few choruses of "It's a Grand Old Team". That was a great night, one of the best get-togethers. We wanted to do what we knew Hoops fans would be doing in Glasgow that night. Even though you are 5,000 miles away, you still want the same festivities and the same banter.

'A lot of the guys who came down for the game had arranged to meet their wives and girlfriends afterwards, but suddenly they all wanted to stay out and celebrate. The brave ones said, "She knows if Celtic wins, I won't be home." Others were on the phone straight away leaving messages at the hotel to say that they wouldn't be home, knowing that they would get a serious ear-bashing later.'

LOCATION: ONTARIO, CANADA

DATE: 21/11/06

TIME: 17.22 P.M.

The tremors of a European night travel far and wide, reaching across continents and oceans, stirring the hearts of many. The Ontario Celtic Supporters Club now boasts 180 members and is a hive of activity on European nights. The Manchester United game will live long in the memory. Jacky Meehan, president of the North American Federation of Celtic Supporters Clubs, recalls, 'We were watching the game in the Celtic club at St Catherine's, which is five minutes from Niagara Falls. The university is right next to it, and we get a lot of students over from Glasgow University on exchange. I remember that night well, because we had four or five Japanese students in the club watching the game due to the Naka factor. When Nakamura scored, all the boys crowded round them, sank to their knees and started chanting, 'We're not worthy, we're not worthy.' There's always a great atmosphere in the club, but that night was special. The game finished at around 5 p.m., and the place was absolutely bouncing.'

The Ontario CSC is part of the NAFCSC, which testifies to the commitment of supporters in following their team regardless of geography. The NAFCSC was established 15 years ago and now has 72 CSCs under its auspices, some of which have been going for 40 years. Meehan was brought up in Castlemilk and worked in the Clyde shipyards before deciding to start a new life in Canada in 1974. Deprived of his regular Celtic fix, he suffered withdrawal symptoms. In those early days, he and a few friends used to crowd round a wireless and listen to the results coming in on short-wave radio. Thanks to the media age, every game is now shown live. With an estimated support base of over 1 million, it is little surprise that interest in Celtic has mushroomed in North America.

LOCATION: RIO, BRAZIL

DATE: 21/11/06

TIME: 19.22 P.M.

. . . .

'Viva A Revoluçaõ Verde' is the motto of the Fergus McCann Rio Celtic Supporters Club. It could just as easily be 'Where there's a will there's a way'. In a city of over 6 million inhabitants, the members of the Rio CSC have pulled together to ensure they never miss a kick of the ball when Celtic are playing. The 'Bhoys from Brasil' regularly take over the Lord Jim Pub in Ipanema, and 21 November was no different. 'It had been raining most of the day,' recalls Jim Dunnett, president of the Rio CSC. 'Due to the time difference, the kick-off was at 5.45 p.m. local time, so the usual stock of excuses for bunking off work – dentist appointments, visits to the vet and deathbed relations – could be saved for another day. However, a combination of our guys' heavy working schedules and a Bhoy on walkabout in New Zealand left me wondering

how many of the regulars would turn up. So, it was with some trepidation that I went to the home of the Rio Fergus McCann CSC in the Lord Jim Pub that day. I needn't have worried, as the place was filled with a healthy complement of the regulars and a large contingent of travelling support who were backpacking and/or holidaying in South America. The game itself was on ESPN Brasil, so the commentary was in Portuguese.'

Dunnett remembers little of the first 81 minutes (which is unsurprising, given how instantly forgettable much of it was) except 'sharing anguish with fellow club members Drewsão, Brucinho, Raimundão and Stanaldinho. Our anguish was more often driven by Raimundão's constant 'Ooohing', 'Aaahing' and 'Fer feck saking' at every ball kicked – as he does during every game – than at the actual events on the pitch.

'It must've been about 80 minutes when Jiří made his run/turn/fa' doon move that will forever in my mind typify his time at the club. As Naka placed the ball, the thought crossed my mind, "This is a carbon copy of the Old Trafford free-kick. No . . . surely not." Well, it was a bit further out, I suppose. The actual free-kick seemed to take an eternity, and I'm sure that most people in the pub that night aged years between time of impact, flight of the ball and it hitting the net . . . Mayhem!

'Much jumping, hugging, kissing, spilt beer – and in Drew's case a burst hand from punching the ceiling. If the previous 80 minutes had seemed long, the next part of the game seemed like 80 hours. Then it was over. I have vivid memories of people rushing out to the next-door off-licence and buying bottles of cheap bubbly to celebrate with after we finished the pub stock. Then there was the usual cacophony of calls and texts, including our walkabout Bhoy, who had found an Auckland bookies where he could watch the game. Wild talk of booking flights to Athens [for the 2007 Champions League final] ensued, and a honeymooning couple from Dublin said that this had made the trip worthwhile. The rest, as they say, is history.'

LOCATION: JOHANNESBURG, SOUTH AFRICA

DATE: 21/11/06

TIME: 11.22 P.M.

The barbecue smoke wafted through the Irish club in Johannesburg. Chattering voices filled the air, drifting to the street outside, where the warmth of the summer's evening still lingered. They were all in tonight. All 60 members and a few more besides. Hoops as far as the eye could see. Manchester United tops, too, and even a couple of people with Rangers shirts on. That was fine. Come one, come all. It was that kind of place. That was what was so great about it. No aggro. President Bill McIntosh took a bite of his burger and shook his head. 'It's a bit too far out . . . it's against a great goalkeeper . . . nah, he can't score from there, can he?'

O ye of little faith. McIntosh's comment would become the catchphrase of the Johannesburg Celtic Supporters Club. 'Every time Naka steps up to a free-kick, we all turn to each other and say, "He can't do it again, can he?"' McIntosh says, chuckling. 'The amazing thing is how often he has done it again, although not from that distance.

'When the ball went in, the whole club went upside down. We might have been 6,000 miles away, but we were going off our heads just the same. I was driving through the half-empty streets of Johannesburg on my way home and felt like beeping my horn and shouting out of the window. At that time of the year, it is usually daylight by 5 a.m., and most people are up by 6 a.m. So, on a night like that, you end up pretty shattered from the night before, but we were high as kites. After the game, the music went on and the whole place was going bonkers.'

McIntosh was born and bred in Castlemilk and left for South Africa in 1976. Now, with satellite television and all the games screened live, the only thing he misses is 'fish suppers'. Having moved to a different culture himself, he is full of admiration for Nakamura's ability to acclimatise to the Scottish way of life.

'Nakamura is just a class act. It must have been a real culture shock for him to come to a place like Glasgow. No disrespect to Glaswegians, but they are one-offs. He wouldn't be able to understand a word they were saying, even if he did understand English. But he's stuck it out. It's a real testimony both to him and to the people of Glasgow, who have really taken to him.'

Interest in the Johannesburg CSC has been growing for the last decade, and McIntosh, appropriately given Celtic's origins, combines his passion for the Hoops with a social conscience. Over the past couple of years, the club has been running Bhoys for Africa, a campaign to help disadvantaged youths throughout the African continent. They began by asking fellow CSCs to send old Celtic and football kit to be distributed to poor communities in Africa. Now they receive boxes of kit from all over the world on a regular basis. The first aim of the campaign is to help out the township youth of South Africa, and the second is to aid children elsewhere in Africa.

'I started it ten years ago, and we try to make a little difference,' explains McIntosh, an accountant by trade. 'Most of these kids have nothing. Recently, we got some strips from Benburb, the junior club in Glasgow. We travelled up to the border with Zimbabwe to give them out there. It was really funny to see these wee kids running about in the jungle with Benburb shirts on. We also take second-hand clothes, and I am going up to the Congo soon to hand out more stuff. It's very humbling to see how little these kids have got. It gives you a real perspective on life.'

LOCATION: SAITAMA, JAPAN

DATE: 21/11/06

TIME: 6.22 A.M.

Martin Burns had not slept a wink. His eyes were out on stalks, and he was perched on the edge of his seat. It had been a long, long night. The drama had started even before kick-off, when he couldn't get his Internet link to work and had been forced to listen to the game on Channel 67. The secretary of the Tokyo Celtic Supporters Club had taken in the match at his home in Saitama, a couple of hours on the train from the capital city. Daylight had begun to peek through the curtains in his bedroom – 6,000 miles away, Nakamura stood under the fierce glare of Celtic Park's floodlights.

'My wife gets up at around 6 a.m. for work, and the game was finishing around that time,' he recalls. 'She was sitting in front of me, putting her make-up on, and then I heard them saying, "Celtic have got a free-kick, and Naka is going to take it." Then Paul Cuddihy, the commentator for Channel 67, went berserk. Then I went berserk. I was screaming and shouting and managed to wake up my whole household, including my mother-in-law, sister-in-law and my dog Jack, who ran away to hide under the bed.

'Amazingly, less than 30 seconds after the goal, it was being shown on Japanese TV. It was screened on the news bulletins, and I remember the presenters saying, "We're not really allowed to show this, but we're going to anyway . . ."'

LOCATION: CELTIC PARK, GLASGOW, SCOTLAND

DATE: 21/11/06

TIME: 9.22 P.M.

. . . .

'He takes all kinds of free-kicks, so which of the 57 varieties are we going to get here . . . Oh, that's a good one . . . It's there . . . Nakamura . . . Parkhead erupts. One . . . single . . . swift . . . blow . . . A typical Nakamura free-kick. Well, they [the Celtic fans] can hardly believe it, but it is in the back of the net.'

Archie Macpherson, the doyen of Scottish football commentators, broadcast Nakamura's famous free-kick to the nation in typically exuberant fashion. He recalls the emotion of the night and the moment of dead-ball genius which inspired yet another legendary commentary. 'The greatness came from the execution but also the context,' says Macpherson. 'Neither side looked like scoring, and you did think that it would take something exceptional to win it. Just prior to him striking the ball, I remembered a comment from someone who had said that Nakamura could open a tin of beans with his left foot. So I said, "I wonder which of the 57 varieties we are going to get here." Then the ball hit the net.

'The other one I remember was Davie Provan's famous free-kick in the Scottish Cup final in 1985. Just before he hit it, I remembered a statistic and said, "Only twice in the history of the Scottish Cup have goals been scored direct from free-kicks. I wonder if this will be another bit of history? IT IS."

'I have been very lucky with free-kicks. You dream of the moment when not only does something happen on the pitch, but you are up to the job of recording it for posterity. The other one of mine was for the Archie Gemmill goal [against Holland in the 1978 World Cup]. My commentary for that was actually used in the film *Trainspotting* in the background to a sex scene. You always hope that something happens in a big game and you can really let fly and say something memorable.'

PREAMBLE

A 3–2 victory for United in the first match at Old Trafford three months previously had been a pulsating affair. Jan Vennegoor of Hesselink opened the scoring in the 21st minute before Louis Saha struck twice to put United in front. Nakamura then equalised in the 43rd minute with an expertly taken free-kick, an uncanny precursor to his decisive blow in the return match. The outcome was eventually decided by Ole Gunnar Solksjær's goal two minutes after the interval. Sir Alex Ferguson had rather ungraciously dismissed Celtic's performance, but the team had drawn much hope from their display at Old Trafford and nursed a quiet belief that they could get a result in front of 60,000 at Celtic Park.

The scene was set, the anticipation was huge, but surprisingly Strachan's selection policy reflected a cautious approach. In a bid to nullify United's embarrassment of midfield riches, including Paul Scholes, Michael Carrick, Cristiano Ronaldo and Ryan Giggs, not to mention a bench packed with international alternatives, the Celtic manager left Aiden McGeady, Shaun Maloney and Kenny Miller on the bench. The defensive-minded Evander Sno was deployed alongside Neil Lennon in central midfield, while Thomas Gravesen was stationed on the right and Nakamura switched to the left.

In defence, Bobo Baldé was brought in for only his second appearance in seven months in place of the injured Gary Caldwell. The Guinean defender, rusty from his spell on the sidelines, caused palpitations in the 36th minute when he surrendered possession to Ronaldo. His recovery challenge snuffed out the danger, although United felt they had a decent penalty claim.

At half-time, Strachan struck a more enterprising tone when he introduced Maloney and Jarošík and pushed Gravesen into a more advanced role. It gave Celtic a greater share of possession, but they had not really created a genuine scoring opportunity until the 81st minute. Cometh the hour, cometh the man.

POSTSCRIPT

The euphoria is punctured minutes later when Shaun Maloney is penalised after Paul Scholes's free-kick appears to strike him on the arm inside the box. The referee gives a penalty, Louis Saha steps up to take it, but Boruc plunges to his right to save the Frenchman's effort. Madness descends once more. Parkhead is rocking. Then it really is all over. Celtic have done it. They have reached the last 16 of the Champions League for the first time in the club's history.

THE BEST EVER?

So just how good was the free-kick? Matt Le Tissier, one of the greatest free-kick takers of the modern game, was left awestruck.

'It was a sensational goal, one of the top five free-kicks ever scored, if not the best,' said the former England international who is now a Sky Sports analyst. 'To get the ball up over the wall and still manage to put so much power in the shot was unbelievable. No goalkeeper in the world would have kept it out.

'Nakamura scored a fabulous goal in the first game at Old Trafford, but the one at Celtic Park was better, because it was from that much further out. People say Paul Gascoigne's goal against Arsenal in the FA Cup semi-final in 1991 is the best ever, but I always felt David Seaman should have saved it. Roberto Carlos's one against France takes some beating, because it changed direction about five times in mid-air, but there isn't much to choose between them.

'The other goal that sticks in the mind is David Beckham's free-kick for England in the last minute against Greece, just because of the sheer magnitude of the occasion. The best one I scored was against Hans Segers at Wimbledon when Jim Magilton flicked the ball up to me and I volleyed it into the top corner. I don't think I ever came close to getting one as good as Nakamura's.'

When I contact Le Tissier a year later to discuss the free-kick further, he insists on watching the strike again on YouTube to relive the majesty of it before offering additional analysis. He does not waver from his view that it remains the best execution of a dead ball he has ever seen. 'I sometimes think that these days there are too few moments in football that make you sit up and say, "Wow." However, I remember seeing that free-kick by Shunsuke Nakamura and thinking just that,' he reflects. 'It had me off my seat. My professional life now sees me watch a lot of football, but I must admit I hadn't seen a lot of this guy. But it was the type of strike that grabs the attention, which probably led to me saying that it was the best ever. It was the perfect free-kick in terms of technique. It was a fair distance out, too – further than the one at Old Trafford – and you could argue that Edwin van der Sar could have learned a lesson from the first one, but the credit goes to the taker. As far as the defending side goes, from that far out, you hope that your wall will do their job, but the perfect direction meant it whistled just over their heads. The Americans talk about the 'upper 90 of the soccer net', but we speak about the 'postage stamp'. Shunsuke hits that spot at pace, and when you do that it's impossible to stop.'

'Supporters have a tendency to see it their way, but when someone such as Le Tissier, with all his experience and expertise, says that it's the best he has ever seen then it means even more,' adds Jim Kerr. 'We have seen guys such as David Beckham scoring great free-kicks, but as soon as the ball hit the net I just knew that it would be hard to better.'

John Hartson's momentous strike against Liverpool in Celtic's UEFA Cup run of 2003 saw him inscribe his name in the folklore of the club. Of the 109 goals he scored for Celtic, it is the one he is most remembered for. The Welshman says that Nakamura will be able to dine out on the strike for the rest of his life. 'He can tell his grandchildren about it. He will take it to his grave. It was no fluke. You can't pull someone out of the stand to do that. Naka can do that six or seven times out of ten.'

Bertie Auld knows more than anyone about the far-reaching impact of making an indelible mark on the club's history. The former Celtic midfielder was part of the Lisbon Lions side that became the first British club to win the European Cup in 1967. It has become the most celebrated moment in Celtic's history. He believes Nakamura's free-kick marked another seminal moment. 'People will be sitting around tables in pubs talking about that goal for years to come. It will become exaggerated, and people will say that it was even further out than it was, or that there were eight or nine people in the wall. But the great thing is that you don't have to exaggerate it, because it was a simply magnificent goal.'

The impact of Nakamura's strike also captured the imagination of Scott Brown, who signed for the club the following summer. 'Against Manchester United in the Champions League, the floodlights were on, the fans were singing, Nakamura scored from about 35 yards and I thought, "What a player that boy is."'

Last word to Aiden McGeady. 'It's got to be up there as one of the best ever. He just whips it in that way he does. It couldn't have been any more in the top corner. Just incredible.'

FINAL SCORE

The dead-ball expert inhabits a world of isolation. In the moments of hushed anticipation which precede the striking of the ball, a million eyes bear down on him, searing through the back of his skull, willing him, urging him. The momentary vacuum of sound before the strike can seem like an eternity. He becomes aware of his heart beating, his breath quickening, his palms sweating. This is his moment.

'There was a wall of silence before the wall of thunder,' reflects Jim Divers, vice president of the Celtic Supporters Association. 'Then, everything that Nakamura wanted to happen, happened. He looked at the goal, looked at the wall, looked at the goalkeeper and then hit it. As time goes by, the legend will grow. In 20 years' time, people will be saying that he hit it from so far out that he was almost in his own half! Not only did it go in, but it went in with style.

'It's not the best goal in Celtic's history. You would have to say that the two goals against Inter Milan in 1967 were the best. But in the modern era, for a goal that was so significant and so vital, in that it took us through to the last 16, you would be hard pushed to say that it is not number one. If football is the beautiful game, then the poetry of that goal was mind-boggling. The ball floated along, and when it hit the net it encapsulated the essence of modern Celtic. It took Celtic to a higher level globally. It was just a truly magical moment. When someone has that sort of expertise, it is something to behold. His free-kicks are an art form. He is like Jonny Wilkinson in the sense that he is a total specialist. You almost expect to see him do the hands thing before he kicks it.'

Football's ability to produce moments of extreme beauty should never be underestimated. In football, as in other creative pursuits, imagination is what separates the artists from the artisans.

'Nakamura has talked about playing against Roberto Baggio at 37,' adds Divers. 'OK, he was older, but he still had imagination, and that is what Nakamura loved about him. Against Dundee United [during the 2006–07 season], he chipped the ball over Derek Stillie. He has the imagination to see that and then execute it. When the pressure is on, that is when great players step up and say, "This is what I do." He did it against Manchester United and against Kilmarnock. It is a habit. Against AC Milan [in the group stage of the 2007–08 Champions League, when Nakamura helped set up Scott McDonald's late winner], there was a wee wiggle that helped create space in the box for McDonald to score.

'He has the weight and confidence of the Celtic support behind him. When Nakamura is not playing, there is something missing. He is a ray of hope. Fans can see when they have got a special talent. If he makes a mistake, the fans don't shout at him, because it is just a mistake. It's not a lack of talent. Nobody would slag off Naka. He is quids in till the day he dies.

'Legendary status comes from the ability to produce moments of brilliance. Lubo Moravčík is a legend. How long was he there? Four seasons? Someone can blossom in a short period, and that goes for Nakamura. Billy McPhail was only at Celtic for two seasons but will always be remembered for the 7–1 game. His younger brother John was a very famous player for Celtic, but Billy is remembered basically for one game. We shouldn't try and quantify someone like Nakamura. We don't try and quantify Vincent van Gogh. Nakamura is an artist, and you just have to appreciate him.'

Inevitably, any discussion of great Celtic goals of the modern era leads back to Henrik Larsson. The iconic Swede's deft lob over Stefan Klos in the 6–2 defeat of Rangers in August 2000 is a rival to Nakamura's best effort. 'Time seemed to stand still when Larsson chipped the ball,' says Kerr. 'It had a loop to it. Like Nakamura, the only man who didn't seem surprised by what he had just done was Larsson. But millions of kids will now watch Nakamura's free-kick on YouTube, and it will be remembered perhaps more than any other goal.'

INJURY TIME

The euphoria had finally subsided, the floodlights had been switched off and the stragglers from the hospitality lounges had been chased into the cold November night. The players had all gone, having trickled out in dribs and drabs, families in tow, faces flushed with success, minds filled with memories of a historic evening in the east end of Glasgow. Memories that would last a lifetime.

Neil Lennon, the triumphant captain, patiently attended to his media duties, clenched a meaty fist in salute to the fans gathered outside the stadium and then vanished into the inky darkness. Gordon Strachan, the manager, slipped out of the side entrance as supporters chased him down – some to secure his squiggle on autograph books, others to take pictures, but the majority just to thank him for making their lives better, more bearable, for giving them memories to pass on to future generations.

An eerie calm had descended on Celtic Park – 11 p.m. had been and gone. Still they waited. Where was Shunsuke Nakamura? The posse of Japanese journalists commissioned to follow the midfielder's every move continued to wait patiently. They couldn't leave. They would take up residence in the car park if they had to. But they couldn't leave. It was more than their jobs were worth, particularly tonight of all nights, the greatest of their professional lives.

Two hours had passed since Nakamura had scored the best and most important goal of his career. Two hours since Celtic Park had erupted in a cacophony of joy and hysteria. Two hours since Shin Toyofuku had jumped out of his seat in the press box after being caught up in the swirl of euphoria. Now, a Far East audience of millions were depending on him and his colleagues, hanging out for news of their hero. David Beckham? Hidetoshi Nakata? Yesterday's news . . . With one elegant swing of his left boot, Nakamura had become the undisputed sporting superstar of the Far East. But where was he?

Just then he appeared: mop of boyish brown hair still damp from the shower; soap-bag tucked under his arm. Dignified, understated, underwhelmed even. Where had he been? Celebrating with teammates in the dressing-room? Slugging champagne with the directors in the boardroom? No. He had been in the gym. In an effort to quicken his recovery time, he had headed for a workout. As his colleagues cavorted around the dressing-room, singing songs loud enough for their vanquished opponents to hear, Nakamura had slipped out unnoticed. History had been made, but the midfielder had a post-match routine to follow. It was a winning formula, and now was not the time to change.

Only he did change it. Exhausted at the end of the game, he resolved to spend even longer on his routine to further quicken recovery time. It was the kind of unseen dedication that had combined with his exquisite natural talent to produce sublime moments such as his 81st-minute free-kick that evening. A moment of genius, as his manager had labelled it, but a moment which belied days, months and years of toil. And anyway, the moment was gone. Nakamura's thoughts had already started to drift to the next game, he told the Japanese journalists. Onwards and upwards; bring on the next challenge.

This had become the creed of his career ever since he had been discarded by Yokohama Marinos, his home-town club, as a 15 year old for being too small; ever since he had moved to Italian club Reggina and been written off as a ball-playing luxury; ever since Philippe Troussier had dumped him from the Japanese World Cup squad in 2002 for lacking strength and stamina; ever since he had disappeared without trace in his first Old Firm game in Scotland and been written off once again. At every step along the way, he had been forced to prove his critics wrong, convert the unbelievers one by one. A pursuit of consistency had become his driving force, his *raison d'être*. And here he was at the very summit of the football world, for an evening at least, but with an acute awareness that it was a long, long way down.

TWO

....

Who is the
Real Nakamura?

'HERE LIES GORDON STRACHAN. AT LEAST IT'S BETTER than Bratislava'. The Celtic manager has joked that the epitaph on his gravestone will be an eternal reminder of the darkest night of his managerial career. It was arguably the most traumatic induction any manager has faced.

Strachan's first competitive match in charge of Celtic was the second qualifying round of the Champions League on 27 July 2005. The club was four matches away from a £10-million jackpot. Five years of sustained achievement under Strachan's predecessor Martin O'Neill had left Celtic supporters acquainted with, even used to, European success. Expectations were high, belief was strong. Artmedia Bratislava were no cannon fodder, but neither were they anywhere near approaching the quality of some of the teams Celtic had dispatched in previous seasons.

Reaching the group stages of the competition was a realistic, achievable ambition. The embers of O'Neill's reign were still glowing. John Hartson, Chris Sutton and Alan Thompson were not the forces of nature they had been, but they were still influential; Stan Varga and Bobo Baldé in defence were not world-beaters, but they were solid, dependable characters; Neil Lennon and Stiliyan Petrov were in midfield, and new signing Maciej Żurawski, an established Polish international, was up front. The new recruits at full-back, Paul Telfer and Mo Camara, were still finding their feet, but Celtic had enough about them to see off Artmedia. Surely.

STRANGLED AT BIRTH

The Tehelné Pole Stadion is one of European football's most inhospitable outposts, a scar on an otherwise captivating Bratislavan landscape. Suffocating humidity and 80-degree temperatures compounded the hostile environment facing the visitors. Attributing failure to peripheral issues is never an appropriate response, yet in the heat of sporting battle strange patterns sometimes do emerge that seem to suggest that 'It's not your night'. Just 13 minutes into the game, Sutton accidentally collided with Lennon and was stretchered from the field with a facial fracture. The loss of the influential Englishman, deployed as an attacking midfielder, immediately handed the initiative to the home side, and they enjoyed the best of the opening half.

Artmedia were set up to attack, their expansive formation consisting of a couple of quicksilver strikers, Juraj Halenár and Branislav Obžera, supplemented by two flying wingers, Branislav Fodrek and Blažej Vaščák. Just as it seemed as if Celtic would reach the interval without conceding, the opener arrived in the 43rd minute. Ján Kozák's slide-rule pass took out Varga and exposed Camara, who had failed to track Vaščák's diagonal run. The winger broke into the box, hoodwinked David Marshall and squared for Halenár to tap home. Celtic's anxiety intensified when Artmedia doubled their lead 12 minutes into the second half. This time, Halenár crossed for Vaščák to tap in at the back post.

Strachan, keenly aware of the importance of an away goal, threw on Shaun Maloney for Żurawski and Jérémie Aliadière, the on-loan Arsenal striker, for Thompson. It was a gamble that backfired horribly. McGeady contrived to miss a glorious chance after being set up by Maloney, and from then on things went from bad to worse. With 15 minutes left, Halenár's searing volley from 22 yards made it 3–0. Moments later, substitute Martin Mikulič made it 4–0, and Halenár completed his hat-trick towards the end with a fifth.

Few could forget the shell-shocked look on Strachan's face as he faced the media afterwards. Disbelief, shock, despair . . . he did not need to speak. The rawness of his emotions were etched all over his features. The worst night in his 33-year involvement in professional football, the worst result in the club's European history, this was not the type of ground he had wanted to break in his first competitive outing. Strangely, Strachan's watch that he had worn for the previous five years stopped working during the game. He continued wearing it thereafter, refusing to forget. Making other people do so would become his prime motivation. Every domestic trophy, every unforgettable European night, every Manager of the Year award, he hoped would rub one letter at a time off that gravestone. But it would always be there, lurking malevolently in the background. Artmedia. Not so much the night a team died but were strangled at birth.

COME IN, NUMBER 25

Where did Strachan go from there? It couldn't get any worse. He needed a break, a diversionary tactic – someone or something to take the attention away, to remove the heat from him. Enter Shunsuke Nakamura. The Reggina midfielder had been linked with Celtic since the start of July, though they were reported to face competition from Atlético Madrid and Deportivo La Coruña. Talks had rumbled on for three weeks before, finally, on 25 July, 48 hours before the first leg against Artmedia, Celtic announced that a deal had been agreed. Peter Lawwell, the Celtic chief executive, said,

'Nakamura is a player Gordon Strachan was especially keen for us to secure, given his superb pedigree in the game. This is a player who has played in Serie A for the past three years, who is a mainstay of the Japanese national side, with over seventy caps, and who is one of the biggest footballing icons in Far East football.'

Strachan was effusive. 'Shunsuke is a very special talent, and once he's out on the pitch I'm sure our fans will realise very quickly why we were so keen to get him,' he said.

Nakamura chipped in, saying, 'Celtic are an enormous club with an extremely passionate support. This was one of the main reasons I signed, and I can't wait to get started and show the fans what I can do. I'm confident of a successful season, both in the league and in Europe, and look forward to meeting up with my new teammates later this week.'

So, Naka was on his way and all was right with the world at Celtic. The problem was that no one accounted for the butchering in Bratislava. Amid the wreckage of the 5–0 defeat, everything was thrown into flux. Celtic had agreed a deal with a player who had a stated ambition of playing at the top level of European football, and now Celtic faced the very real possibility of not even making the UEFA Cup, never mind the group stages of the Champions League. 'Would Nakamura still sign?' asked the Celtic supporters in the turbulent aftermath of their trouncing. Sure, a deal had been agreed, but he had yet to arrive in Scotland, yet to complete a medical and yet to sign on the dotted line. A 5–0 hammering by a minnow of European football would hardly inspire confidence in him that he had been right to choose the Scottish Premier League ahead of Spain's La Liga. He would not be the first footballer to complete a volte-face. The ripples of anxiety were keenly felt.

However, less than 24 hours after Artmedia, Nakamura proved himself to be a man of his word. On Thursday, 28 July, he ambled through the arrivals gate at Glasgow Airport looking like he did not have a care in the world. Mayhem ensued. Dozens of media crews converged on him, cameras flashed, Dictaphones were thrust in his face and dozens of supporters slapped him on the back. Police escorted him back onto the tarmac to avoid the huge crowd and, eventually, whisked him out of a side door to a city-centre hotel.

Prior to boarding the plane from Japan, though, Nakamura had moved to clear up any uncertainty over whether he would sign. 'I am a man of my word and would not have gone back on my decision to sign for Celtic,' he said. 'I heard the team's result just before I got onto the plane to Glasgow, and it's very disappointing. It's a disaster for Celtic, but that is just the way football goes sometimes. There is nothing that I can do about the second leg, because I cannot play in it. But I really hope that the team put in a great effort and get the result they need.

'Last night's result was a setback, but if Bratislava can win 5–0 at home, then I'm sure Celtic can. It will be very difficult, but the team will do everything possible to overturn last night's result. I am praying they do well, but the Champions League is not the only reason I signed. I still very much want to play for Celtic, and I am looking forward to the challenge.'

A remarkable 48 hours for the club were completed the following day when Nakamura was formally unveiled at Celtic Park. Faced with 20 Far Eastern news crews and a battalion of print journalists, together with a party from the Japanese consulate, Nakamura spoke slowly and deliberately through his interpreter, Makoto Kaneko. 'I know Celtic are always at the top of the league, so I do not want the team to go downhill while I am here. When I was at Reggina, the team managed to stay in Seric A until last season, so I think I did a good job there. I would like to do my best here to help Celtic do better than last season and get the title back. The stadium is really big, and the fans are really good in terms of their knowledge of football. I know that because of that I cannot just play normally – I have to play really well here. When I was in Italy, I had the number 10 shirt, so I was under some kind of pressure there as well. But football is a team sport, and I am here

to help support the other players. It's not all about the individual.'
The Celtic years had begun.

So, Strachan's first bout of pressure had been partially offset
by the arrival of a player who would become a keystone in his
side for the forthcoming years. But pressure is a permanent state
when managing Celtic. At Celtic or Rangers, they say you are
only ever one game away from a crisis and two away from the
sack. Strachan needed to get it right. Quickly. Celtic's first league
game of the 2005–06 season was against Motherwell at Fir Park,
the venue of the final-day collapse three months before in which
they had relinquished their league title. The Japanese midfielder's
lack of match fitness meant it was too soon to hand him his debut.
Unsurprisingly, Strachan made three changes to the side who had
capitulated in Bratislava. McGeady replaced the injured Sutton,
Stephen McManus came in for Baldé and Maloney started ahead
of Żurawski. An afternoon of see-sawing fortunes ensued.

Hartson opened the scoring for Celtic in the 14th minute, then
Motherwell's Brian Kerr equalised six minutes later. The Welshman
added another just after the half-hour mark and completed his hat-
trick with a penalty just before half-time. Game over? Not quite.
In the 58th minute, Jim Hamilton pulled one back for Motherwell.
Two minutes later, the home side equalised. Suddenly, from a
position of apparent invincibility, Celtic were on the ropes. With six
minutes left, Willie Kinniburgh scored Motherwell's fourth. Celtic
were in deep trouble, but Craig Beattie rescued a point, and their
blushes, in the last minute. Another inept defensive performance
had moved the pressure on Strachan up another notch.

'You do take it personally, because that is your team. You have
to take it personally,' he lamented. 'What we don't want to do is
panic. That would be the worst thing to do. Our defending is not
at its best and needs to be sorted one way or another. To lose goals
as simple as that is hard to take. We have got a problem, there is
no doubt about that. It needs to be rectified quickly. I don't think
there is too much thinking to be done. It is obvious – really obvious

– where we need to sort things out. Defensively, today it didn't work, so we will have to think of something else for Tuesday.'

Tuesday was the return leg against Artmedia, a game which Celtic hardly approached in rude health. A Thompson penalty midway through the first half inspired hope, which blossomed further with strikes from Hartson and McManus before the hour mark. Beattie's 82nd-minute goal set up a rousing finale, but Celtic just came up short. It was 2 August, and they were out of Europe. It was arguably as close to a crisis as Strachan would experience over the next two and a half years. He needed to start getting results, but he needed more than that.

He needed his defenders to start concentrating. He needed his midfielders to take command of games. He needed his strikers to start finding the net on a regular basis. He needed a break. He needed Nakamura. So, Strachan's bugle came out, and a little Japanese knight appeared on the horizon. Nakamura had not played since the Confederations Cup in June. He was not fully match fit. But Strachan needed him, maybe more than he would ever need him. Dundee United were the visitors to Celtic Park on 6 August. And so, against a backdrop of disarray, Nakamura made his debut.

Expectation hung heavy in the air that sunny afternoon in August. Legions of media had arrived for the historic day and were greeted with Japanese signs directing them to their seats. An estimated audience of 3 million in Nakamura's homeland burned the midnight oil to watch his first appearance in a Celtic shirt.

An appreciative roar greeted his name before kick-off. The Celtic support needed a saviour, and the 27-year-old midfielder fitted the bill. With pressure heaped on his slender shoulders, he faced his first test of character.

If someone were to make a DVD of how to win over supporters on your debut, then they would simply show footage of Nakamura's performance that afternoon. Celtic started like a team possessed, and their new signing almost opened the scoring after 65 seconds.

Nakamura, Thompson and Żurawski exchanged passes before the Pole's cross reached the Japanese midfielder, who directed a downward header on target only for Stuart Duff, the Dundee United defender, to hook it off the goal-line. The Celtic fans were off their seats. This is what they had been waiting for.

In the 17th minute, he showcased his creative abilities with a delightful pass over the top of the United defence to put Żurawski clear, but the Pole's shot was blocked by the legs of Derek Stillie, the Dundee United goalkeeper. Midway through the second half, he won a free-kick on the edge of the box after outfoxing Mark Kerr with a wonderful trick. He took it himself, curling it towards the top corner only for Stillie to claw it over the bar. Soon after, he trapped a cross-field pass on his thigh and cheekily played keepy-uppy as United players converged on him. The Celtic fans were in raptures.

By then, every double shuffle and moment of exquisite control was being greeted with 'oohs' and 'aahs' of appreciation. Five minutes from time, he was substituted to a standing ovation. Moments later, it was all over. Celtic 2, Dundee United 0. Back on track; crisis . . . what crisis? Man of the Match? Who else but their Japanese saviour. 'I thought that was as good a debut as I have seen for a long, long time,' purred Strachan. 'There was lots of pressure on him, not just here, but at home, where he is a big star. I can tell the Japanese people that he did very, very well. I just told him to go out and enjoy the game, enjoy the atmosphere.'

Nakamura was also delighted with his Parkhead baptism. 'That was my first match, and everything I wanted went well. That was the best thing,' he said. 'When there is good play, the supporters cheer, so that was good for my confidence. I received the Man of the Match award, so I thank the supporters for that.'

The late Tommy Burns, the Celtic first-team coach, was intimately acquainted with the fluctuating fortunes at a club the size of Celtic. As a former player and manager, he basked in the highs and donned the tin hat for the lows. Therefore, when asked to reflect on the dreadful start to the 2005–06 season, he was philosophical but quick to acknowledge the contribution of Nakamura in helping to lift the collective gloom. 'That is what happens at big clubs. If you get two or three bad results at a club like Celtic, you can be in the doldrums, but it can also go the other way. Bringing Naka in at the time we did lifted the whole support. He did really well on his debut, and we knew very quickly that he would certainly be a very effective player in Scotland. In fact, he would go on to prove himself to be a better player than even the manager originally thought.'

As club captain, Neil Lennon was feeling the pressure of their abysmal start to the season as much as anyone. The Northern Irishman had been an integral part of the club's success over the previous five seasons, which meant it was particularly galling for him to experience such tribulations. The gradual decline of Martin O'Neill's side had left a talent deficit that was glaringly obvious in those early outings. The introduction of Nakamura injected some much-needed quality into the squad and created a huge buzz off the park. 'When he arrived, he brought a mini entourage with him,' recalls Lennon. 'As well as all of the media, there were supporters coming over from Japan every day and congregating around the entrance. He was, and probably still is, like the David Beckham of Japan. I had never seen anything like that before. We had superstars such as Henrik Larsson in the past but not someone who commanded that sort of attention. He made a big difference when he came, because we had had a bad start to the season. We had lost against Artmedia and then drew 4–4 with Motherwell, and there was a lot of doom and gloom around the club. Straight away when he came in, you could see that he gave us something different, a bit of quality and flair, and he did really well on his debut against Dundee United.'

Nakamura's debut is indelibly printed on the mind of Jim Kerr, who marvelled at the player's immediate impact. 'Even inside the first ten minutes of his debut, he was outstanding,' says Kerr. 'We were at the game, sitting with some of the Japanese people who were through from the consulate in Edinburgh. Some players turn up at Celtic Park and the whole thing is too big for them, or they take a few months to get their heads around it. But he was straight in there, stroking the ball about.'

Kerr also had a particular interest in Nakamura's success. That day, he was accompanied by his long-standing Japanese friend Yumie Suga, whom he had indoctrinated with a love of Celtic on previous visits. 'She has been a friend of mine for about 15 years. She loves Scotland. I took her to Celtic Park a few times, and she became infatuated by the fans, the team and the stadium. For six or seven years before Nakamura came, she developed an in-depth knowledge of the club. Japanese people have a habit of really getting their teeth into something. They get to know the minutiae. So when Naka signed, she was in heaven.

'The weekend Nakamura made his debut, Peter Lawwell, who had met Yumie previously and had marvelled at her knowledge, invited us along. Before the game, we were chatting away to Gordon Strachan. The last two or three times I had seen him was down at Southampton. I remember him saying that he loved the pace of life and the peace and quiet down there, so I was surprised when he ended up at Celtic. He seemed a bit of a fish out of water at that stage.

'Nakamura was the big focal point. Afterwards, we got the chance to have a few words with him. Yumie started giving him a crash course on the history of the club. She was saying to him, "You need to know that this is more than a football club. This is a cultural movement. You need to look after yourself. This is a tougher league than Italy. You have to win every game." She probably didn't go as far back as Brother Walfrid [the Irish Marist brother who founded the club in 1888], but she seemed to be giving him the lot!

'She is about ten years older than Nakamura, and he was very respectful. He stood there nodding away, very seriously. I remember thinking, "If my old granda' could see this!" Naka must have been thinking, "What the hell is this?" She actually got her photograph taken while she was talking to him, and it ended up on the main sports pages back in Japan.'

A more muted performance against Falkirk the following weekend, in a 3–1 victory for Celtic, was partially attributable to an injured thigh, which required him to take a late fitness test before the match. He had barely trained all week but, as Strachan reflected afterwards, had shown considerable character in passing the test in filthy conditions at the club's training ground that morning. 'Shunsuke missed a lot of training with his injury but showed a great attitude to tell me he was fit to play. He had a fitness test at Barrowfield at 10.30 a.m. before the match. The rain was lashing down and conditions were not pleasant, but you could see he wanted to make it.'

The match also showcased an aspect of his game that would prove pivotal as the season progressed. Celtic had fallen behind to a first-half penalty by Darryl Duffy, but they had the left boot of Nakamura to thank for helping to restore parity early in the second half. A coruscating cross from the left found the ever-reliable pate of Hartson, who bulleted a header into the net to inspire Celtic's comeback. 'A lot of positives came from him, and he put in a fantastic cross for John's goal,' Strachan said after the match. 'If he wasn't playing and not around to put in that cross, the game might have been different.'

Nakamura would surely have preferred more time to acclimatise to the blood and thunder of Scottish football before taking his Old Firm bow. He didn't get it. In only his third outing in a Celtic shirt, he was thrown in at the deep end along with another eight Old Firm debutants. For most of the match, he was a virtual spectator. Amid the usual debris of the Glasgow derby, you could almost see the thought bubble above his head: 'Well, I suppose this is football, but not as I know it.' A couple of set-pieces, including one that Baldé failed to convert and another that flew inches wide, were the sum total of his contribution. With Celtic having had Thompson sent off midway through the first half, Nakamura was a luxury they could not afford, and he made way for Maloney in the 54th minute with his side two goals down.

Mercifully for Celtic and Nakamura, another of Strachan's marquee signings had started to acclimatise to Scottish football and was ready to assume some of the burden of turning the Hoops' season around. Maciej 'Magic' Żurawski finally arrived as a Celtic player at the end of August in a league match against Dunfermline the week after the loss to Rangers. The Polish striker ran the Fife side ragged, scoring twice in Celtic's 4–0 win. He also provided an assist for Nakamura, cutting in from the left wing and slanting the ball across to the Japanese midfielder, who slammed it home from close range. Nakamura had broken his duck, and Żurawski had found his shooting boots. Suddenly, shards of hope started to emerge from the rubble of Celtic's opening couple of games.

A goal, an assist and an auspicious debut is a decent return from a new signing in his first five games, but Nakamura still had a way to go to fully establish himself. Never was that more apparent than in Celtic's 1–0 win over Hibs at Easter Road on 18 September. That match encapsulated the good and bad sides to his game. He started the match in sprightly form and split the Hibs centre-backs, Chris Hogg and Gary Caldwell, with a wonderful pass to release Petrov, who scored after five minutes. Celtic created and spurned a hatful of chances thereafter, with Nakamura hitting the post from a free-kick in the 48th minute. They failed to kill Hibs off, and Strachan had grown concerned about the performance of his star signing. The midfielder had become increasingly erratic as the game elapsed, chasing the ball around aimlessly and failing to stick to the game plan. In the 73rd minute, the Celtic manager replaced him with Maloney and criticised his display afterwards.

Strachan said, 'It was a good start for us. We had a nice shape, but when it was only 1–0 at half-time we knew it was going to be a hard game in the second half because Hibs sensed that they were still in it. Nakamura played very well in the first half when he kept his shape. I allow people freedom to a certain point, but there is a point after that where it is not very efficient. And because we dropped back so deep, I felt that we needed legs to run the ball from our own half, and Shaun was excellent. When we kept our shape, we were better.'

If Nakamura was not fully functioning as part of the team yet, then at least he continued to make decisive contributions. In his next match, an extra-time victory over Falkirk in the CIS Insurance Cup, his cross found the head of Hartson for Celtic's winner. A tense home league win against Inverness three days later saw him claim another assist with a well-timed ball to Craig Beattie, who galloped 40 yards to score. Against the Highlanders, Nakamura was central to everything Celtic created and confirmed afterwards that he had begun to adjust to life at Celtic. 'I really enjoy playing at home. The stadium is always full, and I don't feel any pressure. I'm also getting used to the rhythm of life in Glasgow, and I like to go out with the other players for dinner.'

However, Nakamura did not find all aspects of Scottish football easily digestible. The more physical nature and faster pace of the game in Scotland can be a culture shock to new arrivals. There is little doubt that he took time to adapt to the rigours of the game, but there is also evidence to suggest that the Celtic supporters took time to appreciate fully the subtler nature of his talents. Against Kilmarnock at Rugby Park in mid-October, Petrov was the difference between the sides in a stodgy, physical encounter, while Nakamura was a peripheral performer. Beside the thoroughbred that was Petrov, Nakamura looked like an unsteady young foal.

Where Nakamura was concerned, memories of Eyal Berkovic still remained. The Israeli midfielder joined Celtic in the summer of 1999 for £5.75 million. Soon after he signed from West Ham, his former manager Harry Redknapp admitted that he could not rely on Berkovic in away games. An artful, inventive talent, Berkovic did not have the character to make a sustained impact in Scotland and was eventually sold by O'Neill. Would Nakamura prove to be a similar liability?

After the Kilmarnock match, Strachan was asked about the Japanese midfielder's uninspired performance. 'Who is the real Nakamura? Nobody knew about him until he came here. All I know is that if you look at his assists and chances created, he's ahead of anybody else at the club. He takes responsibility and always tries to play the forward pass, the hard pass. That's why I brought him here. We play him in a position that allows him to roam at times, because we know that he can create and dig things out. He does things no one else can do.

'Just because he doesn't go about making crunching tackles, it doesn't mean he's not working hard. The people who really matter are his teammates and the coaching staff, and they're all really pleased with him. Nakamura is a smashing fellow. It may sound like a small thing, but the weather here compared to what he has been used to is really something else. Just walking into training and warming up in the rain is totally different. So, it's not easy for him.'

On the basis of Nakamura's early contributions, it was hard to argue with Strachan's robust defence of him. He had already established himself as one of the side's creative fulcrums, but the questions being asked were also partly justified. He had the skill and the vision, but did he have the character? Would he stand up and be counted when the Scottish winter set in? Where would he be when an Old Firm game hung in the balance? Who was the real Nakamura?

After the chastening experience at Fir Park on the opening day of the season, Celtic's next match at Celtic Park against Motherwell was a test of character for Strachan's side, but they responded in style. And Nakamura's performance was a firm rebuke to his doubters. 'Celtic 5, Motherwell 0 – Nakamura runs Well ragged' read one of the headlines. A glorious 30-yard Nakamura free-kick in the second half, followed by a burst of Aneka's 'Japanese Boy' over the Tannoy, capped a scintillating individual performance. Raking cross-field passes, eye-of-the-needle defence-splitting balls, the Japanese midfielder ran through his full repertoire of tricks and set up Petrov's third. The victory also marked the first real glimpse of Strachan's utopian vision for the team. The Celtic manager wanted to turn his players into a more fluid, mobile, attacking unit than they had been under Martin O'Neill. After their dreadful start to the season, it had looked like a hopelessly idealistic notion, but he had gradually started to impose his own style.

Despite the Bulgarian international scoring his first hat-trick for the club against Motherwell, the majority of reports gave Nakamura the Man of the Match award. It marked his first successful free-kick for the club and another step in his gradual immersion in Scottish football. 'I've had great chances to score from free-kicks in many games so far, but I hadn't managed it, so it was big relief finally to do so,' Nakamura said. Strachan added, 'He did that because he practises all the time in the wind and rain. It's the same as when I played with Eric Cantona [at Leeds]. He used to stay behind after training and practise his volleys.'

Nakamura maintained that there was more to come from him. 'I still feel that I'm only playing at 60–70 per cent, though. In our first five games, I played in the middle, on the left and on the right. But we have a more settled team now, and we know we're always playing 4–4–2, so it shouldn't be long before I'm up closer to 80 or 90 per cent. I've finally found a house, and I'm waiting for my family to come over next month. We have a baby boy, so I will be training in the morning and then looking after him in the afternoon.

'The language is obviously very different in every country I have played in, as is the food and the environment. In terms of football, I believe Scotland and Japan are similar. In Italy, there are so many fouls in the matches. But I don't find communicating with my teammates too difficult. I know a few words, and it's a case of making them into sentences. Anyway, in football you communicate with the ball. When I spoke with the manager, he didn't talk so much about the style of play. He told me it was important to enjoy playing and that I'd be able to do that.'

Strachan highlighted the cultural differences that a foreigner such as Nakamura had to cope with in making the transition to Scotland. 'We have a culture where we do everything quickly. We eat quickly, and we drink quickly. That's the way we are. If you go to France, they take two hours to eat a meal. We take 20 minutes maximum, and nobody speaks to each other. We just keep our heads down and rattle our way through it. If you go to America for a game of golf, it takes five hours. Over here, we fly around like maniacs, and it takes two and a half hours.

'I can see what the fans want. They want the ball in the box and action. But there are different ways of getting the ball in the box. Fans are the same at every club. It's just that there are more Celtic ones out there, and you hear them a lot more. Even having to put up with this weather is difficult compared to what he is used to. We have had everything recently. We had the tornado season three weeks ago, and now it's the monsoon season. It's not easy for him. Even compared to Southampton, the weather here is night and day, and it does affect your training schedule.'

At first glance, Lennon feared that Nakamura's physique would make him prone to a sudden gust of wind, never mind a Barry Ferguson bone-cruncher, but he was impressed by how quickly he adapted. 'Initially, in some of the games away from home, he maybe struggled with the tighter pitches, but he soon got used to it. Every day in training, you could see him getting better and stronger. He had such a slight physique, and it is so difficult for a player to arrive in an environment in which the pace and the style of the game is so different. But he took to it like a duck to water, and he was able to do that because he is just a natural footballer. The great thing about him was that you could give him the ball in any situation and he could manipulate it with his left or right foot. He was also popping up in little areas and looking for the ball.'

By then, the Celtic fans were relatively content that Nakamura was no Berkovic. He had already proved that he could stand up and be counted, that he would not wilt in the face of adversity. What was he, though? They had been weaned on a diet of strong, hard-running midfielders such as Thompson, Petrov, Lennon and Sutton. Whatever he was, Nakamura was not that. 'Naka plays in the position where he can pick up the ball when he wants it,' explained Hartson. 'It is not like he is in the middle of midfield, where he constantly has to be involved in the action. Because he was out wide and in a little bit more space, Gordon was able to say, "Give him the ball whenever he wants it." He doesn't have to get involved in the nitty-gritty, but he can still be involved in the game enough.'

In the bipolar world of Scottish football, Old Firm games are often used as the yardstick by which to judge players. Never mind that they have performed like a world beater in the other 34 games of the season. If they fail to sparkle in an Old Firm game, their character is often questioned. 'Never done it in an Old Firm game,' is the familiar refrain directed at players who do not cover themselves in glory in the famous Glasgow derby. In that respect, Nakamura had already accrued one black mark against his name when he was withdrawn in his first Old Firm game after an ineffective performance. In many ways, his derby debut has become a stick with which his critics have beaten him ever since. A closer analysis tells a different story. His second outing against Rangers, in the CIS Insurance Cup in November, produced a far different outcome. For starters, Celtic won convincingly. Maloney's magnificent long-range strike from 30 yards proved to be the highlight of a game that the home side dominated throughout. Victory was sealed in the latter stages when Stefan Klos fumbled a deep cross from Nakamura under pressure from Baldé to make it 2–0. In a midfield populated by players more than capable of mixing it physically – Hamed Namouchi, Fernando Ricksen, Barry Ferguson and Ian Murray – Nakamura more than held his own, his close control and vision marking him out as an inspiring beacon along with Maloney and McGeady.

Nine days later, Celtic faced their old rivals once again, this time in the league. Again, a Celtic side bristling with midfield inventiveness dismantled an increasingly forlorn Rangers side, in doing so opening up a 15-point advantage in the league. The three-goal winning margin reflected Strachan's side's overall dominance and further established Nakamura's reputation as a player of considerable substance. Fresh from draining international duty, he was at his impish best, personifying the verve and dynamism of Celtic's attack. He added another to his tally of assists with a delightful curling cross from the right wing that Bobo Baldé nodded home for Celtic's second in the 56th minute. Five minutes later, Nakamura and Petrov combined on the right to allow the Bulgarian to spear in a low cross that McGeady touched into the net to seal victory. Nakamura had also been involved in the build-up to Hartson's first-half opener. It was another indication of his growing appreciation of the nature of Old Firm matches. It also left Celtic fans wondering where Roy Keane would fit into the midfield, following the club's pre-match statement that they would be interested in opening signing talks with the Irish midfielder.

If the success of Nakamura's first season should be measured anywhere, it is in the 'assists' ledger. The midfielder might not have grabbed many games by the scruff of the neck, but his gilded left boot was becoming an increasing source of devastation as the season elapsed. A murky day in Aberdeen was precisely the sort of game that Nakamura might have been expected not to fancy. When Celtic fell one behind to a Jamie Winter goal, he would have had further reason to surmise that this was no platform for his subtle talents. The opposite was true. Celtic suddenly burst into life, and Nakamura was the creative spark. Three minutes after conceding, his cross spread panic in the Aberdeen rearguard, and some penalty-box pinball ended with McGeady restoring parity with a thumping shot. Two minutes later, Nakamura picked out Hartson, who spun off Zander Diamond and fired in a powerful shot that was spilled by Ryan Esson. Petrov was onto the rebound and put Celtic into the lead. Telfer claimed Celtic's third goal in eight minutes when he took control of a Nakamura corner and lashed a low, angled drive into the far corner. 'He was outstanding,' admitted Strachan of Nakamura.

In contrast, Celtic's 3–2 victory over Hibs at Parkhead the following weekend was exactly the sort of game in which Nakamura was expected to flourish. Tony Mowbray's visiting Hibs side had earned a reputation for attacking football, and they came to Celtic Park full of confidence. It was the kind of game to make the purists purr with delight, particularly in the opening quarter of the second half. Celtic had taken a first-half lead through a Hartson header from a Nakamura cross. The Japanese midfielder started on the right but frequently drifted into central areas, where he had greater licence to create. Significantly, on the stroke of half-time, Nakamura was scythed by Derek Riordan and looked as if he might limp out of the action. Instead, it was Riordan, booked for the challenge, who was substituted at the interval, replaced by Ivan Sproule. Guillaume Beuzelin brought Hibs back into the game with a header from a Kevin Thomson cross, then Steven Fletcher's angled drive gave them the lead. Celtic came raging back, and four minutes later Maloney scored a masterful free-kick after Nakamura had been fouled on the edge of the box. Hartson then gave Celtic the full points haul after tapping home when Maloney's shot came back off the post.

Strachan declared himself delighted with Nakamura's performance. 'Shunsuke is brave. He's prepared to take the ball,' he said. 'He has great intelligence, sets up counter-attacks and assists with goals.'

Lennon grew to a fuller appreciation of the Japanese midfielder's contributions as the first season progressed. 'Although he wasn't blessed with brilliant pace or physicality, he was so intelligent. He had brilliant vision and a great range of passing. As his first season went on, players such as Maciej Żurawski and Shaun Maloney, who made a lot of runs, really benefited from him. He could play little short passes or 50- and 60-yard ones right onto someone's toe. He was on the same wavelength as his teammates, and although he didn't speak any English he spoke the language of football.'

Celtic would end 2005 on a high, thanks to the timely intervention of Nakamura's increasingly prized left boot. Livingston were the visitors to Celtic Park on Boxing Day and proved themselves uncompromising opponents. It was the type of afternoon on which everything that could go wrong did. First, Roy Keane's official introduction to the Celtic fans before kick-off was delayed by 50 minutes after an electrical failure plunged the stadium into darkness. Then Baldé gift-wrapped the visitors a second-half equaliser by conceding possession to Robert Snodgrass, who fed Paul Dalglish to cancel out Maloney's penalty opener. With embarrassing malfunctions on and off the park and nerves increasingly apparent, Celtic might have been forgiven for settling for a point. That they eventually squirreled all three was down to their increasingly influential Japanese playmaker. With three minutes left, Paul Telfer found Nakamura on the right. On collecting the ball, he made his way along the edge of the area before lashing a powerful shot off the near post to claim victory. 'Anxiety took over,' Strachan admitted. 'However, we are lucky that Nakamura can rise above all the nervousness.'

'That is why you pay big transfer fees for players,' said Paul Lambert, the Livingston manager. 'Nakamura's goal shows that good players win matches.'

A match of relentless intensity against Hearts on New Year's Day proved another pivotal moment in the title race. Strachan's side had fallen two behind inside eight minutes through goals from Edgaras Jankauskas and Steven Pressley and still did not look like salvaging anything when Stephen Pearson pulled one back. The eventual outcome centred around the 76th-minute dismissal of Takis Fyssas, whose last-man challenge had stopped Maloney in his tracks. With the home side down to ten men, Celtic capitalised.

The equaliser came in the 87th minute. Nakamura was again the provider, McManus heading home his free-kick. In the dying seconds, Paul Hartley was judged to have brought down Nakamura. His delivery cannoned off Baldé and into the path of McManus, who swept a low shot into the net from six yards out.

On 14 January 2006, Roy Keane made his first appearance at Celtic Park. All eyes were on the Irishman, who had endured an unfortunate debut in the surprise Scottish Cup capitulation to Clyde the previous week. At one end of the stadium, hundreds of fans held up orange, white and green cards to form an Irish tricolour. The stage was set. Enter Nakamura at his thunder-stealing best. Only a couple of minutes had elapsed when he curled a mesmerising free-kick into the postage stamp for Celtic's opener. When Maloney scored a penalty ten minutes later, the game was effectively over as a contest. Thereafter, the Nakamura–Maloney show had the fans in clover. Man of the Match? Nakamura, of course. Roy who?

That Nakamura's influence waned in the second half of his opening season is undeniable. The heavy schedule of domestic games combined with his exacting international commitments and lack of summer break led to him developing niggly injuries. If he lacked the fitness to remain a major influence through to May, then he still contributed. A steady flow of assists continued to carry Celtic towards the league title. McManus converted a Nakamura corner at Easter Road in March to give them a 2–1 victory, and the Japanese midfielder set up Żurawski for two goals against Livingston at Almondvale later that month.

Celtic's impressive 4–1 destruction of Kilmarnock at Rugby Park in April owed much to the influence of Nakamura, who opened the scoring with yet another magical free-kick and added another eight minutes from time. 'He has the touch of an angel,' said Strachan. A free-wheeling performance in the 1–1 draw with Hibs at Parkhead in mid-April, on the day Celtic were presented with the Premier League trophy, confirmed Nakamura's intention to finish the season on a high.

With the title done and dusted, the final Old Firm game of the season was a dull, meaningless affair, enlivened only by Nakamura's introduction after an hour. The match ended goalless, and Strachan admitted later that he had made a mistake in not starting with Nakamura: 'Naka was excellent. He helped us to be a better side, that's for sure. If you look at the performance, you would probably say dropping Nakamura maybe wasn't a good decision.' The Celtic manager then reflected on Nakamura's contribution to his debut season. 'His touch and vision were outstanding. I thought that Fabrice Fernandes, who filled a similar right-sided midfield role for me at Southampton, was the bee's knees in these respects. But I would say that Shunsuke is ahead of him. I loved watching him, possibly more so than any other Celtic player. The changes to Celtic's style of play made him a crucial player for us, because when we were knocking the ball around you could rely on him not to miss any opportunities to penetrate the opposing defence. Being able to pass the ball is one thing – to be able to play the pass that is going to give your team a scoring opportunity is another. In goal assists, I really do not think there is a player in Scotland to touch him.'

So who was the real Nakamura? At the end of his first season, it was obvious that he was no Berkovic. He was no Sutton, Thompson or Petrov, either. Instead, he was something different, something unique. He was a free-kick specialist; he was a provider. To the diehards, he had proved he had character. To the purists, he had become a ray of hope. To the stattos, he had made his case in black and white.

Games: 38; goals: 6; assists: 10; medals: league, CIS Insurance Cup.

THREE

The Icing on the Cake

'My family were waiting for me with a cake, and I had a nice night with them at home. It was a good way to celebrate, and I made sure we took some photographs with the trophies, because they are now in Celtic Park.'

Shunsuke Nakamura

*T*HE TRAFFIC LIGHTS CHANGED FROM RED TO THE WEE *green man. The drivers peered disbelievingly through their windscreens as he skipped across the road in front of them. He was wearing a tuxedo and appeared to be carrying a trophy of some sort as he made his way up Sauchiehall Street. 'Nah, it couldn't be,' they thought. It was a warm evening in Glasgow city centre, and the Sunday-night revellers were drifting out of the pubs en route to nightclubs. A group of teenage girls stopped and stared; a clutch of young men on the corner caught sight of him, too. Surprisingly for Glasgow, no one shouted, no one heckled. Instead, quizzical looks were exchanged as he slipped off into the shadows.*

Shunsuke Nakamura was in a world of his own, oblivious to it all, his mind racing with the events of the day. The trophy he was clutching was the Scottish Professional Footballers' Association Player of the Year award. Earlier that evening, his fellow professionals had voted him the most influential player of the season. What a feeling; but it was better than that – much, much better. Less than 12 hours had elapsed since he had scored the goal against Kilmarnock that had won Celtic the league: an injury-time free-kick; his trademark; his specialty. The eyes of the Scottish football world had been on him, and he had nailed it. What a feeling; what a season. Then there was the free-kick against Manchester United and the hat-trick against Dundee United . . . endless highlights flashed through his mind as he quickened his step. He would be home soon.

He had left his teammates behind, left the hubbub of the Thistle Hotel in Glasgow in his wake, left them all to it. He had made a quick speech, exchanged handshakes and pleasantries with well-wishers, posed for photographs, and done everything required of him, all the while hatching his escape plan. He wouldn't bother hailing a taxi; the short walk would take him five, ten minutes maximum.

He turned the corner of his street – nearly home. He could see the light on in his apartment. His wife had baked him a cake; his son would still be up, too, waiting for him. He broke into a quick jog as he climbed the small hill. He fumbled in his pocket for the key, placed it in the lock. Home. Now, for the modest Japanese football star, the celebrations would really begin.

Shunsuke Nakamura's first season at Celtic had been a success on any terms, but the second was when he learned how to fully integrate his individual talent into the team. The Player of the Year season was the moment when all the hard work came together to create a platform for his creative gifts to fully flourish. With two thirds of his career behind him, Nakamura might never again hit the heights he achieved then.

Significantly, the platform for their expression was one of hard work, endeavour and physical toughness. For every Player of the Year vote he received for his sumptuous technique and wand of a left foot, he received another for his work ethic and mental and physical toughness. Scottish football likes good foreign players, but it loves the ones who fully embrace the unique challenges of life north of the border, which include coping with the frequently bruising physicality of the game.

Gordon Strachan would make an atrocious poker player. His emotions are writ large across his face. An interviewer can usually tell at first glance what kind of mood the Celtic manager is in. When he needs to get something off his chest, his face visibly twitches and he appears preoccupied. On such occasions, every question directed at him is a complete waste of time until he finally decides to uncork his grievance. After Celtic's 2–1 victory over Aberdeen on 17 February 2007, Strachan entered the small press room at Pittodrie looking like a man whose cat had just been run over by the ice-cream van.

Yes, yes, he was happy with the three points. Yes, yes, it was a good run-out before the forthcoming clash with AC Milan. His face continued to twitch. 'Had he been impressed with his team's battling qualities?' enquired one journalist. Strachan's eyes suddenly flashed. 'When we had to fight and scrap and do the right things, we did them. And I mean everybody, even Naka,' insisted Strachan. 'He's meant to be light, and if you give him a tackle, then you scare him, and he runs away. If people are going to make comments about some of my players, then at least look at what we do. Now I realise why I don't read papers. Naka was fantastic.'

Aha. Now we were getting to the bottom of it. Strachan, who usually claims to avoid reading press coverage of Celtic, had caught sight of a column by his former Aberdeen teammate Stewart McKimmie in the Aberdeen *Evening Express*. McKimmie had commented, 'Shunsuke Nakamura will present the biggest danger to the Dons. I'm convinced if they are brave enough to really hit him with a heavy tackle early in the match, he won't cause them too many problems.' Strachan had been rightly outraged at the comments, which were so clichéd and untrue as to be almost laughable. Nakamura had long since proved himself to be no shrinking violet, and McKimmie's comments betrayed a peculiarly Scottish mentality that chooses to focus on a perceived lack of physical strength rather than revel in technical ability.

Nakamura, who presumably is not an avid reader of the *Evening Express*, was oblivious to the rammy. Appropriately, however, his performance that afternoon in the north-east took the form of an eloquent 90-minute rebuke to McKimmie. Less than ten minutes had gone when he threaded a neat ball down the right for Craig Beattie, who galloped into the Aberdeen box and planted a shot into the far corner of the net. When Aberdeen captain Russell Anderson was judged to have fouled Vennegoor of Hesselink on the edge of the box after 20 minutes, a smile crept onto Nakamura's lips. One flourish of the midfielder's left boot later, Celtic were two in front.

Even Celtic's vanquished opponents had the good grace to salute Nakamura's performance. 'I haven't thought about my Player of the Year yet, but Nakamura would be up there,' said Aberdeen midfielder Scott Severin. 'He was criticised in the past for his work rate, but he knows how to control a ball and bring others into the game. Their midfield is very clever. They take up positions that are hard to mark, and we were afraid to fly in, because they can play a one-two around you. They keep the ball well, and at 2–0 up they had ten minutes when they just passed around us and killed the game.'

Tommy Burns explained the subtle changes they had tried to make to Nakamura's game between the first and second season. 'The Scottish game is not so very physical. Players are a lot more protected now than they were 20 years ago, so that is a bit of a myth. Nevertheless, Nakamura showed great character to blend in as well as he did. He has a great temperament and great composure. I don't think we expect guys like Nakamura and Aiden McGeady to run about making crunching tackles, and there are games when we just leave them to do their thing. But there are other games when we expect them to get back into position or fill a hole to prevent the opposition getting forward. Sometimes the creative players are the ones who do the most running, because they are constantly looking to drift into wee areas of space.

'Sometimes the players who are exalted for their work ethic are the ones who run up and down the field like mad men, but Nakamura has a fantastic attitude in other aspects. Sometimes you need your creative players to take the ball even when things are going against them. The Stewart McKimmie comments were a one-off. He had probably only seen Nakamura three or four times before he made those comments. He was not in a position to say what he said. We watched Nakamura every week, and we knew what he was about.'

Nakamura agreed with Burns that the physicality of Scottish football is overstated. 'When I was in Italy with Reggina, there were so many really bad challenges and tackles. So, I have found that there is fair play, cleaner play, here in Scotland. I have been tackled hard since I came here, but when someone hits me I just get on with it. You cannot allow yourself to lose focus. I have found it easier to adapt to playing in Scotland because people try to pass the ball, and you are protected by the referees in this country as well. In Italy, you can take a bad tackle, and the person who committed the foul doesn't get booked. But here if you make a bad tackle, then you get booked. I've always found that the football environment here is very, very good. The Celtic supporters know their football. They watch games and notice even the smallest piece of play, and if it's good, they applaud. It's really nice for players to hear that. In Italy, you don't get applause for that. You get applause for good tackles and goals. I am not criticising Italian football at all. There is just a different approach to the game in this country.'

Only a couple of weeks after the Aberdeen game and Strachan once again had cause to reflect on Nakamura's physical robustness.

In their 2–1 win over Dunfermline at Celtic Park, visiting midfielder Owen Morrison – who presumably believes everything he reads in the *Evening Express* – poleaxed Nakamura inside the first few seconds. Afterwards, the Celtic manager praised his Japanese midfielder's ability to bounce back. 'Our bravery on the ball was good, and it had to be because we took a few heavy tackles. Their self-discipline was absolutely fantastic. It was like going back to the '80s with some of those tackles and decisions. We tell the players who play the game that they are going to get tackled. We tell them to get up and get on with it, not to retaliate. But they do need protection themselves. The tackle on Nakamura in the first few seconds was like going back to the '80s when you got the first one free. That was like when Neale Cooper put Charlie Nicholas up in the air after three seconds at Pittodrie. They'd only just kicked off, and the ball didn't get out of the circle. It was going back to that. If that tackle was in the 70th minute and the game is tight, I think he's off. So, Nakamura's done brilliantly in picking himself up and playing with a broken hand and getting that kind of stick. We're helping referees out. If Nakamura had gone down and rolled about, there might have been trouble.'

Craig Burley, the former Celtic midfielder, had viewed Nakamura's initial impact in Scottish football with scepticism, claiming in his Sunday newspaper column that the Japanese star was 'in danger of becoming a luxury'. However, he was quick to acknowledge that Nakamura's subsequent impact in Scotland, particularly in his second season, was based on an ability to withstand physical punishment. 'When he first came in, he faced the language barrier and a completely different culture, so it must have been doubly difficult for him,' says Burley. 'He did need a bit of time to adjust. There were never any doubts about his quality or ability, but I felt at times near the start that he wasn't in games enough. But he adapted very quickly, and he became used to the thought that people would try to kick him up and down the park as an avenue to stop him playing. The more challenges that went in, the more he just seemed to bounce back up and brush himself down. He never complained. I think he understood that his was the style of play that would attract that sort of treatment and just got on with it. There have been so many whingeing foreigners in British football, but I have never witnessed Nakamura whingeing about anything. When Celtic have been able to get him on the ball in the final third, he has nearly always managed to make space for himself and get the ball into the box.'

In his first season, he would occasionally stand on the periphery of the action with his hands on hips, gazing on with a bewildered expression on his face, waiting for the ball to arrive. That all changed in his second season. From the first whistle of the first game of the season, Nakamura ran all the time – back and forth, up and down. Teammate Aiden McGeady laughs when the subject is raised. He explains that whereas he and most other players run for short bursts during a game and then stop, Nakamura is constantly on the move, gliding up and down the right flank – perpetual motion. 'He's very fit,' says the Republic of Ireland international. 'When we do the ProZone, which tells you how many metres you have run during a game, he is always one of the best. He runs well over 12 kilometres a match.'

McGeady relates to the development of Nakamura's game, because he too underwent the same process. A similar creative talent to the Japanese star, it was not until the arrival of Strachan that McGeady started to function as part of the team. The Celtic manager explained that it was no longer enough for the talented winger just to be an asset in the final third of the pitch. He expected him to work the left wing, chase back, put himself between opponents and make tackles. And so, as McGeady ploughed an increasingly impressive furrow up and down the left, he looked over at Nakamura undergoing a similar transformation on the right. 'He might have come here as a luxury player who would maybe play behind the front two, but not many managers let players play in that position and not do any defensive work,' explains McGeady. 'He had to adapt. He now knows he has defensive duties, and although he might not win a lot of tackles at least he sticks his foot in. In the first season, he wasn't doing as much as he does now.'

Burley also grew to appreciate his work ethic and compares Nakamura to his former Chelsea teammate Gianfranco Zola. 'One of the best playmakers I have ever played with was Zola during my time at Chelsea. He was a guy who could play wide or off the front, but you never had to worry about playing him in away games. Zola was one of the hardest-working, best team players I have ever played with. Because of that, he was also one of the best individuals.'

Nakamura also worked to improve his stamina. 'I would have to say that my fitness level is the main thing that has improved a lot. On the training ground, we do a lot of running, and I am always out of breath. But then, when it comes to the actual match it makes it much easier to play the 90 minutes. The games themselves are very tiring, because play rarely stops. In Italy, you find that the play stops regularly because of tackles and players needing to receive treatment, so it is easier to cope during the game, because you have a chance to catch your breath.'

Tommy Burns combined his role as first-team coach at Celtic with head of youth development. He was first to acknowledge that Nakamura had made his job a lot easier. As Burns argued, you can do everything in your power to indoctrinate players with the right habits and attitudes. 'Eat the right things, live the right way, practise, practise, practise,' was Burns's mantra to his young charges. But they were only words. Some seeped in, others fell on deaf ears. In Nakamura, however, his words were made flesh. Instead of hammering home his message in a lecture theatre, he could just point out of the window to the wee Japanese guy still on the training field in the driving rain hours after his colleagues had left – practising, honing, working.

'We all say to the young players that guys such as Nakamura and Beckham didn't achieve mastery of the ball during normal sessions. They managed that by the 40 minutes, an hour spent after everyone had left. These guys work out a certain way of striking the ball. They look for advantages in little areas. They practise extremely hard. There have been examples before Nakamura. Pierre van Hooijdonk was a great specialist at free-kicks. Once you put that message across to young players, then it is up to them. For some of them, it doesn't register, and a couple of years down the road they are lost to the game.

'I am presuming that Naka's is the character of the Japanese people. He's come to Scotland and wants to show everyone the type of people he represents. He has a huge love of the game and an incredible professionalism. Long after the other players have gone, he will still be on the training pitch, hitting free-kicks, trying wee things with the ball. He has shown by his honesty and that quiet glow he has about him that he is here to do a job. He's a great example to the young players at the club, but, even more than that, he is also a great example to the senior players.'

Darren O'Dea, the club's 21-year-old centre-half, is more used to preventing goals than making them but admits that Nakamura's mentality has rubbed off on all the young players at Celtic. 'You've only got to watch him in training. He practises every single day and keeps working on his technique. I stay behind regularly after training with some of the younger lads, and he's down there taking free-kicks as well. Normally, he just aims at an empty goal, but there are times when he sticks his interpreter in there. We realised the first day he came to the club just how good he was in training, and he has produced the goods on the big occasions as well. No matter how good he gets, he'll always keep putting in the time. He feels he can always improve, and that's something we should take note of. He is a match-winner, and I'm sure guys such as Shaun Maloney and Aiden McGeady have picked things up from him.'

At Reggina, Nakamura had been used in several different positions, including behind the strikers and as a deep-lying midfielder. The presence of Neil Lennon and Stiliyan Petrov in the centre of Celtic's midfield, plus Shaun Maloney or Aiden McGeady on the left, meant that Strachan decided to play Nakamura on the right of midfield. It was another transition, but Hartson believes that Nakamura's deployment there actually allowed him to acclimatise quicker. 'I wasn't surprised that he adjusted,' he says. 'I am never surprised when great players do anything. Naka can adapt to any situation. He has got the mentality for it. Naka plays in the position where he can pick up the ball when he wants it.'

For a foreigner, the transition can be just as arduous off the park as on it. Dozens have come and gone from Scotland over the years, disappearing as quickly as they arrived amid complaints about inclement weather and unappetising cuisine. For Nakamura, the previous three years had been spent in the small seaside city of Reggio Calabria on the toe of the Italian boot. Prior to that, he had lived his entire life in Yokohama, on the outskirts of Tokyo. Whichever way you look at it, moving to Glasgow must have been a major culture shock. His initial attempts at putting down roots in Scotland were not helped either by his family's failure to settle. More than a year on from joining the club, after a victory over St Mirren in which he had provided an assist for Celtic's opener and played a part in the second, he revealed that his wife and young child had returned to Japan after an unsuccessful attempt to relocate to Glasgow. The only contact he was able to have with them was through video messaging, and their return to Scotland depended on his wife securing her international driving licence. 'Of course I miss my family, but, in a way, I'm used to it after being in Italy as well. My wife is learning to drive and trying to get an international driving licence. That's the problem with coming over. She's finding it quite hard, so it might be another month or so. Obviously it would be better with her and my kid.'

It is not many footballers who move to the goldfish bowl of

Glasgow and revel in their anonymity, but such is the case with Nakamura, who reflects on the serenity of his life in Scotland compared to Japan. 'During my free time in Japan, when I go out somewhere I usually get people following me, hiding behind walls and doors, taking pictures of me with their phone cameras without asking me. They follow me everywhere, and, as you can imagine, that can be difficult at times. It is just completely different to what I have experienced in Scotland. Here, when I see fans, they just ask for a handshake or an autograph.'

Lennon expected Nakamura to depart after his first season but was pleasantly surprised that he stuck around and signed an improved deal. 'I thought maybe if a club from Spain came in for him at the end of the season that he might go and play there. I thought the pace of the game and the more technical nature of it might suit him better, but he stayed and had a fantastic season, which he capped off with the winning goal against Kilmarnock. I think he enjoyed the second season even more than he did the first. He has a God-given talent. You could give him the ball more or less anywhere on the pitch, and he was able to get out of a wee hole or create something for us. He just gave us something a bit different that we maybe hadn't had for a few years.'

Nakamura's willingness to stick it out in Scotland, despite being separated from his family, spoke of his determination to adapt and made the achievements of his second campaign all the more impressive. However, the one thing that was missing was his ability to communicate. Even by the end of his second season, Nakamura had made little progress in his bid to learn English, but, as Lennon pointed out, he was not ostracised because of it. 'You could make small talk with him and ask him about his trips to Japan, that sort of thing. The lads loved him. He was very quiet, and he always had his interpreter around. It was like "me and my shadow". Even during Gordon's team talks, he would be talking away to Naka and translating what he was saying. On the pitch, you communicated more by sign language. He understood what you were trying to say to him, and he also realised when you were not happy and taking him to task about something.'

During his second season, Nakamura also moved from the suburbs into the centre of Glasgow, where he rented a plush apartment with panoramic views over the city. His decision to move had more to do with his keenness to be as close as possible to Celtic Park and the Barrowfield training ground, rather than a desire to indulge in Glasgow's nightlife. The city after dark was not a place the abstinent midfielder was interested in experiencing. He made one of his only forays into a pub on the team's Christmas night out in 2005. As Lennon explained, however, the night ended in tears for the clean-living Nakamura. 'He had a couple of beers, and then I offered him some Swedish chewing tobacco, which is quite strong,' Lennon said, laughing. 'He had never had it before, and after a wee while he was just sitting with his head almost between his knees, so we had to send him home in a taxi. From then on, any time I offered him some, he would just give a wee nod of his head.'

Nakamura's increasingly iconic status was reflected in the unseemly scramble for his shirt by Dumbarton players after their Scottish Cup tie with Celtic in January, in which he had set up Żurawski to score twice in a 4–0 win. 'The lads at Dumbarton wanted strips, but they all wanted Nakamura's, so it shows you that footballers rate him as well. But we couldn't get 20 or more Nakamura strips,' says Strachan, laughing.

'WE ARE LUCKY ENOUGH TO HAVE A GENIUS IN OUR RANKS' – GORDON STRACHAN

So, Nakamura now had the work ethic allied to the natural talent, but what did that add up to? Strachan draws to a contentious conclusion about his midfielder's unique fusion of tenaciousness and technique. The Celtic manager's body language changes when his player's name is raised. His back straightens, his eyes flash excitedly and a smile creeps across his lips. He simply adores Nakamura the footballer and is similarly in thrall to Nakamura the man. He is never less than fulsome in his praise of the Japanese star he plucked from Reggina in the summer of 2005. He has become the player most closely associated with the kind of flowing football Strachan has pursued at Celtic. In his relations with the fourth estate, the Celtic manager has rarely succumbed to hyperbole, so there is added weight to his repeated assertions that Nakamura is a genius. It is quite a claim, but the Celtic manager is in no doubt. But is he really a genius?

It is an overused phrase in football, a term more closely identified with, and perhaps more suitably applied to, the creative arts. Mozart sat down at a piano aged four and instinctively knew how to produce beauty. He was a pioneer, a creative force who broke new ground in his field. The same can be said about great artists such as Vincent van Gogh and Leonardo da Vinci. Their unifying ability was being able to produce something exceptional from a blank canvas. It is harder to quantify genius in sporting terms.

'Exceptional intellectual, creative or other natural gifts,' is how the *Oxford English Dictionary* defines someone in possession of genius. The term implies 'high or particular gifts of nature', according to *Webster's Dictionary*. There are not varying degrees of genius. You either are a genius or you are not. It cannot be attained by perseverance. It is innate.

Talent is defined as a gift that can be developed. It is a more general expression of creativity. There are varying degrees of talent, and it can be attained by mental or physical training. It is easier to analyse an individual's talent than it is to lay claims to genius.

When we think of footballing geniuses, we reflect on those who have redefined the sport, who pushed the boundaries. A 17-year-old Pelé announced his arrival on the world stage at the 1958 World Cup and did things no one had ever seen before. Johan Cruyff was a technical and tactical visionary who changed football irrevocably during his decorated club and international career. He was the first of football's great thinkers. Diego Maradona produced a mixture of skills, power and explosive pace that made him the undisputed best player in the world during the 1980s. His greatest achievement is widely accepted as being the 1986 World Cup, where he almost single-handedly won the trophy for Argentina. His goal in the quarter-final against England remains one of the best individual strikes ever. However, Maradona's role in Napoli's two *scudettos* is arguably an achievement on a par with the World Cup triumph. Zinedine Zidane redefined the role of the midfield playmaker in the 1990s, his sublime technique and metronomic style raising him onto another level from his contemporaries. Most of all, he did it when it counted. It was the Frenchman who led his country to their World Cup triumph in 1998 when he scored twice against Brazil in the final. And his goal against Bayer Leverkusen in the Champions League final will be remembered as one of the greatest in the competition's history.

The common strand between the four men is that they all did it over a length of time and on the biggest stages, raising the beautiful game to an art form in the process. It is clear that Nakamura is not in that category. On the evidence of his performances in Europe and in the 2006 World Cup, he has not produced at the very top level on a consistent basis, which undermines Strachan's claims that he is a genius in the broader sense.

Nevertheless, Celtic's 2006–07 Champions League campaign was studded with memorable team performances, particularly at Parkhead, and Nakamura more than played his part. In their second group game, a 1–0 home win over FC Copenhagen, he was excellent, as were the whole team. The Japanese midfielder made a decisive contribution to the winning goal, which Kenny Miller scored from the penalty spot. With 36 minutes gone, Thomas Gravesen sprayed the ball to Nakamura on the right of the penalty box. He cut inside, bamboozled Copenhagen defender Michael Gravgaard with some deft footwork and was dumped to the turf. Penalty. Nakamura sprang to his feet and clenched his fist in delight. Afterwards, Strachan half-joked that Nakamura had a better claim to hit the penalty than Miller, who, in fairness, tucked the spot kick away confidently. 'Kenny decided this morning that he would take the penalties,' said Strachan, smiling. 'I think it was only because Shunsuke Nakamura couldn't understand what Kenny was saying that no one argued with him over it.'

In the magnificent 3–0 destruction of Benfica in their next group game, arguably the high point of Strachan's stewardship, Celtic were once again inspired against supposedly technically superior opponents. Shaun Maloney was in irresistible form on the left flank, and Miller scored twice, while Nakamura had a hand in two of the goals. For the opener, Nakamura's scuffed shot fell to Miller, who stabbed home. For the third goal, his parried shot fell to Stephen Pearson to score. He had proved he was able to flourish in the rarefied setting of the Champions League, but there were also glimpses of his limitations. In both group games against Manchester United and in the home game against AC Milan in the last 16, Nakamura was unable to impose his will on proceedings during general play. Similarly, in the away leg against the Rossoneri, he again performed competently without taking the game by the scruff of the neck.

Burley believes that Nakamura falls below the standards set by the very best. 'I do think that against big players of real quality he has struggled. His effort cannot be questioned, but I do think there are times when he has not done enough in big Champions League games. I suppose the question is, "What level could he step up to?" I don't think it's an ability thing or a physical thing, but he is not the quickest. He doesn't have the pace to get the better of players and get the ball in. For me, that is the only thing that is missing. I think he would get a game for the likes of Everton or Newcastle, a team in the middle tier of the Premier League. Petrov is a player who has struggled to cope with the physical demands of the Premiership. They talk about the Scottish league being physical and fast, but I have played in both, and England is faster. At this time, I think there are more questions than answers in terms of his ability to step up a level.'

Burns agreed that Nakamura had been found wanting at the very top level. 'I think it is down to the physiological side of it. The games he has struggled in have been the huge European games when he comes up against a different type of player. At that level, players are fitter and stronger. We have seen flashes of him, but he has not been outstanding over the course of 90 minutes the way he has been in the Premier League. Against the AC Milans, the Benficas, the Spartak Moscows, it always seems that he is a wee bit short.'

The free-kick against Manchester United at Celtic Park might have been the highlight of his career, but, significantly, Nakamura admits that he had failed to perform to his capabilities prior to his match-winning strike. 'I was very pleased to score, and it was nice that it was at Celtic Park, but I also made a lot of mistakes. In the first half, I made so many mistakes, which wasn't so good, and I gave the ball away. But it was probably the most important goal of my career, because it was such a big game.'

Jim Craig, the Lisbon Lion, believes that Nakamura's failure to dominate on the big stage is a major flaw. 'I think he is a very talented player who cannot do a lot of things, a bit like David Beckham,' says Craig. 'In big games, he is often not there. I'm not interested in what he does against St Mirren and Inverness. He needs to stand up and be counted in Rangers games. That is when you need players of his ability to have a real stormer.'

A conversation with Luigi De Canio, the Italian who managed Nakamura in the 2002–03 season at Reggina, sheds further light on his limitations. Asked to reflect on Nakamura's impact in Italy, De Canio was blunt. 'It was only a social phenomenon, really. He was a good player but not an exceptional one. Technically, he was excellent, but he wasn't a player who would win you games. He doesn't have great physical qualities. Even when he goes by a man, he's quite easily caught. He never manages to be a match-winner. I had to play him further back in the midfield because of that weakness. An attacker in my team has to be productive – there must be an end product. When a player does a trick for its own ends, there's no point. Admittedly, I've not seen him for about a year.'

Lennon disagrees that Nakamura has failed to perform on the big stage and points out that the true measure of his greatness could only be quantified if he was playing alongside other exalted talents on a consistent basis. 'I think you would have to put him in that environment. Maybe if he went to one of the world's top clubs, you would see even more of him. All I know is that he came to a big club like Celtic and starred. They say that players become better with better players alongside them, so it's possible that he could go into that environment and be comfortable.'

If Nakamura does not rank in the same echelons as world-class players, then where does he sit? John Hartson has played with Henrik Larsson, Lubo Moravčík and Dennis Bergkamp, so he knows a sublime talent when he sees one. He believes Nakamura is their equal. 'Naka's a fantastic talent. He has got an appreciation for the game. He has just got immense talent. It's his weight of pass, his dead-ball delivery, his vision – they are all second to none. He is as good as anyone I have played with. Celtic fans always take to a really big talent. Look how they took to Lubo and Henrik Larsson. If a foreigner comes in and he oozes talent like those guys, then the fans will back them.'

McGeady claims Nakamura's vision is what makes him truly special. 'The biggest thing I would say about him is that he sees things before other players. Sometimes his teammates aren't on the same wavelength. There was a game [in the 2006–07 season] against Kilmarnock at home, and I expected Naka to play the ball to my feet, but he played it in behind the defender instead. I didn't even realise that the ball was on, but I ended up running behind him, and I scored from it. Nobody else would have seen that.'

Bertie Auld, the Lisbon Lion, believes that when Nakamura plays, Celtic play. 'Naka's quality rubs off on players around him. He makes other people play. He has tremendous vision, but he also has a good engine. Scott Brown has not played with him for as long as some of the others, but he will come on tremendously from playing alongside him. Nakamura gets people off their seats, and the Celtic fans have always loved entertainers. Right back to the days of Bobby Collins, Charlie Tully and Kenny Dalglish, Celtic have always had players who can do something a bit different. Jock Stein would have loved Naka, because he has the ability to unlock defences, and that is what you need at the top level. He has been a great addition to the Celtic family.'

The Player of the Year season was sprinkled with special moments that showcased his unique talents and earned him his end-of-season recognition. The game against Dundee United on the afternoon of 14 October was one of personal glory for Nakamura. In 14 unforgettable second-half minutes, he orchestrated the destruction of Dundee United with a sublime hat-trick. After Noel Hunt opened the scoring for United, Nakamura began his one-man rout. Pushed into a more advanced role in the absence of Thomas Gravesen, and with Evander Sno and Neil Lennon holding the midfield, he ran riot. His first, within seconds of half-time, was a stabbed effort from six yards out following a Jiří Jarošík knock-down. The second saw a Lee Naylor throw-in flicked on by Jan Vennegoor of Hesselink to the back-post area, where Nakamura side-footed the ball home. The third was a thing of beauty. Exchanging passes with Jarošík, Naka took one touch to move the ball out of his feet and with his second curled a delightful shot into the top corner for his first hat-trick in eight years.

'This is something I have always wanted to do,' he said. 'Previously, Stiliyan Petrov went forward from the midfield, and when he did that I had to come back a bit. It is the same with Gravesen. But against United we had Evander Sno and Neil Lennon sitting quite far back, and I managed to get forward more often. I am always trying to maintain the balance and shape of the team, so that means I cannot always get forward, and I'm sure the fans appreciate that. But I have been trying to get goals more often, and this will be a great memory, as I don't get many hat-tricks.

'The last one was for Yokohama when I was just twenty years old, but one of them was a free-kick, and this time I managed to score all the goals from open play. I don't know why, but I couldn't kick the ball properly before I scored. Maybe it was the ground, I'm not sure, but next time it is something I can improve on, because I know I wasn't playing that well.'

Strachan said, 'The third and fourth goals got me excited out there because of their beauty. It was that kind of enjoyment of going back to just being a football fan and enjoying the game. Nakamura has so much trust in his ability and his first touch that you never see him panic – and what he did out there for his goals was great.'

Boxing Day 2006 and Celtic Park sounded like a public library. Celtic had lost Bobo Baldé to a broken leg in the first half, and two goals in the opening hour from Dundee United had silenced the home fans. United looked on course for their first victory at Parkhead in 14 years. Celtic were in a deep hole, but Nakamura was about to throw down the rope ladder. With twelve minutes remaining, Celtic won a free-kick on the right, and he curled in a sweet delivery to the edge of the six-yard box, where Darren O'Dea, who had replaced the stricken Baldé, ghosted in to plunge a header into the net.

Two minutes later, Nakamura produced the goods once again. Sno, deputising for the suspended Lennon, shuttled the ball to Derek Riordan on the right. He laid the ball inside to Nakamura at the angle of the box, who looked up and flighted a glorious chip beyond Derek Stillie. Celtic could even have nicked it with the last kick of the game when Riordan's shot from outside the box came off a post, trundled along the goal-line and ran to safety. 'His personality decided the game for us,' said Strachan of Nakamura. 'He decided, "We'll not get beat here," when some of the others were thinking, "Is it going to be our day?" He's a fantastic player. His goal was pure genius. I don't know what else he can do other than carry the rest of the players around on his back. He was the one who saved the game for us.'

Even Stillie was moved to heap praise on Nakamura's delightful strike, which had wafted tantalisingly beyond his grasp. 'I thought I was getting to Nakamura's effort, but it stayed up there. It was a great bit of skill from a fantastic talent, and it is great to have a player like that in our game. He can win you matches out of nothing. At Tannadice earlier in the season, he was having a quiet day, then within ten minutes he scored a hat-trick.'

But a genius? Nakamura himself rejects the label. 'I don't think I'm a genius – geniuses don't make mistakes. Some people say I can't make slide tackles or head the ball, but I will always try to contribute using my brain while working to improve those other areas of my game.'

The only time Nakamura has used the word genius is in reference to his teammate McGeady. He is a huge admirer of his Celtic colleague and believes that McGeady is blessed with a greater degree of natural talent than he is. 'I knew he was a really good player when I arrived, but he has improved a lot. I think he is a genius. When I first arrived at Celtic, I was very surprised that he was only 19. I didn't think he would be that young. I was not that good when I was 21. I keep trying every day to be a better player, but I think Aiden has the natural ability.'

'YOU WOULD NEED FOUR LEE WILKIES ON STEP LADDERS TO STOP A NAKAMURA FREE-KICK' – CRAIG LEVEIN

Nakamura acknowledges that he does not have the all-round game of a Zidane or a Maradona, so it is in the area of free-kicks that he shows something that is given to very few. If genius can reside in moments, then a narrower definition of the term would seem to suit Nakamura.

As Hartson points out, Nakamura's ability is God-given. 'His deliveries, particularly from free-kicks, are unbelievable. Both Naka and Shaun Maloney were the hardest-working players at the club. They would be out there for hours on end with a bag of balls. It was no fluke when they did it in games. Naka knows he has a special, God-given talent, like David Beckham. The way these guys strike the ball from free-kicks is just incredible. Because he works so hard at it, he can do things like he did against Manchester United.'

They say practice makes perfect, but, as Lennon argues, to reach the heights that Nakamura has, particularly from dead-ball situations, there must first exist a vast reservoir of natural talent. 'That is just a God-given talent. He obviously stays behind and practises them, but I could stay behind every day and practise free-kicks for three or four hours and wouldn't get anywhere near his level. The one he scored at Old Trafford was amazing, because van der Sar didn't even move. Not only does he get it up and over, but he also hits it so hard. The second one at Celtic Park was even more amazing. The height of the ball and the way it bent away from van der Sar was incredible. It was funny, because it got to the stage that every time we got a free-kick outside the area you could feel a real buzz going around the stadium. He would also look at the position of the goalkeeper, and if he thought the keeper was expecting him to aim for the top left-hand corner, then he would switch and hit it in the bottom right. The great thing was that he did it consistently.'

McGeady has watched his teammate at close quarters and believes his free-kick ability lifts him onto another level altogether. 'You always see him with a ball before and after training. He has a few tricks up his sleeve, but the main thing is his free-kicks. On the first day he came, he was practising free-kicks, and he had a bunch of the young boys in the wall. They didn't realise how good he was, and they just stood there amazed as nearly every shot went in. In terms of free-kick technique, there is no one like him. The only one you could possibly compare him to is Juninho at Lyon.'

Bertie Auld used to marvel at teammate Tommy Gemmell's dead-ball expertise but claims Nakamura is more of a free-kick strategist. 'Big Gemmell used to thunder free-kicks in like bullets, but Naka picks out wee areas that he wants to hit, and he hits them consistently. He's a bit like Charlie Tully in that respect. Tully did amazing things in the days when the balls weren't as light and the parks weren't as good. The people who came to watch us in the 1950s and '60s used to talk about how great Tully was. He was a tremendous entertainer. If Naka's thing is free-kicks, then Tully's was corner-kicks, and there is the great story about him taking a corner-kick and scoring, then being told to retake it and scoring again.' Remarkably, Nakamura has also matched Tully's legendary feat by scoring direct from a corner for Japan.

On a more light-hearted note, he has also proved his dead-ball superiority over Barcelona striker Ronaldinho in a free-kick competition filmed for a Japanese TV station. Now watched by thousands on YouTube, Nakamura triumphed over the Brazilian. 'I have the DVD from that programme,' he said, smiling. 'The television company sent me it, and it was all good fun.'

A look of dread spreads across Jim Jefferies' features when Nakamura's name is mentioned. His Kilmarnock side have suffered more than any other at the hands of the Celtic midfielder over the past three years. Since joining the Parkhead club in 2005, Nakamura has scored six times against Kilmarnock, including the famous goal that clinched the league title in 2007. Five of the half dozen have come from dead-ball situations, so it is little wonder that Jefferies views attempting to stop Nakamura as a task akin to climbing Everest in a pair of flip-flops. 'We've discussed it with our goalkeepers and tried different things,' he says. 'Someone even posed the question, "Is there even any point putting up a defensive wall?" But then you know that he won't take it if there's not a wall. They'll get somebody to bore it in instead. But the boy has fantastic ability to get the ball up and down and put it in the postage-stamp corner, so you have to give him a lot of credit. There will be better teams than us that he will score against. He scored twice against Manchester United in the Champions League against a six-feet-five-inches goalkeeper in Edwin van der Sar. The last time at Rugby Park we thought about trying one or two things, and he put it into an area we never thought he would. We talked all week about it and tried something that Alan Combe [the Kilmarnock goalkeeper] thought might work, but there's nothing really you can do about it. You put someone on the post, then take him off it, and he still scores.'

John Collins was scoring free-kicks for Celtic when Nakamura was still in short trousers. Arguably his most famous dead-ball strike was against Rangers at Ibrox in 1994, a game in which Celtic fans were banned from the stadium. Producing the goods under extreme pressure is the most difficult aspect of taking free-kicks, argues Collins. 'In France, Lyon have Juninho, the Brazilian, who is rated Europe's best, because he replicates the flight of the ball each time. Nakamura has done it twice against Man United and is in the top bracket. He has great technique. Constant practice is the only way to achieve that, but it is one thing to do it in training and quite another to do it in a high-pressure situation in a game.'

Strachan agrees that Nakamura's ability to score sublime free-kicks on the big stage is the key. 'Most football players have instinct, we know that,' says Strachan. 'But when you have time to think, it's different. It's like golf – these guys with the six-foot putts to win championships. They've got a couple of minutes to think about it and all that pressure builds up. It's the same with taking a big corner, a free-kick or a penalty kick. Can you handle that period when you're on your own, you've got to deliver and the whole of the football world is watching you? We've seen them all taking them at training – easy. But when it comes to the nitty-gritty, there's more to it than just ability, that's for sure. To put those away calmly like Nakamura does takes real mental strength. That's why David Beckham has been so successful over the years – he does it at the right time.'

Matt Le Tissier's analysis of the second free-kick against Manchester United is enough to convince anyone that Nakamura has reached a level of expertise in dead-ball situations that is extremely rare. Burns agreed that Nakamura's genius resided in his dead-ball abilities. 'The free-kick against Manchester United was absolutely wonderful. The trajectory of the ball was phenomenal. In that respect, he is a genius. It all depends on what level you put genius. Maradona's dribbling skills made him a genius, the way Cristiano Ronaldo drives at players makes him a genius, even some of McGeady's skills you could say make him a genius. Naka is a genius by one kick of the ball. It is the act itself.'

FOUR

··········

From Tokyo to Tollcross

'Nakamura signed for us in late July ... and made an immediate impact at Celtic, not least because it seemed that every time you opened a cupboard, a Japanese reporter would fall out.'

Neil Lennon

PLANET NAKAMURA HAS ITS VERY OWN SATELLITE SYSTEM in constant orbit. To say Nakamura is big news in Japan is like saying Watergate was a decent front-page scoop. A voracious appetite for news on the 30 year old has resulted in all-consuming coverage of his career, which has, in turn, catapulted him into another stratosphere from other Asian football stars. The beast must be fed, and there are willing workhorses on hand to satisfy the cravings of a Nakamura-obsessed Japanese public.

The media entourage includes a five-strong team (four journalists and one interpreter) permanently based in Scotland who cover his every move for newspapers and web media in Japan. Their numbers are swollen on Champions League nights when more Japanese reporters arrive from London and elsewhere to reinforce the 'Glasgow Five'. The Five are a disparate, eclectic bunch whose livelihoods are bound up with the fortunes of Japan's current football superstar. They are . . .

> **The Exile:** came to Scotland 15 years ago, aged 14, without a word of English. Is now more steeped in Scottish culture than the majority of natives. He interprets, rather than reports, Nakamura's every word from Japanese to English.

> **The Itinerant:** the football anorak who left Japan to cover Italian football and has ended up reporting on every ball Nakamura has kicked for the last six years.

> **The Nightclubber:** the Tennent's Lager-swilling dance-music enthusiast who swapped Tokyo for Tollcross and has never looked back.

> **The Academic:** born in Glasgow, he spent 11 years teaching in Japan and now forms half of the only husband-and-wife sports reporting team in Scotland.

> **The Chef:** born in Japan, married to a Scot, he reports on Nakamura by day and indoctrinates eager Glaswegians on the joys of his native cuisine by night.

THE EXILE

The music starts up, and he strides on stage in full Highland regalia. There is a hushed silence followed by uproarious laughter and pointing. Unperturbed, he begins to dance, kilt swinging violently from side to side, feet an ever-quickening blur. The boy's got rhythm. The boy can dance. The smiles quickly turn to astonishment then admiration. 'Gaun yersel', son . . .' He now has them in the palm of his hand. They are clapping and cheering, whooping and hollering. The music stops, and he exits stage left, cheers trailing in his wake. He has won them round, danced them into submission. The way he does every night.

By day, Makoto Kaneko is the interpreter for the most famous Asian footballer on the planet. By night, he is Scotland's only Japanese Highland dancer. And surely the only interpreter in the world able to express himself even more eloquently with his feet. The 29-year-old Kaneko's life is a fascinating tale of courage, perseverance and talent.

The story begins at a swimming pool in Tokyo approximately 20 years ago. Ten-year-old Kaneko has just missed the qualifying time for the junior Olympics by one second. He is inconsolable. He is also tired: tired of swimming, of the endless lengths of the pool and the relentless early morning training sessions. He wants to try something else, something a bit more exciting. He wants to live a little. Enter Mother and Father Kaneko.

'My parents do what we call folk dancing but with a world perspective,' he explains. 'The dances are in various forms, such as country, American and Spanish. Basically, anything from around the world. They love Scottish country dancing, which is quite big in Japan. I went to a party one day, and I saw someone doing a demonstration of Highland dancing, which is a bit different from country dancing. It involves sword dancing, Highland flings and solo dancing. I thought, "That's great. I want to do that." I was amazed by the sound of bagpipes as well.'

And so the trunks were traded for a kilt, the goggles swapped for dancing shoes, the monotony of ploughing up and down a pool replaced by the thrill of perfecting a Highland fling. Kaneko had the dancing bug, Scottish-style. Blessed with natural ability, he had found not just a new hobby but an all-consuming passion. The Billy Elliot of the Bens was born. His early teenage years whizzed past in a blur of reels and jigs. He was seriously good but wanted to be even better. There was only one answer. Fast-forward three years and with junior high school drawing to a close in Tokyo, Kaneko instinctively knew that his future lay on the other side of the world. To perfect his art, he had to go to Scotland.

So, aged 14, Kaneko left Tokyo for boarding school at Merchiston Castle in Edinburgh. 'When I think back now, I say to myself, "How could I have done that?" But at the time I just wanted to dance,' he reflects. 'It must seem crazy to come to a country like Scotland without English – but because I just wanted to dance perhaps I thought I didn't need to speak. I wasn't even interested at all [in learning English]. My mum [also a talented dancer] had missed the chance to go to America and always regretted it, so she was happy for me to have the chance to go for it.

'I came to Scotland on my own, and it was very difficult initially. I went straight into boarding school in Edinburgh, but because I couldn't speak any English I couldn't communicate with other people and found it impossible to make friends. I cried every night in bed. I didn't go to any classes at Merchiston, so it was more like bed and breakfast. I went to English college in the morning and dancing classes in the evening. Students are not normally allowed to go outside, but I had permission to go to classes. At the weekends, there were competitions and Highland Games. I was basically dancing every day.'

Gradually, the loneliness and homesickness passed. Scotland did not seem such a bad place. The dancing was going well, and the growing collection of trophies on his mantelpiece was a reassuring sign of his talents. Aged 17, he was crowned East of Scotland Highland Dancing champion, a title which qualified him for the World Championships. His English had improved beyond recognition and other avenues began to open up. He left Merchiston and enrolled in a degree course in biochemistry at Heriot-Watt University in Edinburgh. 'It was good, totally different from boarding school, with so much freedom,' he says, smiling. 'I made good friends, and after lectures we would have a few pints in the union and then head out on the town.'

After graduating, he studied sports science at Telford College in Edinburgh for two years then completed his studies with a further year at the same institution, where he undertook a course in different forms of dance. Oh, and Kaneko also learned the bagpipes. His assimilation into Scottish culture was complete. 'I like the Scots – they're naturally very kind and friendly people,' he says. 'I felt that when I first came over. All my Japanese friends who visit Scotland say that they want to stay here.'

The 'real world' loomed, though, and he knew that the magic in his feet was not enough to pay the rent. Initially, he eked out a living by doing written translations of medical documents, but things took an unexpected turn one afternoon in the summer of 2005. 'After a year of translating, I was told that Shunsuke Nakamura was signing for Celtic and needed an interpreter. That was a real buzz. I knew of him because he was really famous in Japan. I was asked to go to Celtic Park the day before the press conference to announce his signing at 9 a.m. He was really nice to me from the beginning. We are the same age, and he sensed I was really nervous, so he spoke in short sentences. I thanked him afterwards.'

Little did Kaneko know just how much his life was about to change. Initial interpreting duties soon developed into a full-time post. Now the pair are joined at the hip. Where Nakamura goes, Kaneko follows. Nakamura's failure to learn English has kept Kaneko in a job and made him a regular fixture in and around Celtic Park. 'I basically follow him wherever he goes. We meet at the training ground, and I go into the dressing-room. When the players talk to him, I interpret. On the training pitch, I stand there and listen to what's going on and then interpret. I am everywhere. During the game, I am usually behind the dugout, although he can usually understand what the manager says to him during the match.

'His teammates, through me, speak to him quite a lot – just normal conversations. They were hesitant when he first arrived, but now they know that I'm there. I even went to the Christmas night out the first year. At the moment, he talks to Massimo Donati the most, because Naka speaks a bit of Italian. Artur Boruc speaks to him a lot, Jan Vennegoor of Hesselink, too, and big Mick [Stephen McManus] as well.'

Kaneko enters into the spirit of the job. On Celtic duty, he wears a club jacket and mixes well with the players and management. He even has a nickname – 'Macca' – and feels like an integral part of Gordon Strachan's side. 'I do feel like I am part of the team. It makes me feel great. I am just an interpreter, but I feel like one of the teammates. When they win, I celebrate with them. When they lose, I feel down as well. I'm even recognised at Celtic Park now. People have asked me for my autograph. Some people think I'm a player, so I always tell them I'm not. A few of them say, "I know. You're Nakamura's interpreter. I still want your autograph!" When fans come up to him in the street, I usually interpret for them, but if I'm not there, they just keep talking to him anyway. Every moment is great in this job . . . on the training ground, match days, abroad for the Champions League.'

However, it does have its awkward moments. Nakamura might be one of Strachan's most prized assets, but he is not immune to criticism. If he has not been performing, the Celtic manager shouts at him as he would any other player. Nakamura will sit typically passive as his manager forcefully tells him where he is going wrong. Kaneko must faithfully translate every word. 'That's quite a difficult moment to be a translator. You must try to translate *everything* he says, of course. Strachan is a very nice and funny guy. He has a great sense of humour. I get on very well with him, and so does Nakamura.'

In Kaneko, the Celtic midfielder has found a best friend as well as an interpreter. He has joked in interviews that if his English improves too much, he risks losing his right-hand man. Perhaps that is part of the reason his English lessons have fallen by the wayside. 'Sometimes, I go to his house and play with his son,' says Kaneko. 'Or we might go for a meal or ten-pin bowling, although he doesn't go out that much. We are good friends. He always says about Glasgow that the weather is too cold, but apart from that he loves it, and so does his family. He even asked me to join his family when they went to Paris recently. We get on pretty well. Of course, he is football mad.

'He is quiet. He doesn't talk a lot, even in Japanese. But he is very caring. I thought a famous footballer would say, "Just do this, just do that." But he's not like that. He is always saying, "Oh, you don't have to do this or that." I really feel that he relies on me. I like to help him, even away from Celtic Park. I don't have to do that, but I'm happy to. I interpret, translate, I go to the bank, shopping, book restaurants, fill in forms. He speaks a little English now, such as "good morning" and "see you later", but he can understand more than he can speak.'

Kaneko has one of the most eclectic CVs in the world: biochemist, sports scientist, Highland dancer, interpreter and translator. He could also add 'goalkeeper'. When Nakamura practises free-kicks after training (which he does every day), Kaneko acts as goalie. Clad in club jacket and with his arms spread out, he stands motionless on the goal-line as balls whiz past his ears. 'I'm not a goalkeeper at all,' he says, laughing. 'Truthfully, I am trying to escape from the ball. I really just stand where a goalkeeper would stand, and I then pick the ball out of the net. He asked me once if I could try and stop one. I would go to one side then he would switch and put it in the other. It was really funny. Once, I actually saved the ball and ended up with a big bruise, so I didn't even try after that.'

Most employees try to avoid seeing their boss on holiday, but there is no escape for Kaneko, particularly when he returns to Tokyo. 'If you go out in the town, there are huge advertising posters of Nakamura everywhere. When you're watching television, he will appear, or I'll be reading a magazine and say, "Oh, it's him again." When I first started the job, I found that very strange. He is everywhere.'

And what does Nakamura think of his friend's Highland dancing? 'He said to me, "I'm not sure about coming to watch you dance . . ." For Japanese people, to see a man wearing a skirt and dancing is a strange thing. He said to me, "Maybe if I see you dance in a kilt, I won't be able to speak to you again!"'

THE ITINERANT

Shin Toyofuku remembers his first taste of Scotland. When a hail of greasy chips slapped him on the back of the head, he knew that he had arrived. The date was 20 August 2005, and Toyofuku had been in Scotland for three weeks, dispatched to cover Nakamura's every movement for an audience of millions in the Far East. He had been impressed with Glasgow, seduced by the friendliness of the locals and the hospitality shown by Celtic. But now . . . now he was sitting in the middle of the main stand at Ibrox and could feel the hostility washing over him. 'It was the game in which Neil Lennon and Alan Thompson were sent off,' he recalls. 'The Japanese journalists were put beside the Rangers fans. I don't know what the Ibrox press officer was thinking. I got such a nice reception from the Rangers fans. Someone threw something, and it hit the back of my head. Someone else wrote in my notebook, "Fuck Nakamura". We were all crying!'

But Toyofuku is laughing at the memory, as if it was just another of the cultural curiosities he has stumbled upon since his Scottish odyssey began three years ago. He resolved that it would take more than a few stray chips to detract from his enjoyment of a derby he had always wanted to attend. After three years covering Italian football, and regular trips to the great Spanish derbies, he considered himself to be a big-game connoisseur but admits that his first experience of the Old Firm match simply blew him away. 'The rivalry with Celtic and Rangers is so famous. The Old Firm game was the one game I wanted to see since I was a young boy. My first time was incredible. The atmosphere and passion was amazing. At that point, I realised that I had arrived in Scotland.'

Toyofuku writes for *Hochi Shimbun*, a Japanese-language daily sports paper with a circulation of 1 million. He is to be found most days of the week with his mobile phone glued to his ear outside the club's training centre at Lennoxtown, pacing around the car park as he phones in his copy in a bid to meet the latest deadline. He speaks to Nakamura every day, even when there is nothing to report.

One example illustrates this perfectly. After Celtic's 1–0 defeat to Benfica in Lisbon in October 2007, the usual phalanx of Japanese scribes waited for Nakamura to pass through the mixed zone, the area reserved for interviews after Champions League games. When he appeared, there was a mini-stampede in his direction. The only problem was that Nakamura had not played. When they asked him to stop and speak, even he looked at them quizzically before obliging.

Toyofuku is in the big time now, living the dream of football aficionados the world over. He watches Champions League games, visits the best stadiums and gets paid for it. But it has not come easily. His journey to the top has not been without its sacrifices. Self-belief and a sprinkling of synchronicity have also played their part. Growing up in Fukuoka, in the south of Japan, his ambition was to become 'an expert on football'. 'When I was young, my father loved football, and it became a big passion for me, too. I started devouring football magazines, and this passion coincided with the launch of the J. League in 1993. From a Japanese perspective, football went global with its launch. World-famous players such as Zico, Gary Lineker and Pierre Littbarski arrived to light up the new league. It was such a new thing for me. I followed every single game of Kashima Antlers and knew instinctively that I wanted to become a football writer. My ambition was always to see the top professional clubs. And travel round the world. And earn money. Which is perfect. Thanks to the foundation the J. League gave me, I am now in this world.'

Very quickly, the teenage Toyofuku was drawn to the lustre of Serie A, which was then undergoing a renaissance. He rhymes off the world-class talents – 'The great Dutch trio of Ruud Gullit, Marco van Basten and Frank Rikjaard, Roberto Baggio, Franco Baresi . . .' – who fired his adolescent imagination and helped establish the Italian top-flight as the greatest league in the world during the late 1980s and early '90s. But he did not just want to watch from afar. Toyofuku wanted to be part of it. Phase one of his master plan began. In his mid-teens, he started to learn Italian. After four years at university in Tokyo, where he completed a business degree, he began phase two. Italy was where he wanted to be, so Italy was where he would go. So began the itinerant years.

'I went on my own to Milan to study. I enrolled in a language course to improve my Italian, and during that year I went to every European football match I could. I was writing some stuff for an Internet site, so I was making a little bit of money, but the big thing was that I could get accreditation for games. That was enough for me. I mostly went to AC and Inter games, but I also went all around Italy to watch matches. Through that, I got to know some sports editors from the Japanese media. After a year or so, I got a break I didn't expect and certainly never planned. Shunsuke Nakamura signed for Reggina, they called me up, we made a contract and I went down to cover him. It was very lucky. My dream had come true.'

If Tokyo to Milan had been a culture shock, then switching from Italy's bustling, industrial metropolis to the tiny Reggio Calabria, home of Reggina, required another transition period. Tentative at first, he was soon drawn out of his shell by the exuberant natives. Every day he turned up to watch Nakamura train, and every day he was besieged by inquisitive locals. 'I made a lot of friends in Reggio Calabria,' he says. 'I would meet people at the training ground, because training is open to everyone in Italy. I speak Italian, so it was not so difficult to make friends. Nakamura had many Italian supporters. Italians would come up to me and say, "Hey, Nakamura!" They are very open and friendly people. The city itself is very, very small. Sometimes it was hard to live there because there are no big-city shops and things like that. Italian and Japanese are completely opposite characters. Japanese people are more silent, but, as time passed, I got to like the Italian way. After four years, I became one-third Italian.'

Before the move to Reggina, he had never met Nakamura, although he diplomatically claims that 'he was my favourite [Japanese] player'. A relationship had to be established, and Toyofuku began to chip away at the midfielder's natural reticence. 'He was cautious at the start. He is a very, very private man. It's not easy to make a relationship with him, because he is not very open-minded. During the first year, I asked questions, and he answered, nothing more. So, the first year wasn't so easy. At first, we weren't friends. He was a player, and I was a journalist, but when I had to interview him we would sometimes go to a restaurant to have something before. Not every day and not every week, but sometimes.'

After two years of covering Nakamura, Toyofuku moved to Florence to report on Hidetoshi Nakata's fortunes at Fiorentina but was reunited with Naka a year later. The protracted deal that brought Nakamura to Parkhead heralded another change of city for the journalist. 'When I came to Scotland, my relationship with Shunsuke was closer, because I was the only one from the Italian period. Now we know each other very well. Following him every day is very difficult because, after a certain time, you run out of questions,' he reflects. 'Usually we ask, "What did you do today?" Or if something has happened in Japan, we will ask his opinion. He follows J. League games and is well-informed about the Japanese football scene.

'When he was at Reggina, I watched him practise free-kicks every day. We are not allowed into training at Celtic, which is very sad. I would like to see training even just once. In Italy and Spain, the training is open. How much I write depends on what is happening. We speak to him every day he is at the club – probably six days out of seven. I work for one of five daily sports newspapers in Japan.'

Swapping the southern Italian sun for Glasgow winters might not be everyone's idea of a good career move, but Toyofuku again embraced the chance to experience a new culture. He knew his history and knew that Glasgow was no ordinary city, Celtic no ordinary club. 'I first went to Milan, one of the biggest cities in Italy, then I went to one of the smallest cities in the country. Then I had the chance to go to Glasgow, which is a very important city in terms of its football history. To be there every day, at a big club like Celtic, was an amazing opportunity. Celtic are 1,000 times bigger than Reggina. Reggina are like . . . Inverness Caledonian Thistle. When you go into the trophy room at Celtic Park, you see the history. It has been a very positive thing in my life. I wanted to come here to improve my English and watch more Scottish and English football. It wasn't only for Nakamura; it was a new culture. I lived in London for a couple of months when I was 18 or 19 and enjoyed British life. When the opportunity of moving to Scotland came up, I thought, "This is my chance.'"

Toyofuku had watched Nakamura's subtle talents make a few ripples in Serie A. The more technical nature of Italian football suited him, but his team's status as perennial relegation candidates, together with the emphasis on defence, thwarted his opportunity for self-expression. More than anything, Nakamura needed a proper stage to allow his talents to flourish, a canvas more suited to his artistic skills. Toyofuku would never have predicted that a switch to the Scottish game could provide the catalyst for Nakamura's leap to becoming a world star. 'When he signed for Celtic, we thought, "This will be very hard for him," because Scottish football, to us, was very physical. We were uncertain about Nakamura's future in Scotland. But, of course, it went very, very well. In Japan, he has always been big, but when he moved to Celtic, and especially season 2006–07 [when Nakamura won both Player of the Year awards], his global value exploded. In Japan, they talked about the "Golden Quartet" of Nakata, Nakamura, Shinji Ono and Junichi Inamoto. Nakamura was second or third in that group when he signed for Celtic. Now he is top . . . top by miles.'

At 28, Toyofuku is young enough to still revel in his itinerant lifestyle. He might be a young man far from his homeland, but he has the opportunity to explore the world and use football as the vehicle. Another country, another language. After three years in Scotland, his English is impeccable, so too his Italian. Oh, and should Nakamura's dream of playing in the Spanish top-flight materialise, he also speaks fluent Spanish. So where next? 'Spain would be great,' he says, smiling.

'The Spanish league has always been Shunsuke's dream. I like Spain, too, and speak Spanish, so it would be easy for me to live there. But I think Nakamura will stay at Celtic or go back to Japan. He wants to go back to Japan before he is past his peak. He doesn't want to go back at 35. He wants to show what he has learned in Europe.'

THE NIGHTCLUBBER

Toyofuku's duck-to-water-like immersion in Scottish culture has been matched only by that of his close friend and colleague Daisuke Nakajima, a reporter for the *Sports Nippon* daily newspaper in Japan. We are sitting in a pub in Glasgow's city centre, near his flat in the fashionable Merchant City district. 'I love Tennent's Lager. It is the best beer in Scotland. In fact, it is the best beer in the world. Some Scottish food is good, but what are you doing frying pizzas?' he says, supping from his pint and dissolving into a fit of giggles.

The 29 year old comes from just outside Tokyo but has found his spiritual home in Glasgow. He is a regular on the Glasgow club scene and wiles away the night hours at The Sub Club and The Arches. 'Dance music does it for me,' he says, dismissing Toyofuku's passion for Belle and Sebastian, the Glasgow-based band who are 'big in Japan'. 'Too melancholic . . . I prefer house and techno,' he says, grinning. 'I like the Scottish people, the beer, the music, the football. Everything is very expensive, and the weather is bad, but I love Scotland. The Sub Club is amazing, and I love Slam at The Arches. I've met a lot of cool people on the pub and club scenes.'

Before, Nakajima was a freelance sports journalist based in Tokyo, where he covered just about every sport imaginable. 'I wrote about football, baseball, gymnastics, synchronised swimming, ice skating and martial arts, but my favourite sports are baseball and football. I was sharing a flat in Tokyo and working practically every hour of the day when the offer of a move to Scotland to cover Nakamura presented itself. I jumped at it.'

From the sophisticated and cosmopolitan city of Tokyo, he moved to Tollcross, a working-class district of Glasgow near Celtic Park. 'I had a limited budget, and I had to find a flat as soon as possible. Why Tollcross? Well, it was very close to Celtic Park, but best of all it only cost me £375 a month. It was just a one-room ground-floor flat. No furniture, just a bed, a TV and a CD player. No curtains.

'I didn't know anybody, but the people were very kind. I used to go to the local pub to watch Rangers games, and everybody was so friendly. The first time I walked in, a guy came straight up to me: "You're new here. I'll get you a hauf [whisky]." They were full of questions: "Where are you from?", "What are you doing here?", "Where are you staying?" When I explained about the flat, they said, "Get yourself a pair of curtains if you want to keep your furniture, son."

'I ended up staying there for six months, and it was a good experience. I cycled to Celtic Park from Tollcross every day to speak to Nakamura and chained my bike up outside. There is no safer place than outside the stadium, because the same people are always hanging around waiting to meet the players. They came to recognise me and knew that I was there to interview Nakamura. But I had no Internet connection in the flat, so I would go to an Internet café to file my stories. I enjoyed my time there, but I have moved into the town centre now to be closer to the clubs.'

Nakajima and Toyofuku have formed a close relationship with Nakamura during his time at Celtic. 'I've played him at Pro Evolution Soccer,' says Nakajima, giggling. 'He has the J. League version. He won every game. I never beat him once.'

They are both immensely proud of the Japanese midfielder and his achievements in Scotland, but Toyofuku describes the relationship as unique. 'When he plays bad, we have to write that,' he insists. 'We are not so close friends, because you have to keep a certain distance. If you become a close friend, that is the end of you as a journalist.'

Nakajima agrees, but there is a clear bond between the journalists and player, who are all roughly the same age. 'Naka likes to talk to the press after games. He just loves talking about football, and we usually speak to him for more than 20 minutes,' says Nakajima. 'He now comes to speak to us before he does his regular gym session after games. He is a very gentle and kind man. Last season, he took all the Japanese journalists out to dinner. He paid, of course.'

Nakajima has also been the grateful recipient of Nakamura's Man of the Match champagne. 'He doesn't drink alcohol, so when he wins the Man of the Match award he will give me the champagne. I go home and drink it and shout, "I'm man of the match!"'

THE ACADEMIC

'Is Nakamura already a Celtic legend?' James Morrison lets the question hang in the air, turning it over in his mind. It is a chin-stroker, a prime subject for a pub debate. Appropriately, he takes a long sip of his beer. Few are better placed to reflect on Nakamura's impact in Scotland than the 37-year-old Glaswegian. Morrison is the senior member of Nakamura's press entourage and straddles both Scottish and Japanese cultures. Born and bred a corner-kick away from Hampden Park, he is steeped in the history of Scottish football, Celtic's in particular. He also knows what it takes to be a Celtic legend. 'It's a difficult one. Would Stiliyan Petrov be classed as a Celtic legend? He was there for seven years and scored plenty of goals, but he didn't have the sublime skills of Naka. I think Naka is halfway there.'

Morrison is a fluent Japanese speaker, having moved to Japan to teach English after graduating from Strathclyde University, aged 22. He planned to stay for two years, but hung around for eleven, marrying a Japanese woman called Yuko. In the west of Scotland, one of the most intense newspaper markets in the world, the Morrisons' names would not draw even a flicker of recognition. It is ironic, then, that the copy they file daily marks them out as two of the most widely read football correspondents in Britain. They work for *Nikkan Sports*, a Japanese daily sports newspaper that was founded in 1946 and commands a daily readership of 2 million. Like his Japanese colleagues, Morrison is also living the dream, but for different reasons. He has what all fans crave: an insight into the inner sanctum. 'I have been able to see the workings of the club I've supported all my life. It's been an eye-opener in more ways than one. Being able to talk to the players and coaches whom my friends idolise is a big thing. I am really happy with the way Celtic have accepted the Japanese press.'

Scottish journalism's only husband-and-wife team first met in the unlikely environs of The Horseshoe Bar, Glasgow's famous drinking house with the longest bar in Britain. 'She was on exchange in Glasgow and was out with a couple of friends. I met her again in Japan, and the rest is history.' It did not take Morrison long to indoctrinate his wife with the history of his team. 'She's now a Celtic fan because of me. We watched the UEFA Cup final in 2003 at 4 a.m. in Japan, even though she was about to have a baby. She enjoys the job, especially mingling with the other Japanese on the Nakamura team.'

When they moved back to Scotland, they began the ultimate job-share. During the week, he is a school teacher and Yuko reports on Nakamura. At weekends, he covers the games. Morrison is a likeable, easy-going character, a friendly, unobtrusive presence around the club. He explains the mechanics of their role. 'We get information from newspapers, magazines or websites here, basically anything in English that deals with Naka. Two or three times a week, plus after games, we will speak to him and get a comment on his condition. I phone in the quotes as soon as possible. On a good day, we get a quote at 1 p.m., which I phone in straight away. That is 9 p.m. in Japan. The sports desk at *Nikkan* take the comments and make them into a story. They will ask for an input in terms of how the team is shaping up, so we report, and they write. That's the way it works for all foreign correspondents. *Nikkan Sports* has 2 million readers a day, but, remember, there are 12 million people in Tokyo alone, 127 million in Japan. The paper is a cross between *The Herald* and the *Daily Record,* maybe more towards the *Record.* The amount of coverage Nakamura gets all depends on what he has done. If he has helped Celtic win, he will be on the front page. After the Manchester United game, there were two or three pages on him, maybe more. In football terms, he is number one in Japan.'

Although he enjoys a cordial relationship with his subject, there were teething problems at the start. 'He took something I said the wrong way. The Japanese way is to start a question and allow him to take over. My style was more Scottish, in that I fired questions at him. I have had to learn to think Japanese as well as speak it. He has ups and downs like everyone else, but he never really shows it. Having said that, if he has had a bad day, you can tell. When he's injured, he's never in the best frame of mind.

'It's difficult following one player all the time. If I jeopardise the relationship with Naka, I jeopardise my newspaper's relationship with him as well, and that becomes a problem. I am also foreign, so I don't have the same relationship as someone such as Shin, who has been with him for six years.'

There is a video of Nakamura aged 18 when he was a young player at Yokohama Marinos. It is a short documentary interspersed with training-ground footage and interviews. In one clip, he is practising his free-kicks on the training ground at night. Endless streams curl over the wall and nestle in the corner. Then, suddenly, the training ground plunges into darkness. The groundsman has switched the lights off on Nakamura. It says everything about the obsessive lust for self-improvement that has driven his career. Later, he is pictured in his house, wolfing down a bowl of rice and rewinding a video of a match.

Self-analysis has been another keystone of his success, as Morrison has come to appreciate. 'A lot of it is about specifics. He has played on two continents now, and he has always looked back and analysed his performances. That is what has helped Naka become a better player. He is fiercely self-critical. If he gets two free-kicks in the one game, he might miss one, but he will get the second – or at least get it on target. A lot of players might look back on games and say, "I had a bad game, and I just want to forget about it." Naka doesn't do that. He looks back at his mistakes and analyses them. He also has copies of his best moments, but it's not an ego thing. It's because he wants to work out what he did right. In the Dundee United game [when Nakamura scored a hat-trick], he didn't do anything the whole match but put the ball in the net three times. He was quite humble and honest enough to admit that he didn't do anything.'

Attention to detail is another vital aspect of Nakamura's character. 'When the team plays in different competitions, such as the CIS Cup, Premier League and Champions League, they use different balls. That is a big thing for Naka. Artur Boruc said that the Champions League ball is very difficult for goalkeepers to catch, but for a player such as Naka it is great because it allows him to put so much bend on the ball. Given his attention to detail, I would imagine he would practise with the Champions League ball before Champions League games.

'When Naka moves on, that will be our stint finished. Hopefully, he will stay for another four or five years.'

THE CHEF

Makoto Sassaki is a novice compared to the football obsessives that are Nakajima and Toyofuku. In many ways, however, he is the responsible older brother to his two young friends. He is also a man on a mission to convert Glaswegians to the delights of sushi. Every Monday, Sassaki, a chef by trade, teaches a night class on Japanese cooking at Langside College on the south side of Glasgow, where he shares the delights of his country's cuisine. Don't mention supermarket sushi, though. 'Crap shite,' he says. 'Don't ever touch it. Sushi is meant to be eaten the same day. It is not going to last two or three days. Good rice is the key to good sushi. You can get fantastic seafood in Scotland, but sushi can be vegetables or even cooked meat. It's basically soy sauce, sugar and *dashi* [a Japanese soup stock].' Not that he is unacquainted with the delights of Scottish cuisine. The 33 year old might be the only man in Scotland to eschew salt and vinegar for lashings of soy sauce on his fish supper. You can take the boy out of Japan . . .

Sassaki has even more strings to his bow than Kaneko. He teaches Japanese cooking at night, works the graveyard shift in Asda and reports on Nakamura for *Sankei Sports*, a Japanese sports daily newspaper, by day. Allegedly, he sleeps occasionally. In October 2007, he travelled to Portugal to cover Celtic's game against Benfica in the Champions League. The match was on a Wednesday night. Sassaki's schedule was as follows. 'On Monday, I worked in Asda during the day and then taught my night class in the evening. Then I got up on Tuesday morning for a 5 a.m. shift in Asda, finished at 10 a.m. and headed to the airport to fly to Lisbon. The last time I went to Lisbon [when Celtic played the Portuguese side in 2006], I met a few Celtic fans on the way. They saw me reading the *Evening Times* and bought me a couple of pints. I had a great time.'

Perhaps it is something to do with Sassaki's impish sense of humour, or his passion for cigarettes, that makes him seem more Scottish than most natives. He met his wife, a Scot, in Japan, where she was teaching English, and jumped at the chance of moving back to her homeland. 'I was fed up in Japan working as a chef in a very small restaurant. I also did lots of factory jobs. I made water gates for canals and dams. I can weld. I can operate forklift trucks. I can drive seven and a half tonnes in Japan. But I wanted a new challenge, and I also wanted to learn more English.

'There was just something I liked about Scotland. Scottish people are very quick with their humour. They are full of cheeky but very funny comments. When I moved to Scotland six years ago, I started studying English at Langside College, and then I got a job working in The Arthouse Hotel. After a couple of years in the kitchen, I had barely seen daylight at all and was getting depressed, so I chucked it. Then I heard Naka was coming.'

Sassaki knew little about Nakamura before he arrived, his only knowledge of football stemming from a passing interest in his home-town team Sanfrecce Hiroshima. Initially, he had hoped to get the job as his interpreter. 'The Scottish Japanese Residents' Association put me forward for the job, but I didn't get it. *Sankei Sports* then got in touch and said, "Do you know someone who can cover Nakamura?" I didn't have a job at the time, so I thought, "Great. I'll do it." I had to learn about football very quickly. I could understand the rules, but it was a case of learning who was who. I kept asking Shin and Daisuke. Going to the games allows you to see the whole thing – Naka's little tricks and vision. I really enjoy watching him now. He was quite reserved at the start, and I didn't ask many questions, mainly because I didn't know what to ask. These days, it is OK. I can ask things. Between the four of us, we always come up with something to ask him. If he is injured, we can ask him how he is that day. If he says, "Same as yesterday," it is just a quick call to the desk.'

Sassaki usually drives their little group to away games. 'When we first went to Inverness, we took the scenic route up past Loch Long, Glencoe, Fort William and then Inverness. By the time we got to Loch Ness, it was dark. Shin and Daisuke wanted to go back the next day and see it in the daylight. I said to them, "All you'll see is a plastic monster. There's no point." But we went back anyway, and they went in paddling. I was tempted to push them right in!'

THE REST ...

Nakamura is not the only Japanese footballer to have his own press pack. Hidetoshi Nakata had reporters following his every move when he first moved from J. League side Bellmare Hiratsuka to Perugia in 1999. Ironically, his poor relationship with the Japanese media led to him refusing to give any interviews. Thus, the reporters who were paid to report on his every word were left high and dry, their only copy being provided by Italian journalists, whom Nakata was more than happy to give interviews to.

When Junichi Inamoto signed for Arsenal in 2001, his introductory press conference was attended by 100 Japanese journalists. If writing about the same footballer every day can seem tedious in the case of Nakamura, then the 'Glasgow Five' can content themselves with the fact that at least their man plays regularly.

At Arsenal's weekly press conference, Inamoto's faithful troop of journalists would turn up and, without fail, ask the same question of manager Arsène Wenger: 'Will Inamoto play tomorrow?' They nearly always received the same one-word answer.

In his one season on loan at Highbury from Gamba Osaka, he played just 149 minutes. As a result, the Japanese reporters were forced to cover games in the FA Premier Reserve League South. Incredibly, the matches were even screened on a satellite channel back in his homeland.

Inamoto's press pack followed him throughout his time in English football, from Arsenal to Fulham, West Brom and then Cardiff City. They then tracked him to Turkey in 2006 when he signed for Galatasaray and are currently stationed in Germany, where he is turning out for Eintracht Frankfurt.

Shinji Ono's £5.45 million move from Urawa Red Diamonds to Feyenoord in 2001 sparked hysteria in the press in his homeland. Upon his arrival in Rotterdam, Ono was followed everywhere he went, and a group of around 40 Japanese reporters would turn up every day to record his every word and movement. They filed stories on Ono every day despite the fact that he rarely gave interviews.

FIVE

· · · · · · · · · ·

Bridging the Divide

SHUHEI TAKAHASHI IS A BRIDGE BUILDER. NOT LITERALLY, but culturally. In 2004, he arrived in Edinburgh to begin a three-year spell as Japanese Consul General. His brief was to find common ground and foster better relations between the two countries. For a year, he chipped away at the coalface, drilling little holes that he hoped might burst forth in a fountain of fellowship between Scotland and Japan. Then one day he received a phone call. It was Peter Lawwell inviting him to Celtic Park for the unveiling of the club's first-ever Japanese signing, Shunsuke Nakamura. Takahashi sat bolt upright in his seat. This was big. For the previous 12 months, he had been trying to make little differences wherever he could. And now . . . now the ultimate Japanese ambassador had landed on his doorstep. His dreams of greater unity could now become a reality thanks to the Far East's biggest football star. Needless to say, he jumped at the chance of going to Celtic Park, where he was taken aback by the hospitality of his reception and the level of interest in Nakamura.

'At his first press conference, I gave many interviews to Japanese television stations. That was the first time I met Shunsuke, and

I was very impressed by his characteristics. He was a very nice person and also very shy. Then we went along to watch his debut with some other members of the Japanese community. He was made Man of the Match, and I still remember the nice comments of Gordon Strachan, who said it was one of the best debuts he had seen.

'At his debut match, I was allowed to bring my whole family and took my son and daughter along. My youngest son was six years old, and we all met Shunsuke at the back of the reception hall after the game. He doesn't smile very often, but when he saw my youngest son he started grinning and said, "Your son is just like my son." Shunsuke's son was only six months old at the time, so there was a big difference in ages, but he saw similarities. That was the beginning of my son's passion for football. He will never be as skilful as Nakamura, but he is second to none in terms of the time he spends playing. He now plays four times a week and dreams of being a footballer like Shunsuke. He changed my son's and my family's life.'

His impact has not stopped there. The presence of Nakamura has also had a positive spin-off for Scottish tourism, and Japanese football fans make regular pilgrimages to Scotland to watch their hero in the flesh. Throngs can often be spotted milling around Celtic Park on match days as they soak up the history and atmosphere of the club, together with a visit to the nearby Celtic superstore. 'A lot of Japanese people come to Scotland to watch Shunsuke play now,' added Takahashi. 'They stay for one match, and the trip costs them £2,000 in total. Many Japanese are fascinated by the beauty of Scotland. As the Japanese consul, I could only do small things, but Shunsuke made a big impact on our cultural exchanges.'

Despite the cultural differences, Takahashi has been hugely impressed by the way the Scottish public, and Celtic fans in particular, have embraced Nakamura and his followers. 'I remember reading an article in the paper about a Celtic fan who had gone to Japan and come back with lots of Japanese food to present to

Shunsuke. The fan was doing his best to make Shunsuke feel at home, and that was a very symbolic thing. Shunsuke has inspired many people in Scotland and Japan to find out more about each other's countries.

'I know that Shunsuke found a big difference between his experiences in Scotland and life in Italy. He was quite badly treated in Italy. He played there for three years, and on his birthday a coach presented him with a yellow T-shirt, representing the colour of his skin. It is abuse by any standard, but he just smiled and got on with it. But in Glasgow he was so well received, and he has told me directly how much he appreciates the efforts of the Scottish people. In my three years in Scotland, I have also come to realise that Scottish people have warm hearts, open minds and charitable spirits. I refer to "Scottish people" in the broader sense, including people who see themselves as Scottish and also those who love Scotland even more than the natives.

'I often feel that Scottish people have more "Japanese-ness" than native Japanese. They consider duty and possessing a warm, kind heart important qualities. Scottish people regard the connection and bond between people as more important than anything else.'

Nakamura's impact has also sparked interest in the Japanese language among primary- and secondary-school pupils in Scotland. The Learning Centre at Celtic Park, run in conjunction with Glasgow City Council, now offers youngsters taster sessions, involving learning to write their name in Japanese, traditional drumming and origami.

Secondary pupils have the opportunity to take their interest to the next level. 'We are now accredited to offer a GCSE course in Japanese language,' explains Tony Russell, the coordinator of the Celtic Learning Centre. 'The impact of Nakamura at Celtic has led to an upsurge in interest in all things Japanese. Initial interest for the CGSE class has been strong. Koki Mizuno dropped into the centre recently, and we hope that Nakamura will make an appearance soon.'

So, Nakamura has sparked interest in all things Japanese among Scots, as well as attracting an influx of tourists into the country. However, his presence has also had a trickle-down effect for the sizeable Japanese community already based in Scotland. Kumiko Hatori is the prime mover in the Scottish Japanese Residents' Association, which now has a membership in the hundreds. She works closely with the consulate in Edinburgh to ease the transition of Japanese people to her adopted homeland. When she is not acting as an interpreter for the NHS, businesses or police, she is teaching Scots how to cook sushi at her weekly classes or organising a wide range of community activities aimed at deepening the relationship between Scotland and Japan. Although she is based in Glasgow's West End, the association's involvement extends throughout Scotland to Japanese residents based in places such as Edinburgh and Stirling. Hatori has lived in London, New York, Tokyo and Amsterdam but has found greater freedom and a better outlet for her creative tendencies in Glasgow. She is married to a Scot and revels in the laid-back lifestyle and natural beauty of Scotland.

'I have been away from Japan for 23 years,' she says. 'In Japan, we have to travel a lot to reach nature, but you can find unspoiled nature very close by in Scotland. Life is lovely when you can be creative. Japan is very compact, a small, heavily populated island. There is no space for a quiet, nice life. I want to work with and for people, to help out in the community. Scottish people are wonderful. I have never had a bad experience. I have stayed in London, New York, Tokyo and Amsterdam, but Glasgow is the most comfortable place to stay. It has good gardens, good parks and you are near the countryside. Glasgow is also less pretentious than most metropolitan cities. Japanese women come to Scotland and enjoy more respect and freedom. Japan is a very rules-based society, and many women have found the freedom to be themselves away from Japan.'

The association has also been galvanised by Nakamura's switch to Scotland. Hatori was invited to attend his first press conference and gratefully accepted the player's offer of six season tickets for the association, which are regularly passed around its members. 'Great is the only word to describe Celtic Park. When I went to a game there, the people around me were singing that song "Turning Japanese" in tribute to Shunsuke. That was amazing.'

Hatori was even suggested for the job of Nakamura's interpreter but was prevented from taking it by one logistical problem. 'Peter Lawwell said to me, "We couldn't give you the job because you would have to work in a room full of naked men!"'

Nakamura's hectic schedule of games and commercial commitments have prevented him from fully integrating with the Japanese community in Scotland. His shyness is also a contributing factor. Both Takahashi and Hatori have extended numerous invites to various social functions, but most have been politely declined. 'I invited him to different occasions, such as the New Year and National Day receptions, but he was always too busy. He promised me once that he would visit my house and have dinner with my family, but his schedule was always too full,' lamented Takahashi. 'He did send his interpreter, Makoto Kaneko, to an event once when he could not make it along, and that was a great thrill for everyone. I was able to say in my speech that we had a representative of Nakamura with us.'

In a wider sense, Nakamura is quick to embrace his position as a role model for Japanese youngsters. Takahashi tells the story of a young Japanese boy with a physical disability whose dream was to meet Nakamura in person. The youngster's story was the subject of a television documentary in his homeland and offers a unique insight into the footballer's personality. 'It is a very heart-warming story. The boy started practising football because he was a fan of Nakamura. He was talented and was selected as a regular in his primary-school football team. He entered junior high and was very successful there as a footballer. But he was not a normal boy. His leg below his right knee was artificial, because the flow of blood stopped when he was in his mother's womb, stunting the growth of his legs, hands and fingers. But he could play football very well with his artificial leg. One of his dreams was to become a professional footballer like Nakamura. The other dream was to meet Shunsuke and play together. The latter dream came true in October 2006. He was invited to Celtic Park to play with Shunsuke. He very sincerely told the boy how to hit a good free-kick. Shunsuke ended up being the one who expressed gratitude, because he got so much encouragement from the boy's story. He promised the boy he would play well the next day, away to Dundee United, and he went on to score a hat-trick in the game. Afterwards, he presented the boy with the Man of the Match champagne, the boots he had worn and the match ball. The boy thanked Nakamura, who said, "It's you who gave me courage. I will keep up the good work." The documentary on the boy was broadcast on Japanese TV and was very touching.

'The boy had been touched by Nakamura's humbleness and the spirit to do his best in every situation. It was this attitude, rather than Nakamura's performance, that inspired the boy to challenge his own limitations and continue to pursue his own dreams. It is well known that Shunsuke is first to arrive at the training ground and last to leave. Many Japanese people are impressed by his characteristics. Shunsuke struggled to make it as a professional because he was not physically strong enough. He went back to high school and practised his skills all the time. When he graduated, he had practised so much that he had become a top player. He had come back like a phoenix.'

Koji Morimoto is another to have experienced Nakamura's impact both in Scotland and in Japan. He spent five years in Scotland working for OKI, the Japanese electronics company, at their Cumbernauld plant and last year returned to his homeland, where he is based in Takasaki. Over a plate of sushi in a downtown bar in Tokyo, he admits that he pines for a return to Scotland. His five years there allowed him to indulge two of his passions: golf and Celtic. He developed the latter after the arrival of Nakamura, and he chatters excitedly about the impact of his countryman in Scotland.

Morimoto watched from high up in the Jock Stein stand the night that Nakamura scored his famous free-kick against Manchester United. He flips open his laptop to show me a commercial for an electrical store in Japan. The advert features Nakamura having a kickabout with some children in the shadow of Celtic Park. He tells me proudly that two of the children are his own.

'One of Nakamura's agents contacted the school, which is based at St Margaret's Academy in Livingston, for young Japanese children in Scotland. My daughter Mayu and son Ryota both attended the school every Saturday. They were making an advert for one of the big electrical stores in Japan, Yamada Denki. I went along with them and got Nakamura's autograph and shook his hand. He has become a hero for my children, and my son now has a big dream to become a footballer player. I would like to return to Scotland, if possible. I would also like my children to go to a Scottish university.' There is an unmistakeable glint in his eye when he suggests St Andrews, coincidentally the home of golf, as a possible option for his offspring's further education.

Parkhead is another sporting venue that holds special significance for him. 'I went to Celtic Park five or six times for games. I took my son along to a Celtic v. Hearts game, and he was really excited by the atmosphere. The Celtic supporters were very kind to us. "Are you Nakamura's brother?" they shouted. One of the supporters gave my son money to buy sweets. It was a much better atmosphere than baseball games. I am a Celtic supporter now and would remain so even if Nakamura left. I love Celtic, golf and Tennent's Lager.'

Good players attract admiration; great players inspire devotion. Nakamura falls into the latter category. In February 2008, he was invited to be the guest of honour at the Celtic Supporters Association annual rally in the Glasgow Royal Concert Hall. The previous guests of honour, dating back to just after the Second World War, have included Danny McGrain, Kenny Dalglish, Jimmy Johnstone, Billy McNeill and Jock Stein. The honour has also been bestowed on more modern players, such as Paul McStay, Henrik Larsson and Neil Lennon. Length of service is one criteria, extraordinary ability is another. Hence the reason that Lubo Moravčík was invited to be the guest of honour despite only being at the club for less than four years. Similarly, Nakamura's invite came after just two and a half years in Scotland. 'That was notable from our point of view,' says Jim Divers, the vice president of the association. 'With the movement of players now, it is harder to judge who to give it to. Lubo Moravčík was special. Henrik Larsson was, too. I think you have to recognise that Nakamura is also someone unique, a Japanese player who has come to this country and will now live for ever in the memory of Celtic supporters because of the goals he has scored. When we sent the invite to Nakamura, we sent a letter confirming that he would also be in our hall of fame.'

Tommy Dornan, the association's head of public relations, emphasises the fact that Nakamura's contributions will live long in the club's history. 'On the same night, an award was given to Billy McNeill on behalf of the centenary team, which won the league and cup Double in 1988, so that tells you what kind of level Nakamura is at. I think people have taken to him not just because of his abilities, particularly from free-kicks, but because of the way he is so laid-back and friendly. You never hear any problems from him. He has a wonderful attitude. Even when he plays a good game, he will often come out afterwards and say, "I don't think I played very well there, and I don't understand why people were applauding me." Then he will go straight to the gym.'

The evening itself was centred around the presence of Nakamura, with Kenichi Suganuma, the new Japanese consul general, and his wife also in attendance and a huge banner hanging at the back of stage with the player's face on it. A boisterous atmosphere prevailed as a variety of acts had the sell-out crowd on their feet, but it was nothing compared to the eruption that greeted Nakamura's arrival on stage to receive his award. An audience of young and old chanted 'Di Di Di Diri Nakamura', the player's signature song to the tune of the classic dance track 'Papa's Got a Brand New Pigbag'. Typically, Nakamura looked a bit embarrassed at the adulation but, through Kaneko, insisted, 'I couldn't do it without your support.' Cacophonous cheers rose up again, and he walked off smiling from ear to ear.

In a basement bar in Tokyo, 12,000 miles away, Nakamura is helping to bridge the cultural divide. It is 4.45 a.m. in Paddy Foley's Irish Bar in Roppongi, the spiritual home of the Tokyo Celtic Supporters Club. On street level, Tokyo's party district is in full swing with a mixture of night crawlers and insomniac Japanese salarymen enjoying the unique attractions offered by the area. Foley's is a haven, a football-friendly joint in a district of fleshpots, and tonight the atmosphere is buzzing.

It is Barcelona v. Celtic in the last 16 of the Champions League, and the anticipation is huge. A 3–2 deficit from the first leg, which all but killed Celtic's chances, has not prevented everyone from rising at an ungodly hour of the night to support their team. As the teams prepare for kick-off, a chorus of the Celtic anthem has the walls shaking. Ryuji Mizuno, a businessman by day and Celtic enthusiast by night, leads the singalong. 'You'll Neeeveeer Walk Alooone . . .' he bellows, doing an uncanny impression of a bag of drowning kittens. A predominantly Japanese and female crowd, peppered with expats, joins in with gusto.

Mizuno is a Nakamura devotee, as are all his boisterous chorus line, but his connection with the club transcends the presence of the Japanese midfielder. He is a Henrik Larsson fan and first grew to love the club through following the legendary Swedish striker's career. Then Nakamura signed and Mizuno became a regular at the Tokyo CSC. Now he is a diehard. Tonight he is wearing a Celtic away strip with 'McManus 44' on the back. 'McManusss . . .' he screams as the camera pans past the Celtic captain before kick-off. 'I like his strength, his leadership skills and the way he captains the team,' says Mizuno, smiling, when asked why the rugged Celtic captain had won a place in his affections. 'I love Celtic and went over for the Old Firm game [in January 2008], but it was cancelled because of Phil O'Donnell's death. It's great having Nakamura there as well. What's impressed me most about Nakamura is that although he's Japanese, his heart and soul is Celtic.' The same could be said for Mizuno.

The Tokyo CSC was established in 2001 after a couple of expat Celtic fans decided to congregate with some like-minded folk and raise a glass to the successful early years of the Martin O'Neill reign. Ronnie McMillan, one of the founding members, tried his luck by putting an advertisement in Tokyo's *Metropolis* – a local free sheet for the expatriate community – and so the Tokyo CSC was born. Back then, there were no webcasts or coverage of the Scottish Premier League on Japanese TV. The members asked fellow CSCs in Scotland and America to send them videotapes of the matches, which usually arrived a fortnight after the games had been played. Around a dozen of them would meet in Paddy's for a few pints of Guinness to watch a game they already knew the score of.

At the 2002 World Cup, Paddy's reputation began to spread, and the pub became a second home for supporters of the Irish national team. In 2003, Andy Ferguson, the president of the Tokyo CSC, made a forty-four-hour return trip to Seville along with five other members for Celtic's appearance in the UEFA Cup final against Porto. Then, in the summer of 2005, Celtic announced the signing of Nakamura, the club's first-ever Japanese player, and interest levels went through the roof. Suddenly, every match was shown live in Japan on SKY PerfecTV!, and the club's profile was increased by regular features in the Scottish press. They also built an impressive website, which is now run by an Australian journalist called Anthony Fensom, who used to be a staff writer for the *Daily Yomiuri* and has now moved back to his homeland. The club started out as a small gathering of folk, but it began to attract more and more Japanese people eager to follow the fortunes of their country's number one soccer star. Now, the club is 70 per cent Japanese, sprinkled with a mixture of different nationalities. It is also a haven for celebrity Celtic fans and has been visited by bands such as Mogwai and The Fratellis when they are on tour in Japan.

On the night of the Barcelona game, the usual gathering of Japanese fans, around 60 per cent of whom are women, have staged their usual boisterous occupation of Paddy's. As the camera follows Nakamura before kick-off, a cheer goes up, but a louder one greets Aiden McGeady, while Artur Boruc is also a popular figure. As well as the McManus-loving Mizuno, another Japanese fan has a shirt with Evander Sno's name and number on the back. Nakamura's legacy has been to create a genuine interest in Celtic beyond his own popularity. 'If Nakamura left Celtic, a couple of them would fall away, but most would stay. They would miss the *craic* too much,' says Neil Day, the manager of Paddy's and a Celtic fan from Ireland. 'Even if the diehards can't be here, then the Japanese fans will still sing the songs and cheer them on in the same way. The core of Japanese people will always run the club. You see girls here at four, five, six in the morning, and they are willing to come to Roppongi, which is a district that can be a bit dodgy, because they know this pub is safe. It's growing every year. When Nakamura is playing, more and more will support the team. Koki Mizuno joining will create even more interest.'

'Close him down,' barks Martin Burns, the Tokyo CSC's own Vesuvius, whose dulcet Glaswegian tones provide the soundtrack to the first 20 minutes of the game. Celtic find themselves 1–0 down after three minutes, and Burns is not happy. If the Japanese contingent are the life and soul of the Tokyo CSC, then Burns is the smiling face. Or the booming voice. He was born in Coatbridge and left Scotland at the age of 21 for London to pursue a career in acting. There, he converted to Buddhism, fell in love with a Japanese woman, moved to Saitama and has never looked back. Well, that's not quite true. He admits to serious pangs of homesickness when he moved to Japan five years ago, but his transition was eased by the camaraderie he found in Paddy's. 'I was so happy to discover the Celtic Supporters Club when I came out here,' says Burns, who grew up idolising Kenny Dalglish. 'I was so homesick for Scotland, and this place felt like an oasis. I could come here, drink beer, shout at the TV, and eat pie and beans.

'The interest levels now are phenomenal. Japanese people come here because they are interested in Naka, but they stay because they have such a fun time. The AC Milan game in the last 16 of last year was the best night we have had in here. The build-up was huge, and we had people come down who had never been here before. At one point, we were all playing football outside, and the police came down and told us to be quiet. They were filming for the ITV show *Champions League Weekly*, too, and it was an amazing atmosphere. Once a month, we have an official get-together, and there are usually 30 to 40 people. The majority are Japanese. If it is a Celtic and Rangers game or a cup final, then we will fill the place, which means more than 100 folk.'

Burns cut his acting teeth in shows such as *Taggart*, *Rab C. Nesbitt* and *The Bill*, and is about to fulfil an ambition by playing the lead role in a stage version of *Richard III*. 'I formed a theatre company with like-minded people, and at the end of this year I will play my dream role. I feel I am now at the right age and stage of my career to do it. I once held a record on *Taggart* for the amount of takes for one shot. I was playing a car thief, and the scene took 22 takes. Twenty-one were because of technical faults, and one was my fault, because I slipped.

'I was getting into acting at the same time as Robert Carlyle. He was a mad Rangers fan, a lovely guy. He said if I wanted to be a good Scottish actor, then I should stay in Scotland, but if I wanted to be a good actor, then I should leave. I left for London and got hardly any work for about five years. I think his plan was to get rid of me and become the darling of Scottish cinema.

'As well as acting, I teach English to Japanese children and indoctrinate them in the Celtic way. Sometimes I wear my Celtic shirt, and when I do they all come running up to me and shout "Nakamura!" The Japanese mentality is that when someone moves abroad, they become even bigger. If Nakamura buys a bag of chips, it is reported here. He is the big soccer idol in Japan.

'People say he disappears in games, but I don't think that. The opposition put two or three men on him, and he can hardly move. He's a fantastic player, one of the most skilful we've got.'

Despite Barcelona passing Celtic off the park, the atmosphere remains good-natured, with one well-oiled backpacking couple from Dublin conducting the Japanese crowd in various singalongs. Liam O'Hare, a 19-year-old Celtic fan from Maryhill in Glasgow, sups his pint at the back of the pub and laments Gordon Strachan's refusal to introduce Scott McDonald to the Celtic attack. O'Hare left Hillhead High School in the summer of 2007 and is working at the Iwatake Ski Resort in Hakuba as part of his gap year. His far-flung location has not prevented him from following his team, though. 'I stay in the dormitories at the ski resort, and we worked out that if we went to one of the windows in the corridor then we could pick up a faint Internet connection from one of the nearby hotels. I have managed to get about 10–15 foreigners together – Aussies, New Zealanders and English – as many people as I can persuade to get up at that time in the morning. We sit beside this window with our laptop watching games such as Celtic v. Inverness Caledonian Thistle or St Mirren. It's a rubbish Internet connection. You get about two minutes of action, and then it spends the next two minutes buffering. That's the lengths you go to to see your team, though.'

SIX

· · · · · · · ·

If at First You Don't Succeed...

THE MODERN, HIGH-RISE BUILDING SEEMS TO STRETCH FOR ever into the Yokohama skyline. The bright lights of Tokyo glint in the distance. At the foot of the apartment block, tourist cruisers drift lazily down the river, showcasing the attractions of the port city to newcomers. Its favourite son will one day become the centre of attention. Some time in the future, a Nakamura nameplate will be screwed to the door of one of the luxury apartments. The Celtic midfielder has already acquired one of the properties in anticipation of a return to his spiritual home. It is a luxurious space in a new part of the city, with pleasant sea views, but its significance lies elsewhere for its soon-to-be occupant. From his flat, Nakamura will be able to overlook the impressive Yokohama F. Marinos training complex. He will return to the club that first nurtured him at some point, before his powers have started to wane, and when he does he will only be a corner-kick away from his place of work. 'He will be able to look out of his window and see whenever there is a game of football on,' says Hiyushi Kanbayashi, the director of the Yokohama Football Association.

He is only half-joking, because Nakamura is, above all else, a football obsessive. Everyone says so. It is a fact to which all his former coaches and old friends in Yokohama constantly return. The 30 year old goes back to his home city on a fairly regular basis, and when he does he always pops into his old club to have a kickabout with his old youth coach, Fuyuki Nishitani. 'We have a game of football, and when all the Marinos kids realise who it is they come rushing over,' he says, smiling. 'The last time, one went in goal, and Shunsuke [pronounced Shoon-Skay in Japanese] hit a free-kick. The young goalkeeper saved it and said he would never wash his hands again. "Shun" is his nickname here, not "Naka". The kids love him. He is their idol.'

It does not take a stretch of the imagination to see Nakamura gazing out of his window high up in the tower block and being tempted to join in with one of the games on the training pitches below. If he has the time, he might grab his boots. If he has family duties to attend to, then he could always watch from a distance. 'He is always thinking about football, unlike the ginger Nakata,' says Nishitani, laughing. 'Football, football, football . . . He is like a child in that way.'

Marinos is the club that produced Nakamura. It is also the club that rejected him. Before he joined their ranks, he was a key member of Misono FC, a junior club. A skilful, talented playmaker with a sumptuous left foot, he was the talk of the town and joined the youth set-up of Nissan FC, which became Yokohama Marinos after the launch of the J. League in 1993. Aged 12, the move took him from being a big fish in a small pond to a tadpole in an ocean. He had magic in his feet, but it was rendered meaningless, as he was ill-equipped to handle the physical side of the game. Photographs from that period confirm his lack of physical stature. In one team picture, he is at least four inches smaller than the majority of his teammates. His skinny limbs add to the impression of a boy among men. 'When he was 12, he was the champion of his junior club, Misono FC, but by the time he got to the Marinos junior group he could not play well against the bigger players,' says Nishitani. 'He was so nervous and worried. He had ball skills and technique, but he was slender, weak and made little impression. He would beat one man but the next one would always get him.'

Nakamura suffered in silence, but there was always a rage burning within him. His coaches remember him as a shy, diffident youngster – 'top secret' as one puts it – but his own frustration at a lack of physical presence ran deep. When the Marinos junior side won the championship one year, they held a celebration party for everyone connected with the club. As the evening passed, Yoshio Noji, then head of the Marinos youth set-up, noticed that Nakamura was not present. 'Everyone was there – the coaches, the players and the parents – but Shunsuke was outside crying,' he says. 'He had not been a regular player in the team and was frustrated and angry at being unable to contribute more. I was angry too and told him that he must attend. He came in eventually – after he had stopped crying.'

However, his physical shortcomings did not stop him from honing the dead-ball skills that would become his trademark in later years. 'He did a lot of self-training, even back then. Before the team training and after, he would practise free-kicks for 30 minutes. He loved hitting free-kicks,' adds Nishitani.

Takayuki Nakamaru (known as Takayuki), an affable 30 year old who is now a youth coach at Yokohama FC, played with the Celtic midfielder in the Marinos junior ranks and then in the first team years later. He was also part of the same Yokohama select team, a collection of the city's best players born in 1977 and 1978, who toured the former Soviet Union in 1990. Takayuki is a year older than Nakamura, but recalls that the younger man had few physical problems at that stage because his contemporaries had not yet started to grow. Over the next few years, Takayuki grew up, filled out and captained the Marinos junior and youth teams to great success. Nakamura, meanwhile, languished on the periphery. 'I used to watch him hit free-kicks. He had the control, but he was hitting weak shots because he did not have the power in his legs. He played behind the centre forward or on the left side of midfield, but he did not have the power to make his technique work for him at that stage,' recalls Takayuki.

As he hit his mid-teens, Nakamura's fledgling career reached a crossroads. The step up from the junior ranks to the Marinos youth team necessitated a cull. It came as no surprise that Nakamura, still small, frail and on the fringes of the team, did not make the grade. It was the first, but certainly not the last, major rejection of his career. For a football-mad kid, it must have come as a brutal blow, but Noji insists that the decision was reached by consensus. While the Marinos coaches gently guided him towards a future away from the club, there was also a crushing realisation on Nakamura's part that it was time to try to progress his career elsewhere. 'My advice to him was that he would find it very competitive in the Marinos youth team,' explains Noji. 'I said if he joined us, he wouldn't be a regular player. He would maybe be a substitute or not even that. I said to him that if he chose another team, he would have more of a chance. He was still very small at that time. He chose to play more. He made the choice himself, and he selected Toko Gakuen High School.' It was arguably the best decision of his career.

Nakamura believes that his problem at that stage was not just physical but mental. 'I had a bad experience when I was younger that I've never forgotten,' he says. 'I was playing for the junior team of Yokohama Marinos and was really satisfied with myself. I was 15 or 16 years old and had the number 10 shirt. I had some skills but was really small and couldn't run fast. Yet I thought I was a really good player and would do a lot of backheels. The real problem was my mentality. When the squad went up a level, only ten players could progress, and I wasn't selected. I could see that others had improved while I had stood still. I went back to high school and joined the football team there. I did my best from then on to work my way back to Marinos. I was worried that I might never make it as a professional. I think that was the moment that changed my career.'

On first impression, opting to play for his high-school team might have seemed like the second-best option, but it proved to be the first of Nakamura's many shrewd career moves. Competitive sport enjoys a huge profile in many Japanese high schools, where talented youngsters can dovetail sporting achievement with academic success under a similar system to that of the USA. Kato Tsuneo, a gentle, statesmanlike man, has taught at Toko Gakuen for a quarter of a century and coached and mentored Nakamura during his high-school years. He explains the way the system works in Japan. 'High schools in Japan have a different history from Europe,' he says. 'After the Second World War, no one was happy. The economy and education became the two most important things. Education for all was the key, and then sport fed off that. Through education, talented sportsmen and women learned how to live their lives properly. The Premiership clubs in England have now done a similar thing with their academies. This was to ensure that young players who might have been at risk from temptations such as drink and drugs, or might have struggled to get a job after retirement, had a sound foundation. So, sport in Japanese high schools is based on the academic side first. For those who applied themselves, they could also develop their sporting potential. In the case of football, the high-school tournaments have a great reputation. The national high-school final can attract a crowd of 40,000 and is also screened live on TV.'

Rather than lose out after leaving Marinos, Nakamura gained access to top-of-the-range coaching and facilities. 'When Shunsuke was at high school, their set-up was actually better than the clubs,' admits Takayuki, who was progressing rapidly through the Marinos ranks at that time. Tsuneo expands on the school's impressive infrastructure. 'Toko Gakuen High School had a physical trainer, an athletics trainer and a sports psychologist from a university. Shunsuke worked with all of them, and they would give him feedback from each day's training. The same happened for every player, but especially Shunsuke, because he was so talented. He always worked very hard.'

Football was an all-consuming passion for Nakamura. In an effort to make the grade, he began to invent his own training techniques. 'When I was really young, I would use a normal size ball, but I made it smaller as I got older,' he says. 'When I was in the bath, I would practise my kicking technique. I would stand and pretend to kick a ball against the resistance of the water. I thought it would help me. I did a lot of small things to improve when I was younger. On my way to school, I would jump up onto higher steps to improve my leap. I played with a team called Misono FC when I was in junior high. We would have free-kick competitions, and whoever lost would carry back the bag of balls. On the way home from the ground, I would try never to touch the ball with my hands. I would only use my feet. Even when I came to a big hill, I wouldn't hold the ball. I would be running down a steep slope, trying to keep control of the ball. I just thought it would help me.'

Nakamura could not have failed to be inspired by the launch of the J. League and the galaxy of stars who lit up domestic football in Japan as he tried to make a career for himself in the game. Yet he revealed that his commitment had less to do with dreams of individual glory and more to do with maximising his talent at something he loved doing. 'I never had a big dream. I went step by step, and I never really looked at what I wanted to do long-term. I just practised to become a better player. Looking back, it was all worth it. But I must also say that I wouldn't have achieved anything without the advice from all the coaches I've worked with.'

Nakamura's three years at Toko Gakuen were make or break as far as his aspirations to turn professional were concerned. If he had not applied himself, he would likely have slipped through the net. The school is based in the city of Kawasaki, a lengthy daily commute from Nakamura's home in Yokohama. Tsuneo talks through his protégé's punishing regime. 'He would leave home at 5 a.m. every day. It would take him two and a half hours to travel to school on his own and then he would begin self-training at around 7.30 a.m. for one hour. After the school day, he would come to after-school training, which I would take, and when that was finished Shunsuke would continue for another two hours. He often wouldn't finish until eight or nine at night, which meant he wouldn't get home until close to midnight. He did that every day. He was different from other players. His self-training was about working on his weaknesses. He was already good on his left foot but wanted to work on his right. Normally, a youth player only kicks with one, but Shunsuke was determined to kick with both. He would constantly challenge himself.

'He did a lot of free-kick training. We had a free-kick board made up of five dolls, and he would practise continually. His father was also a key influence and took a video of every game he played and showed it to him afterwards. His father is president of the Toko Gakuen Supporters Club and is also a company president. He helped Shunsuke in any way he could. He was the passion behind him. His mother also knew a lot about nutrition, which helped. He is such a clever person. He could have gone to university and become a doctor, but it was just football for Shunsuke.'

At high school, Nakamura also began to practise qigong, a set of breathing and movement exercises often taught in conjunction with Chinese martial arts. 'Qi' refers to energy and 'gong' means exercise, so 'qigong' can be roughly translated as 'breathing/energy exercises'. In a similar way to t'ai chi, qigong's slow external movements help stimulate the internal organs by promoting the flow of the body's internal energy or qi. The benefits are many. Qigong allows someone to manage their breathing for health maintenance purposes, such as stress reduction. More pertinently for athletes such as Nakamura, it also enhances both stamina and the body's ability to mobilise energy quickly.

Golfers such as Tiger Woods and Colin Montgomerie frequently carry out breathing exercises before hitting big shots, but more relevant is the example of someone such as David Beckham, who shares Nakamura's world-class ability in dead-ball situations. Before striking a free-kick, Beckham goes through a rehearsed routine, involving deep-breathing exercises and visualisation techniques. The aim is to channel the body's energy into completing the task in hand, namely to beat the goalkeeper.

Colin Orr, a chief instructor at the Tai Chi Qigong Health Centre in Norfolk, says, 'Nakamura would definitely benefit from qigong in terms of being able to go inside himself to concentrate on the task ahead. The idea of it is to centre the energy in your body. When it is practised consistently over time, it is something that you are then able to do as and when you need it. It makes the body completely relaxed and ready to spring into action. When he is ready to take a free-kick, he is able to go into that state and centre himself ready to strike.'

Nakamura was doing everything possible to carve out a career as a professional, but his hopes rested on one area over which he had no control: his physical stature. Thankfully, Mother Nature obliged. 'When I first met Shunsuke, aged fifteen, he was five feet four inches tall,' says Tsuneo. 'That was when he joined the team. My first impression of Shunsuke was that he was the most skilful player on the team but everything would depend ultimately on the physical side. One year later, he was five feet six and a half inches and eventually he finished up five feet ten inches.'

While hardly a giant, Nakamura could now hold his own with players his own age. The change had not gone unnoticed. 'I saw Shunsuke in second grade at high school, and I said to him, "You've got big!"' recalls Noji, who relayed news of the youngster's growth spurt back to Marinos.

Toko Gakuen were also experiencing success and reached the final of the high-school championship in 1996. With the exposure offered by success in the high-school championship, Nakamura's name began to be dropped by scouts around the country. Out of seeming failure, he had picked himself up and become one of the country's most promising young talents. He owed much of it to the sanctuary offered by Toko Gakuen. His three years at the school were the making of him, and he has not forgotten it. Every time he returns home, he takes in a visit to his alma mater, which continues to churn out top-class footballers with impressive regularity. 'We have produced a minimum of 20 players who have gone on to play in the J. League,' says Tsuneo proudly. 'Two players have been involved with the Olympic squad, but Shunsuke is the most successful. After they graduate, a Japanese student and their teacher always keep in contact. The teacher is like a father. The Japanese school is like a family. The students always come back to the school to say, "Hello, how are you?" Every time Shunsuke comes back home, he visits the school and meets with the young boys. The last time he gave the students a lot of Adidas balls and played a game with them. He doesn't talk a lot, but he shows himself through football.'

With Nakamura approaching graduation and having established himself as one of the brightest young talents in the country, club scouts were hovering. Inevitably, Marinos renewed their interest, but a clutch of upwardly mobile teams in the newly created J. League were also eager to secure his signature. 'He had offers from Júbilo Iwata, Tokyo Verdy and Gamba Osaka,' recalls Tsuneo.

For Nakamura, it was time for the next major decision. Previously, he had chosen high school instead of being on the sidelines at Marinos. In many ways, he had chosen the more difficult path. He could have continued on the fringes of the Marinos youth team but instead decided to push himself to the limit at Toko Gakuen. He had chosen boldly and, with half the J. League now chapping at his door, had been vindicated. This time around, he could opt for one of the offers from his new suitors or return to the club where he had failed to make the grade. He went to the club he felt would best allow him to maximise his talent.

'He chose to return to Marinos not for sentimental reasons but because he thought they were the most professional club at the time,' says Tsuneo. 'Other clubs suffered from a bad image – lazy players and a lack of professionalism. But at that time Marinos were the best-performing club for young players. He sensed they wanted success, and that was why Shunsuke wanted to go back. He thought that if he performed at his best, he would be given his chance.'

Takayuki was not surprised that he chose to return to his former club. 'That is Shunsuke's style. I think he wanted to prove he could make it at the club that rejected him, to prove to everyone that he had advanced in football terms. He had plenty of time to make himself a player at high school. He did it himself and proved to everyone – himself, his family and friends, and the Marinos coaches – that he could do it. But crucially he got bigger.'

When Nakamura finally signed for Marinos in 1997, Takayuki was impressed by how the boy had become a man. His success at Toko Gakuen had also earned him a call-up to the Japan national youth-team squad, which reached the quarter-final of the FIFA world youth tournament in 1996.

'Shunsuke's experience with Toko Gakuen and with the national youth side had changed him,' explains Takayuki. 'Through his experiences in those years, he gradually became the hardest worker. It was a step-by-step process. His mentality was stronger than before. He was a survivor. He was always training himself.'

Nakamura also had a crucial advantage on Takayuki. He knew what it felt like to fail. Takayuki had moved easily through the junior and youth ranks at Marinos. He had been the captain and best player. He had lifted all the trophies and attracted all the plaudits, while Nakamura had been the runt of the litter, the skinny kid who could not get a regular game and was left crying outside the team party. He was the one who had been rejected, who had experienced the crushing blow of having to leave his contemporaries and friends behind to start again at high school. The bitter experience had

Nakamura (back row, far left) gives the thumbs-up. Despite the trophies,
his size prevented him becoming a regular in the Marinos junior ranks

Nakamura (bottom row, far left) celebrates success
in the Yokohama Marinos junior ranks

Nakamura playing for his high school, Toko
Gakuen, where his performances reignited his
hopes of becoming a professional

As a young player in the
Yokohama Marinos first team

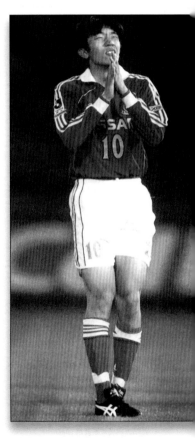

In action for his home-town
team, Yokohama Marinos

Nakamura's body in a perfect arc as he strikes a free-kick against Japan's Yokohama F. Marinos during a friendly match at Yokohama's Nissan Stadium (© Getty Images)

With Reggina's oldest fan, Nonna Maria, who is in her 90s (courtesy of Takashi Yuge)

Celebrating in style after another priceless goal for the Serie A minnows, Reggina

The Reggina Ultras hail their Japanese
hero (courtesy of Takashi Yuge)

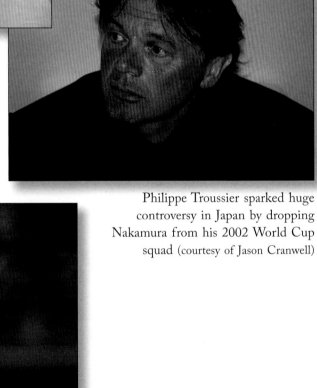

Philippe Troussier sparked huge
controversy in Japan by dropping
Nakamura from his 2002 World Cup
squad (courtesy of Jason Cranwell)

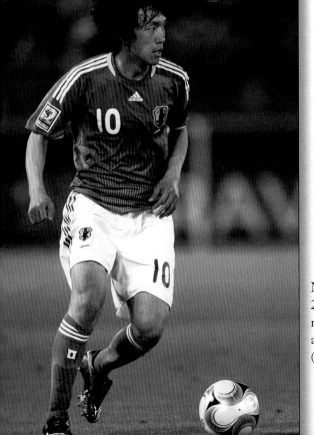

Nakamura in action during the
2010 World Cup Asian qualifier
match between Japan and Oman
at the Nissan Stadium
(© Getty Images)

Nakamura's faithful press pack. Left to right: Daisuke Nakajima, Shin Toyofuku, James Morrison and Makoto Sassaki (courtesy of the author)

Nakamura holds the Premier League trophy aloft (© Getty Images)

Nakamura celebrating after scoring against Manchester United at
Old Trafford in August 2006 (© SNS Group)

The Tokyo Celtic Supporters Club belt out a chorus of 'You'll Never Walk Alone'
(courtesy of Jason Cranwell)

Nakamura with his top off, celebrating after scoring the free-kick against Kilmarnock to win Celtic the league in 2007 (© SNS Group)

As guest of honour at the Celtic Supporters Rally, alongside interpreter Makoto Kaneko and club captain Stephen McManus

Nakamura's muted celebration after Celtic beat Spartak Moscow to reach the group stages of the Champions League in 2007. The midfielder missed a penalty and several chances, and felt he had let his teammates down (© SNS Group)

changed him, strengthened his resolve and made him hungrier to taste what Takayuki had always taken for granted.

As a consequence, when the pair reached their late teens and prepared to take their first steps into a professional career, Nakamura exploded into the first team and seized centre stage. Takayuki laughingly recites an anecdote that perfectly illustrates the difference in the two players' mentalities at that time. 'Me and my friends from the first-team squad would often relax and have a barbecue and a few beers near the Marinos training ground. We would all be standing about drinking beer and saying to each other, "Why are we not in the first team? It is very unfair." Then, as we were standing around complaining one night, Shunsuke ran past us doing laps of the track. We pointed at him and said, "That's why we're not in the first team!"'

Nakamura's motivation might have come from within, but a visit to Barcelona with Marinos inspired him to try and reach the very top level. 'I went to Barcelona as an 18 year old as part of a youth-training camp when I was at Yokohama Marinos. We were just training in the city and playing against different local teams. We went to a Barca game. Rivaldo was the big star, and he was the most impressive player I saw. It was my first football game outside of Japan, and it was incredible.'

Steve Perryman, the former Tottenham midfielder, enjoyed a successful seven-year spell coaching in the J. League, and his time there coincided with the emergence of Nakamura at Marinos. By then, the J. League had been established for almost five years, and the honeymoon period was over. The influence of the foreigners was starting to diminish, to be replaced by home-grown talents such as Nakamura.

'Nakamura was a perfect model for clubs to prove that they could make their own players,' said Perryman, who coached and managed Shimizu S-Pulse to notable domestic success. 'He broke into the team as a youngster, and by the time I left he was established in the national team. He was not big or strong or powerful, but what technique he had. He was a very, very difficult opponent to play against. We didn't man-mark him, but we always had someone very close to him when he picked the ball up, because we knew how dangerous he could be.

'Marinos were a top-four side back then. They won championships before Nakamura came in, they won one with him there and they have won some since he left. A lot of it was about not giving away free-kicks in dangerous positions. At corners and free-kicks, his deliveries were very special. Spurs had some great midfielders during my time there – guys such as Glenn Hoddle and Ossie Ardiles – and he could manipulate the ball in a similar way to them.' Comparisons with Ardiles are particularly acute, as he was a midfielder of similar stature to Nakamura and had been a huge success in British football.

In his first season at Marinos in 1997, Nakamura scored five times in thirty-one appearances and proved he could handle the demands of full-time professional football. The following season, when he scored ten goals in thirty-seven appearances and made an impressive number of assists, he began to be viewed as one of the brightest prospects in the country. His influence continued to increase in the forthcoming years, but it was not until the arrival of Ardiles as manager in 2000 that he experienced his first taste of success. The Argentine had managed S-Pulse with Perryman between 1996 and '98 before moving to Croatia Zagreb and then returning to Japan. In his first season at Marinos, he led them to the J. League first-stage championship. (Until 2004, the J. League was played in two stages, with the winner of each meeting at the end of the year in a home-and-away play-off.) Perryman believes that his former colleague was the perfect man to bring the best out of Nakamura, who also went on to win the J. League's MVP in 2000. 'There was an Argentine influence at Marinos, with guys such as Ramón Díaz and then Ossie,' explains Perryman. 'Ossie really liked Nakamura even before he went to Marinos. He was a great spotter of talent, and I remember him talking about Hidetoshi Nakata a couple of years before he really made his name. Ossie is the kind of guy who really loves pure talent. He coached and managed in a similar style as he did as a player. His training sessions always moved very quickly. Ossie was a World Cup winner, but he believed that confidence was the main thing for a footballer. He knew how easy it was to knock someone's belief, so he felt the clue was to give a player confidence. Some coaches rant and rave after defeats, and that can affect a player's confidence, but Ossie never did that. He would always keep his counsel, and I think Nakamura, being the type of person he is, appreciated that. Ossie and Nakamura were a perfect match for one another.'

Nakamura continued to produce an impressive level of consistency, with five goals in thirty-one appearances in 2001, helping Marinos to J. League Cup success. A goal in every two games before he left for Reggina in 2002 confirmed his status as Marinos' key man. Perryman has followed his career closely and been impressed by how he has developed his game. 'He was a typical Japanese footballer, in that he didn't switch off because he had talent. There is a lot of Brazilian, Spanish and Italian football shown in Japan, so despite all the attention the top players such as Nakamura received, there was a realisation that they were not at the same standard as some of the players at the clubs they watched on TV – such as Barcelona, Real Madrid, AC Milan and Palmeiras.

'The mentality of Japanese players is to learn something new every day, to work on their technique. Nakamura had energy and legs, if not real power, but you always felt there would be two or three moments in the game when he would really hurt you. But as he has approached the mid-years of his career, he has been able to produce these moments more consistently. It was a great move for him to go to Celtic. If he was in a less strong team, he would not be able to play to his strengths so much.'

Noji was delighted that Nakamura had fought his way back to Marinos and proved himself in the J. League, but he was adamant that domestic football should not be the pinnacle of his career.

He believed that Nakamura had to get out of Japan to continue his football development. 'I welcomed him back to Marinos, but I also said to him that it depended on where he went next. If he kept playing in the same league with the same players and half-full stadiums in Japan, nobody would challenge him. He would be the number 10 and everybody would shake his hand and say that he was a genius, a local hero. He had to push himself again.'

After five seasons and the disappointment of not reaching the 2002 World Cup, the time was right for the 24-year-old Nakamura to move out of Japan and take his career to the next level. His choice of Reggina, the small Serie A club in the deep south of Italy, marked another key decision in his career. Noji believes it was yet another example of Nakamura taking the tough route to better advance his career. 'He chose to go to Italy and push himself to the limit in that sense. European football is harder work. In the beginning, he wanted to go to Spain, but then he changed his mind and chose Italy. It would prove to be a wise choice. Then when he moved to Scotland, the focus was more on attack, and he was ready to take that step.'

Nakamura remains Yokohama's greatest sporting export, and there is no doubt that he will return there one day. Despite a long-held ambition to play in Spain, it is likely that the midfielder will return to his homeland after his time at Celtic draws to a close. The 30 year old is proud of what he has achieved in Europe but also keen to return to the J. League before he is too old. There is an unmistakeable pride in his intention to return to Marinos and show his home fans what he has learned during his years in exile. 'I will go back to Japan some time in the future,' he says. 'I don't want to finish my career away from my homeland. Marinos is the club I started my career at, so it would be great if I could go back there.'

Yokohama is Japan's second-biggest city, with a population of 3.5 million. It is located just 20 minutes from Tokyo and has all the attractions you would expect in a metropolis of its size. There are two Yokohama-based teams – Yokohama F. Marinos, Nakamura's old club, and Yokohama FC – but the development of their separate identities is mired in controversy. When the J. League started, the city was represented by two teams: the Nissan-sponsored Yokohama Marinos and Yokohama Flugels, whose backers were All Nippon Airways (ANA). Then, in 1998, it was announced that the Flugels were to merge with the Marinos. In reality, though, it was not an equal merger, with the Marinos owners Nissan taking a 70 per cent stake in the club and ANA left with just the remaining 30 per cent. The new club would take the name Yokohama F. Marinos, and only a few Flugels players would be accommodated in the first team. In effect, the Flugels were to be consumed by the Marinos. 'It was more of a takeover than a merger,' says Steven Tweed, the Scottish defender who played for Yokohama FC for over two years. 'It was the equivalent of the time when Wallace Mercer [then Hearts chairman] tried to take over Hibs some years ago. The decision stemmed from the problems in the Japanese economy, and the executives decided that they only wanted one club in the city for commercial reasons.'

So, a takeover was announced, and that was to be the end of it. Or so the bureaucrats and businessmen thought. In fact, the controversial plans ignited the first real showing of fan power in Japanese football. The Flugels supporters, a hitherto passive bunch, reacted with fury and demanded of ANA executives that the merger be cancelled. ANA had not taken into consideration the ethos enshrined in the establishment of the J. League and which it continued to foster throughout its early years. Saburo Kawabuchi, the founding father, wanted it to be a 'social revolution', with newly formed clubs around the country becoming the focal point for local communities. In doing so, he wanted to shift the emphasis in Japan away from corporate life. ANA's decision rode roughshod over Kawabuchi's vision and harked back to the days when owners ran sports teams only as a sideline to their business to boost their corporate image.

They would not get it all their own way. A 'Save the Flugels' group was formed, and clubs around the country lent their backing to the cause. The group soon gathered over a quarter of a million signatures for their petition, which they presented to Kawabuchi.

ANA continued to stick to their guns, but the Flugels produced the ultimate last act of defiance. At the end of the J. League season, they went on a run to the final of the Emperor's Cup, where they faced Shimizu S-Pulse. Despite going a goal down in the first half, the Flugels came back to win 2–1 and lift the cup. They had gone out on the ultimate high. The players took a bow before the fans at the end and threw their shirts, socks and boots into the stands. It was a stirring spectacle and even moved the opposition fans to chant the Flugels' name.

F. Marinos began the following season in much the same form as the old Marinos. Just three former Flugels had been brought into the squad, and the only visible change was the inclusion of the letter 'F' in the club name.

However, the 'Save the Flugels' were still not finished and went on to form a 'Rebuild the Flugels' group. By the end of 1998, they had brought in 67 million yen (£370,000) and filed an application to start a company. So began Yokohama FC, which was modelled on Barcelona FC's set-up, effectively a private-members club bankrolled by supporters. The fans were now in control of their own destiny and hired German legend Pierre Littbarski as team manager. Yokohama FC started in the Japan Football League (JFL, the semi-professional league under J1 and J2) and continued to grow. By 2001, they had reached J2 and were more or less back to where they started from when ANA 'merged' them.

'The Flugels were reborn from the ashes, and that is why Yokohama FC have got a phoenix on their badge,' explains Tweed. 'They had to start again in the bottom league, but then worked their way back up to the J. League. They now bob between J1 and J2. It was a wonderful experience playing for them [between 2004 and 2006]. They are a very proud and focused club. We could get crowds of 5,000 to 10,000 or up to 40,000 if we played in one of the big stadiums.'

The story of the Flugels has a wider significance. The formation of Yokohama FC and the refusal of the ordinary fan to be dictated to by corporations helped establish football's identity in Japan. Their actions proved that football was no longer a corporate plaything but a community-centred national sport through which people formed a sense of identity.

Even now, Yokohama is primed for Nakamura's return. In the superstore beside the Nissan Stadium, home of the Marinos and venue for the 2002 World Cup final, the 'Nakamura 10' shirts fly off the shelves. On match days, vendors sell posters of him, and his return will transform the club. 'Yokohama is a big city, but it hasn't produced many football players, and no one as big as Shunsuke,' adds Kanbayashi. 'Marinos' attendances just now are 25,000, which means that the Nissan Stadium is 70 per cent empty, but if Shunsuke came back, we would fill it.'

After his playing career is over, Nakamura won't be short of options. Nishitani hopes to persuade him to do some youth coaching, while Kanbayashi believes that Nakamura's caring personality lends itself more to community work. 'I hope to get him involved in working with people with disabilities,' he says. 'There is a rehabilitation centre next to the Nissan Stadium, and hopefully he could be involved in that in some capacity. I would also like him to do some social work. I've enquired as to whether that might interest him, and he has said that it would. There is also an international school in Yokohama, and I would like to get Shunsuke along as a guest coach.'

SEVEN

·············

A League of Their Own

IMPECCABLE TIMING HAS ACCOMPANIED SHUNSUKE Nakamura's rise to the top. They say that talent without opportunity is nothing at all. By virtue of his arrival in the world on 24 June 1978, the Japanese midfielder was afforded every opportunity to fulfil his potential. By 1993, a 15-year-old Nakamura's relationship with the sport was already an intimate affair, but the formation of the J. League that year ensured it would have the chance to be consummated. Regardless of his prodigious talent, he might never have become a professional footballer had it not been for its establishment. It was an organisation that revolutionised the sport in Japan, and every footballer of the current generation – including Hidetoshi Nakata, Junichi Inamoto, Shinji Ono and Nakamura – remains indebted to its creation.

'The J. League has definitely helped,' says Nakamura. 'For years, baseball has been the dominant sport in Japan, but football is becoming more and more popular, and most young boys now prefer it to baseball.'

Prior to the J. League, there was only corporate sport in Japan. Teams were owned by companies, and players were full-time employees. Corporate sport was a keystone of Japan's post-war economic revival as firms attempted to create a culture of company as family, but by the 1990s there was revolution in the air. Society was changing, horizons were broadening and football became the vehicle for a more modern, outward-looking country. So, in 1993 the J. League erupted in a riot of colour and expectations. Stuart Baxter, the widely travelled and highly respected coach, had been enticed to Japan to take over Sanfrecce Hiroshima in 1992, just before the league's launch, and was amazed at its impact.

'It was a much bigger thing then than it is now,' he recalls. 'I think it has become more realistic now, but back then it was like a massive show. It was a total departure from what the Japanese were used to. Sports such as baseball and sumo wrestling are big in Japan, and they are both very regimented. Suddenly football appeared on the scene and supporters were painting their faces, then players started dyeing their hair funny colours. It really captured the country's imagination. I remember for the first round of games there were 9 million ticket applications. The whole season was sold out. Nakamura would have been part of all of that. He would have been a young lad watching all of this stuff happening and would have been able to go along and play in the youth team of his nearest club.'

Overflowing with money, the J. League enticed world-class players just past their peak to play for the newly created teams and spearhead aggressive marketing campaigns. Gary Lineker, Pierre Littbarski, Zico, Dunga, Dragan Stojković and others all arrived amid huge publicity. Multiple sponsors were signed up and an infrastructure put in place for producing the next generation of Japanese footballers. 'What was so impressive about the J. League was that they ticked every box,' explains Sebastian Moffett, author of *Japanese Rules: Why the Japanese Needed Football and How They Got It*. 'They knew they needed to make money. They realised that European football wasn't making any at that time, so they studied American sports and how they marketed themselves. They got involved in the selling of replica shirts, multiple sponsors and got the commercial side of things right. They realised that no one would support corporate teams, so they set about making them home town-based. Then they realised that they had to get foreign players in to bring quality and exposure, but not too many. These older foreigners, ten or so world-class players, became icons for the supporters. The supporters had seen these players at World Cups and on TV for years. Because they were playing locally, lots of people turned out to watch them. They also sprinkled the foreigners around the teams.'

Before the J. League, it was virtually impossible for Japanese players to make football their careers. The one outstanding exception was Yasuhiko Okudera, who left Japan to sign for FC Köln in West Germany's Bundesliga in 1977. He soon established himself as a prolific striker and won the Double in his first season. Despite being a household name in Germany, Okudera was largely ignored by the media in his home country. He spent nine seasons in the German top-flight, playing for Köln, Hertha Berlin and finally Werder Bremen. Okudera returned to Japan to play out the rest of his career. He made suggestions as to how they might improve the Japanese Soccer League (the precursor to the J. League, consisting of corporate teams) but was always met with resistance. It said everything about the insularity of the Japanese mindset, together with the lowly status of football then, that not even their most successful export could find a receptive ear.

The era prior to the J. League is perhaps best encapsulated by the struggles of Kazuyoshi 'Kazu' Miura. Kazu was born in the city of Shizuoka, a football-mad region, but showed little signs of talent from a young age. Fuelled by a fierce desire, he worked to develop his skills and close control. By his mid-teens, he had improved enough to decide to take a leap of faith. He moved to Brazil to continue his football development and found a place in the youth system of a team in São Paolo called Juventus. Staying in a flea-ridden dormitory, he continued to work tirelessly on his technique but, sadly, was often subjected to racial taunts and lost confidence. Switching from Juventus to XV de Jáu, a small club outside São Paolo, he continued to stagnate. During these dispiriting struggles, he considered returning home, but with typical Japanese diligence he stuck it out and eventually found enough form to be offered a professional contract with Santos, Pelé's former club. Disappointingly, in his first six months he only played two matches, and for the next couple of years he flitted around lower-league teams in Brazil, eventually being offered a contract with his old club XV de Jáu. Once there, he prospered, scoring the winning goal against Corinthians in a São Paolo state championship match. 'O Karate Kid do Futebol' read the headlines the following day. A move to Cortiba FC saw him become a regular in the 1988 Brazilian championship, and when they played Flamengo Kazu faced his hero, Zico. The Brazilian legend approached him at half-time, shook his hand and told him, 'You've made it.' The following day, the Japanese papers carried a picture of the two together, prompting Kazu to burst into tears of joy. After spending a further year at Santos, where he scored the winner against Palmeiras in a 1990 São Paolo state championship match, Kazu returned home, where the imminent launch of the J. League would allow him to turn professional. Its genesis ensured that no other aspiring Japanese footballer would have to endure his monumental struggles to fulfil their football dreams.

Participation levels in football were high before the J. League, even rivalling that of the nation's number one sport, baseball, but the 1990s provided the opportunity for talented players to make the step into professionalism. An amateur set-up already existed in Japan, and, given the number of participants in a country of over 127 million, there was a huge pool of natural talent in place without the proper structure to fully develop it. The J. League would provide that vital component. This bottom-up development is a key reason for the continued success of the J. League compared to the North American Soccer League of the 1970s, in which the base of Americans participating and viewing the sport was just not big enough to make the league sustainable.

Every J. League club had a youth set-up, which dovetailed with the excellent high-school football system. The latter offered an alternative showcase for young football talent and also allowed sporting success to be allied to academic excellence. In Japan, where there is an obsessive drive for academic achievement throughout society, aspiring players could remain in the education system until the age of 18, providing a safety net should football fail to provide a full-time J. League contract. Crucially, it also meant that football did not miss out on the academic high-achievers who were also gifted footballers.

The J. League has been hugely instrumental to Japan's success in establishing itself as a credible football nation, and this has been reflected in their qualification for the last three World Cups. Just as the initial fervour surrounding the J. League was dying down, so Japan qualified for their first World Cup in France in 1998. Four years later, together with South Korea, they hosted the finals and reached the last 16, which whipped the nation into another football frenzy. When they qualified for the 2006 finals in Germany, the national team's success had greatly helped the sport gain a permanent foothold in society beyond the initial novelty value associated with the start of the J. League.

Japan was well acquainted with top-level competitive sport before the J. League. Personalities such as Jumbo Osaki had raised the profile of golf in line with indigenous sports such as sumo wrestling, but baseball was, and still is, the number one sport in Japan. Nakamura reflects on its popularity. 'Guys like me and Hidetoshi Nakata are the most famous footballers, but then there's Hideki Matsui, who plays baseball for the New York Yankees. He's still a lot more famous than us. Compared to us, he really is Godzilla [Matsui's nickname].'

Football, in contrast to baseball, did not have a great history or tradition prior to 1993. Nevertheless, the appetite for its introduction was huge. Steven Tweed started his career at the Scottish Premier League side Hibs before leaving for spells at Ionikos in Greece, MSV Duisburg in Germany and then Yokohama FC. He and his family stayed for two and half years in Japan, and Tweed was immediately struck by the country's desire to catch up with the West in football terms.

'I thought the standard was unbelievable,' he says. 'The technique and pace was incredible. The small players have a low centre of gravity and are so dynamic. Their technique comes from training and practising when they are young. Everything is done very professionally. At the first hotel I stayed in with Yokohama, we were sleeping on the floors way up in the mountains. In the mornings, they whipped up eggs and rice and served green tea. No tea and toast like Britain. That was the start of it. You had to get used to it. They had different ways of recovery – bathing, acupuncture – and the whole medical side was a major aspect.'

The all-consuming attitude and intense work ethic of the Japanese towards football reflects their attitude towards work and life in general. In little over 50 years, they had picked up the pieces of defeat in the Second World War and established themselves as an economic superpower. They achieved this by making business the centre of life. 'People go to their work at seven or eight in the morning and are back home at eleven or twelve at night,' explains Les Mottram, the former UEFA referee who spent almost nine years officiating in the J. League. 'When they do a job, they do it until it's finished. That is inbred in their natures. Professional footballers feel privileged to be in such a position, and, as such, they work very hard. I remember going into Rangers to get some treatment on an injury during the Andy Goram and Mark Hateley era. The players would come in at half-ten and go home just after twelve. I know things have changed now in Scotland, but in Japan the players are there for the whole day. They come in at nine in the morning, stop for lunch and then go back out in the afternoon until four, five or six o'clock. The European coaches who were over there couldn't believe how hard the Japanese players worked.'

Nakamura's dedication towards practice and physical conditioning might have been seen as revolutionary in Scotland, but, as Tweed argues, such an approach is routine in Japan. 'The things that Nakamura does to maintain fitness and aid recovery at Celtic are just normal in Japan. The fruits are there for all to see, and 2007 was the first year in eight or nine that a Japanese team, Urawa Red Diamonds, won the Asian Champions League. They are doing something right at club level. There are only three foreigners allowed per team. It's still quite a purist thing in Japan. They have the population, they have the infrastructure, they have the league – it is all there now.'

Tweed was most struck by the importance the Japanese attached to establishing football as a national sport. 'Prior to the J. League, there were company football teams such as Nissan and Toyota. Honda are still in what is now the third league, but they didn't want to go professional. The teams who went for it did so wholeheartedly. Yokohama Marinos [previously Nissan FC] built a new training complex right across from Nissan headquarters. It's probably one of the most expensive land sites in the world. Right in the town centre and the centre of the business world, there's this land with pitches and clubhouses on it. It's like having it at Queen Street Station in Glasgow. Off the field, once the Japanese say something, it's done. They never say, "It's not in the contract." Your word is your bond. There's no freedom of movement with players. It's the old system, whereby a tribunal has to be set up if you move between Japanese teams. It's the kind of atmosphere where everything is above board. It is how business used to be, which is nice.'

Gradually, a more sober culture also built up around football, in contrast to baseball, in which the tradition is for the victorious team to drench each other in beer. No one reflects the professionalism surrounding Japanese football more than Nakamura. He does not drink alcohol, and during his time in Italy he only went to a nightclub once with his teammates and left after an hour. The next day, he woke up to discover he was front-page news in the local paper, *Gazetta Del Sud*. 'Surprisingly, Nakamura Went to Discoteca!' read the headline.

Tweed, who now plays for Second Division Scottish side East Fife, was enticed to Japan by his former Duisburg coach Pierre Littbarski, one of the J. League's first foreigners. Some friendly early advice from the German legend offered a keen insight into the important contributions foreigners were expected to make. Littbarski explained that they were regarded as shining examples of how to do things properly, and Tweed quickly realised that he was part of an influential chain that started with players such as Zico and his German manager and continued with coaches such as Arsène Wenger, the present Arsenal manager who brought a cerebral, scientific approach with him during his three-year spell at Nagoya Grampus Eight. 'Littbarski said to me before my first training session, "First impressions are so important with these guys. You've got to do it properly. You have to run at the front of the group. You can't just settle for being in the middle. Maybe you can run in the middle after a couple of months, once you have been accepted, but you have to be up the front – leading." I made sure I got my football vocabulary first and then my "learn to live" vocabulary later.'

The importance of conveying the right image is huge in Japan. How others perceive them, and how they perceive themselves, is a fundamental part of the Japanese mindset. 'In their lives, it is very important that they are seen to be diligent,' explains Stuart Baxter. 'If you work in a bank, there is a competition at night to see who leaves last. Some businessmen sit in their cars after work before going home so that people will think they have been working longer. They want to be seen by other people to be working hard. Their footballers put the time in on the pitch. They want to constantly improve. Once you get an idea of what makes Japanese players tick, they are easy to coach. The idea was to give them a structure and make sure that they knew their place within it. Japanese players don't feel good if they do not know what is expected from them. When they realise what is expected of them, they will take it as far as they can go.'

Just as foreign players and coaches played a key part in Japan's football revolution, referees such as Mottram also had a pivotal role. 'The ethos was to bring in foreign players, foreign referees and foreign coaches, learn from them and then replace them with Japanese,' said Mottram. 'That has happened to a great extent. Japanese players, coaches and referees have all improved greatly. On the playing side, teams are not allowed to field any more than three foreigners, including the substitutes. So out of fifteen or sixteen players, you have a maximum of three foreigners. That has allowed young players to come through. It is not like Europe, where the Bosman ruling allows coaches to fill their teams with foreign journeymen, which prevents their young indigenous players developing in the team.'

If the J. League recognised the necessity for world-class players to raise its profile, then it also deserved huge credit for choosing the right ones. They did not want just any old foreign stars; they wanted ones with a genuine passion for developing football in Asia. No one would make a greater contribution in that regard than Brazilian legend Zico. In 1989, he had brought the curtain down on an illustrious career in which he had scored an astonishing 68 goals in 89 games for his country. He had been voted South American Player of the Year, World Player of the Year, won just about every domestic honour and competed at three World Cup finals. Zico was a bona fide legend. He was also addicted to football. After a short spell as sports minister of Brazil, he was drawn back to it. Zico came out of retirement and joined Sumitomo Metals, a team in the Second Division of Japan's corporate amateur league, two years prior to the launch of the J. League. It seemed a strange move, but Zico had taught football classes on previous trips to Japan and had been struck by the infectious enthusiasm of the

Japanese people for the sport. With the launch of the J. League, Zico began a one-man mission to drive up standards and make it more professional. Most of all, he taught Japanese players how to take the game seriously. Players found laughing or joking after a defeat would feel the lash of his tongue. He even insisted that his interpreter used the same admonishing tones as he did so that nothing would be lost in translation. By then, and largely thanks to Zico, Sumitomo Metals, now renamed Kashima Antlers, were one of the best teams in Japan.

Zico continued to be heavily involved with the club after hanging up his boots, occupying the post of technical adviser for a spell, as they went on to win three J. League championships. They honoured his contribution by erecting a bronze statue of him outside the stadium. He would go on to coach the Japanese national team between 2002 and 2006.

'Zico helped develop things a lot by showing what a professional does,' observes Sebastian Moffett. 'I saw an interview with Yutaka Akita [the former international defender] recently speaking about the influence Zico had on him. When Akita was young, he was a bit of a lad and went out boozing a lot. But when he saw the way Zico lived his life and approached the game, he changed his ways. Zico provided an example of how the best professional players should take their talent seriously.'

Zico was also the catalyst in Nakamura's international career. Following his omission from the 2002 World Cup squad by Philippe Troussier, the Brazilian not only restored Nakamura to the squad but gave him the number 10 shirt and built his team around him, describing him as 'the soul of our midfield'. The two have also joined forces off the park and appeared on the front cover of the Japanese releases of Konami's Pro Evolution Soccer video game series.

The J. League was never going to be able to sustain the intensity created by the initial fanfare, but, significantly, it had put enough structures in place to ensure long-term development. In the initial stage, which lasted for around three years, people flocked to stadiums to watch the leading foreign stars, such as Zico, Littbarski and Lineker. In the next stage, it would have been easy for the project to crash and burn with the departure of the stars, but the teams that had thrown themselves wholeheartedly into the sport, such as Urawa Red Diamonds and Kashima Antlers, flourished even when the initial interest levels started to fade. In the third stage, those same teams have been the ones that have gone on to be very successful, commanding crowds of around 40,000, which rivals attendances at most of the top leagues in Europe.

The social significance of the J. League should not be underestimated. At its inception, the founding father, Saburo Kawabuchi, described it as a 'social revolution . . . different from just making Japan good at football'. Most of all, he was committed to shifting the emphasis in Japanese life away from business to a more community-centred approach.

Perhaps it also served a more significant if less obvious function. Expressing patriotism had become an uneasy emotion for the Japanese. Prior to the Second World War, Japan had been an imperial power with a long military history. However, post-war, with its military officially redundant, it was left to Japan's economic might to provide the country with a source of pride. By the 1990s, the time was right not just for the J. League, but for a successful national football team to give the Japanese a natural, benign outlet for their patriotism. The performances of the national football team in reaching the finals of the World Cups of 1998, 2002 and 2006 have cemented Japan's place in world football, cause for much justifiable national pride. Football and its true importance is almost universally exaggerated but perhaps this is an example of the powerful, unifying force it can be at its best.

If the J. League had learned the lessons of the failed American experience, it shrewdly picked up on its strengths, particularly its family emphasis. Mottram had come from a British football culture, where he carried out his refereeing duties to a soundtrack of almost constant abuse from supporters. On arrival in Japan, having just officiated at the 1996 European Championships, the family friendly atmosphere inside football stadiums took him aback. 'The thing I noticed was how many of the crowd were female and that there was a big family atmosphere. When you heard roars from the stands, they tended to be high-pitched. When I came back to Scotland for Christmas and New Year, some of the Japanese referees would come with me, and I would take them to Scottish games. I remember taking some to a Livingston game, and when the referee made a decision the supporters barracked him. The Japanese referees said to me, "Why are they shouting at the referee? He made the right decision." I said, "It doesn't matter if it was the right decision or not. That is the way it works in Scotland." And they didn't understand why one set of fans was abusing the other. That just didn't happen in Japan, and it points up the difference between the two cultures. In Japan, they go to support their team, not to barrack the opposition.'

The aftermath of a game can be a precarious time for a referee. If he has made a controversial decision that has changed the course of a match, he might be tempted to don a false beard on his way out of the stadium to prevent being collared by irate fans. Not in Japan. Mottram explains how society's emphasis on respect extends to the sporting arena. 'I once went to Hiroshima to referee a game between Sanfrecce and Urawa. There was a Yugoslavian player playing for Urawa, and I cautioned him for dissent towards one of my assistants. He started again over a decision later in the game, so I sent him off. I stayed the night and flew back to Tokyo the next day. As I was making my way through the airport to pick up my luggage, there were two Urawa fans waiting. Had it been in Scotland, and the two fans been Celtic or Rangers fans whose team had just lost the game and had a player sent off, I might have been a bit concerned. But the Urawa fans came up to me and actually apologised for the behaviour of their player. I used to come back on the train from places such as Kyoto with the fans, and they were superb. They just wanted to talk about football.'

If the J. League provided the stage, then the players were the actors, with the famous foreigners initially taking the lead roles and stealing the show in the most lavish of productions. As the league developed, a subtle change began to occur. Instead of aspiring to be the new Zico, Littbarski or Lineker, young Japanese players had a home-grown role model. Enter Kazu.

By that point, he had triumphed over adversity in Brazil and was ready to stamp his personality all over his country's new league. He did not hold back. Kazu's name might not be immediately familiar to a Western audience, given that he spent the majority of his career in the J. League, but he is the most popular Japanese player of all time. 'Kazu is Mr Japan. He is the David Beckham figure. Kazu is God, basically,' says Tweed.

Kazu took the J. League by storm. After scoring, he would perform a Michael Jackson-esque crotch-grabbing routine that became known as the 'Kazu Dance'. He became a huge personality and sex symbol, cultivating his celebrity status by wearing outrageous clothes and marrying a beautiful singer-cum-model. 'Kazu just loved publicity,' says Moffett. He could also play, however, and delighted crowds with his Brazilian-inspired trickery. He held the J. League's scoring record until 2001 and scored 56 goals for the national team. Japan loved Kazu, but part of the attraction was the romance of his story. He had left his home country, made a success of himself and came back to share his talents in his homeland. Through him, the Japanese football dream inched closer to a reality. With respect to Zico and the rest, here was a Japanese idol to look up to.

The pieces of the jigsaw were coming together – they had a successful league, top-class foreigners and a home-grown talent – but they wanted more. From the late 1980s onwards, the Japanese had begun to travel extensively and interact with the West as never before. The heightened status of the national team, and the hysteria generated by their qualification for the 1998 World Cup in France, was a further indicator of their willingness to look outward. As the 1990s progressed, however, what the Japanese really craved was international sporting success. As is the case with South American, African and Eastern European players, the world looks to the big European leagues, particularly the Champions League, as the benchmark of real success. Kazu's impact in Brazil had given the Japanese the briefest taste, but his subsequent one-year spell in Italian football with Genoa was a failure. Japan now desperately wanted to produce an international star, ideally one who would stand out in one of the best European leagues. Enter Nakata.

On 16 November 1997, Japan faced Iran in a crucial World Cup qualifier. Having already won the right to host the 2002 World Cup, the country desperately wanted to qualify for their first World Cup on merit. Four years before, they had agonisingly failed to qualify for the World Cup in the United States, and the nation's hopes rested on beating Iran to reach the finals in France the following summer. At half-time, Japan were a goal to the good, Hidetoshi Nakata's slide-rule pass having picked out Masashi Nakayama to score. Two rapid strikes from Iran after the interval caused panic, but Nakata delivered once more. The midfielder crossed for Shoji Jo to head home Japan's equaliser. With two minutes to go before the end of extra time, Nakata burst from midfield and, as he approached the penalty area, unleashed a left-foot drive. The goalkeeper parried it out to Masayuki Okano, who scored to take Japan to the World Cup finals for the first time in their history. A nation went wild, and in Nakata a star was born.

As the country trained its gaze on the 20-year-old midfielder, it soon became clear that this was no ordinary footballer and no ordinary man. First, he was very intelligent, with an IQ of 129. Second, he did not hold true to the values commonly associated with Japanese society. Nakata was fully aware of his own self-worth and not in the least deferential. In fact, he rejected conventional notions of hierarchy, particularly when associated with football. 'When you're on the pitch, the players are all equal, and there shouldn't be any hierarchy,' he insisted after a clip from the Iran game showed him shouting at team captain Masami Ihara without the polite suffix '*san*'. Nakata soon emerged as a symbol for a new generation of Japanese, personifying the values of a rapidly changing, Western-facing society.

His football philosophy, meanwhile, was unique. Nakata's analytical mind had developed a new way of approaching the game. 'I like things such as maths and physics in which you use formulae and laws to end up with the only correct answer. It's easy to play football if you think about it mathematically. I go after the ball according to a football "formula". There is always a theory in my head.' Japan, it seemed, had its first philosopher-footballer. He fleshed out his scientific approach even more. 'I am not very skilful, and I'm not very physical, but while I'm playing I can look at the game almost like a third person, and that's very important because it makes you able to judge where to find space to receive the ball, shoot or play a pass.'

He backed up his natural talent with a ferocious work ethic and became fixated with marrying his idea of how the game should be played with reality. Practice was the key to reconciling the two, and he was even reduced to tears of frustration on the occasions that he failed to give practical expression to his theories. 'Japanese people, in general, have this idea, whether it is their craftsmen or swordsmen, to practise something 100 or 1,000 times,' says Moffett. 'They repeat it again and again and again until the action becomes part of the body. It's about incremental improvements, getting a little better every day.'

Nakata's formula for success clearly worked. At that point, he was signed to the J. League club Bellmare Hiratsuka, but his performances before and during the World Cup soon attracted the attention of European clubs. In the end, he chose the small Italian club AC Perugia, who had just been promoted to Serie A. It offered him the ideal launch pad for his career in European football but also a sanctuary. Since his overnight success in 1997, Nakata had become the country's biggest sporting superstar, and he found that his actions were heavily scrutinised by the media. He also felt he had been badly treated by the Japanese press and decided not to communicate with them at all, despite a huge contingent tracking him to Italy. Nakata's problem with them stemmed from the manner in which he believed they exaggerated his every comment. He also had a deep mistrust of their propensity to switch between high praise of him and scathing criticism. As a result, he retreated into his shell.

However, he worked hard to maintain channels of communication with his fans and wrote several memoirs about his thoughts and theories on football. The Internet revolution also came along at the perfect time for Nakata to circumvent the press. Nakata.net became his channel of communication with the world and, at its peak, received up to 5 million hits a week. He explained the importance of his website in an interview with CNN. 'The reason I started was because in 1998, just before the World Cup in France, it was the worst moment [for me] with the Japanese media. It was very difficult to talk because they changed my meaning. So, I said, "I don't want to talk to the media, so maybe I have to have my own media." I started my website, and slowly it got bigger and bigger.'

In his first game for Perugia, against Juventus in the 1997–98 season, Nakata scored twice against a team that included stars such as Zinedine Zidane, Edgar Davids and 'Pippo' Inzaghi. Despite losing the game 4–3, Nakata had proved he could prosper in illustrious company, and Perugia would go on to survive that season thanks to his ten goals – a remarkable haul for a Serie A midfielder.

In 2000, he moved to Roma, with whom he won a *scudetto*. Although he often started games on the bench, his star was still in the ascendancy, and he secured an £18-million move to Parma. Nakata was not only a talent, he was also a commercial asset, and his Italian clubs could count on lucrative Far East shirt sales and sponsorship. Nakata's appeal in his homeland continued to mushroom, and Japanese youngsters were to be seen drifting around the streets of Tokyo in Perugia or Roma shirts. On Monday evenings, highlights of what Japanese players overseas had done that weekend would be broadcast on television, and the players were hailed as ambassadors for a country that was rapidly falling in love with the beautiful game.

As Mottram explains, Japan was proud of its footballing exports, and there was no grumbling when Nakata or Nakamura left the J. League to develop their talents in Europe. 'I spoke to Saburo Kawabuchi, and he has always wanted Japanese players to go abroad. He knows that it will improve them and there will be a spin-off back in Japan. That has happened with guys such as Nakata and Nakamura. Players like that are afforded superstar status at home. When they go abroad, their status goes up even more. Nakamura is a national hero. Japanese fans are perhaps disappointed that they don't see him but appreciate that going abroad will make their players better. It's a wonderful culture in which sports people are built up and everyone does their best to keep them up there. In Scotland, sadly, it tends to be the case that people build them up to knock them down.'

Nakamura has embraced his ambassadorial role. 'The heroes for these young boys playing football in Japan are players who have left the J. League to play in Europe, and that is the ambition for all the footballers still playing in Japan. Guys such as me and Nakata are the most famous footballers.'

Stuart Baxter believes that players such as Nakamura and Nakata's ability to adapt outside Japan reflects a part of the samurai spirit that still resides in the nation's psyche. Samurai was the name given to the military nobility of pre-industrial Japan. They were well-trained, highly skilled warriors who shaped Japanese history for 1,500 years up until the late-nineteenth century. Although perceived by many Westerners as a warrior class, samurais were also politicians, poets and farmers. The samurai's life was ruled by *bushido*, a strict warrior code that placed the emphasis on honour and discipline. It dictated that a samurai serve his *daimyo*, or master, with absolute loyalty. Indeed, the word 'samurai' actually means 'to serve'. It does not take a great leap of the imagination to see how these values still inform modern-day Japanese society and, in this case, their leading sportsmen and women. Both Nakata and Nakamura had their struggles after leaving Japan but showed admirable discipline and endurance to stick with it. Nakata remained in Italy for eight years before moving to Bolton Wanderers and then retiring. Nakamura has been out of Japan for six years. Both see themselves as ambassadors, 'serving' their country by establishing Japan as an emerging football nation.

'I was interested in martial arts before I moved to Japan, and when I was there I wrote a book about the mentality of Japanese sportsmen,' says Baxter. 'Initially, I thought they would struggle to leave Japan, and the comfort and hero worship behind them, to go and be small fish in big ponds. But I realised that they have something of the samurai spirit in them – they buckle down and battle through the pain barrier. It has stood them in good stead. If you go back in history, that has always been a character trait of the Japanese. So, it is less difficult for them to leave their country and leave all that behind. That attitude is inherent. It is part of their history.'

That Nakata was a pioneer for Japanese football is beyond doubt. He blazed a trail that others, most notably Nakamura, were only too happy to follow. It is no coincidence that when Nakamura chose to launch his career in Europe he also plumped for a modest, lower-ranked Serie A side, in his case Reggina. In fact, he revealed recently that he consulted Nakata before making the move. The two also share similar personality traits. Nakata's endless passing drills, in which he would meticulously work out the effect of different levels of pressure from certain areas of the foot, mirror Nakamura's dedicated dead-ball practising. Both are deeply analytical and self-critical, but perhaps Nakamura is less of a strategist and more of an artist. Whereas Nakata broke down every part of his game and successfully put it back together again to form a winning package, Nakamura has emerged as arguably a more spontaneous talent. If Nakata approached football as an intellectual pursuit, Nakamura approaches it with a more spontaneous, creative, almost sensuous touch, trusting that his technique will provide the platform he needs to excel. If Japanese football needed a Nakata to break down barriers, it also needed a Nakamura to provide a more creative and aesthetic approach to the sport.

As people, the two could not be more contrasting characters. While Nakata was unconventional and bucked the system, Nakamura plays by the rules. If the former was more Europeanised, the latter more closely fits the Japanese profile. Mottram gained a unique insight into Nakata's character not long after his arrival in Japan. 'When I went out there at first, he was breaking through. He had extraordinary ability and was a very intellectual guy. He was not a typical Japanese person. He had a mind of his own. Before the season started, the J. League asked me to speak about the wearing of jewellery on the pitch. Nakata always wore a small medallion around his neck, but the J. League wanted me to make the point that no jewellery was allowed. But Nakata spoke up and said, "I wear a short chain, and it would not harm anyone else." I said to him, "Yes, but you could harm yourself. If you are running and something happens, it could cut your throat." He said, "That is my responsibility," to which I replied, "No, it is my responsibility, because if you end up with a cut on your throat on the pitch, I am the one who will get the blame." I watched him in games after that, and whenever a foreign referee was officiating he would never wear his medallion, but he always did when it was a Japanese referee. He knew how to play the system. He was a completely different kettle of fish from Nakamura. When Nakata was thrust into a situation in which he had to do or say something, he would do it and do it very well. I don't think Nakamura would put himself forward in that way.'

Whereas Nakata had refused to interact with the Japanese press, Nakamura embraced them. After a year spent with Nakamura at Reggina, Shin Toyofuku was switched to cover Nakata at Fiorentina. He spent a year chipping away at the midfielder but got nowhere. 'I was with Nakata in 2004–05. Florence is fantastic, much bigger than Reggio Calabria. There is a lot of history and art – very beautiful – but I found it very difficult to make a relationship with Nakata. He had the same attitude to all the Japanese press. Some people say that when he was playing in Japan the press criticised him heavily and because of that he became a press-hater. But I'm not sure why he behaved like that. I asked him to speak, and he said, "I can't say anything." If that counts as a conversation, I had 1,000 conversations with him. If conversations count as something more, I didn't have one with him. When I went on away trips and we were sitting next to each other on the same charter plane I would say "Hi", but he would say nothing. He just sat and read his magazine. It was strange. There was no way to approach him. He wants to be European. He spoke to the Italian press. I would sometimes get the quotes from them. I was there from Japan for Nakata, and I would end up asking the Italian journalists what he said. It was so, so strange, maybe a unique case in football history.'

When Toyofuku was mercifully restored to the Nakamura beat in Glasgow in 2005, the contrast between his two experiences could not have been greater. 'Even after a bad performance, Nakamura will say something to us. I think that is as a professional footballer should be. When Nakamura was playing in Japan, he wasn't like he is now. Sometimes he would run away from the press. Maybe being abroad at some point changed his attitude to me and the rest of the press. I have a good relationship with him now.'

With Nakata, football was never the all-consuming passion it is for Nakamura. Unlike the latter, who often rushes home from training to watch football DVDs, Nakata pursued other interests, most notably fashion. During his spell at Bolton in 2005–06, Nakata reflected on his strained relationship with the sport. 'I wasn't a fan as a youngster. I didn't watch on television or have videos or anything. I don't watch football now, and when I retire that will not change. I don't really understand why people are football fans. I don't like to watch any sport, so I don't understand what makes people do that. I want to play rather than spectate. I'm like that in life. I want to take part.'

Nakata, like Kazu before him, was a flamboyant, strong-willed character. He dressed differently, he dyed his hair strange colours, he had dalliances with supermodels. He was a playboy as well as a playmaker. 'These guys are showmen in the sense that they do things to make them the centre of attraction, and that probably helped to get them as far as it did,' says Tweed. 'Kazu was the J. League Player of the Year once and turned up in a white tuxedo and pink shirt. He wore outrageous clothing to stand out. All the Japanese love their designer gear. It's the culture in Japan. Nakata has his own label, and Kazu was massive on European clothing. A lot of what they do outside of football is fashion, whereas Nakamura doesn't come across as that kind of person. Maybe it just tells you about people in general. Some want to stand out, and some want to melt into the crowd. Nakamura just wants to be accepted.'

Nakata's growing disillusionment with professional football finally resulted in his retirement in 2006, aged just 29. After Japan's 4–1 defeat by Brazil at the 2006 World Cup in Germany, which saw them exit the tournament, he slumped to the turf and cried uncontrollably for ten minutes. Just over a week later, he announced on his website that he was to retire. He has since travelled the world and developed his interest in fashion. Though unreceptive towards his country's press, Nakata has always had a shrewd awareness of his own marketing potential and has gleefully exploited it over the years. He has featured in around 40 major television commercials for brands such as Coca-Cola and Nike. Like Nakata, Nakamura also advertises products in Japan. 'Shunsuke seems to shun the showbiz side of it, unlike Kazu and Nakata, but at the same time he still gets all the commercial endorsements,' says Tweed. 'He's on all the posters. He's the face of Adidas in Japan. He doesn't miss out on all that.'

The Scottish Premier League might not be the most glamorous league in Europe, but it has offered Nakamura the chance to play in the Champions League. If Manchester United are the most popular team in the Far East and Nakamura is the most popular player, then it is impossible to overestimate the impact of the latter scoring a free-kick against the former in football's richest playground. That Nakamura did so twice during the 2006–07 season on club football's greatest stage sent his profile and popularity through the roof in Asia.

It takes a player with incredible mental strength to bear the burdens of an expectant nation. Others before Nakamura have tried and failed. Before the 1998 World Cup in France, the Japan manager Takeshi Okada had picked out the team's young striker Shoji Jo as a key man. He had shown up well in the qualification matches and proved that he was capable of raising his game at the Atlanta Olympics. He was decent in the air, good with both feet and knew the way to goal. Unfortunately, in France, he was also very, very nervous. After spurning a couple of good chances in Japan's opening match against Croatia, Jo was widely expected to score against Jamaica, their weakest group opponents. On two occasions, he had golden chances and fluffed them badly. On the biggest football stage of all, and with the hopes of a nation on his shoulders, Jo had lost his bottle. In a TV interview a few weeks later, he said, 'Before you play football, you have to know yourself and have mental strength.'

Nakata had won a *scudetto* with Roma but was only a bit-part player, his contribution limited mainly to substitute appearances. In Nakamura, Japan finally produced a player of skill and vision, a player who was one of the best free-kick takers in the world and, most importantly, who could do it when it mattered most, when the pressure was at its most intense – in the Champions League with a worldwide audience of millions bearing down on him. That was what made him number one. That was what made him the most successful footballer the nation has ever produced.

If Nakamura represents the culmination of Japan's development as a football nation to date, then the question remains: where do they go from here? In a nation of 127 million, the challenge must now be to produce a world-class talent, a player who can surpass the achievements of Nakamura and take his place among the true greats. Many believe that day is fast approaching. 'I don't think it is far away,' says Mottram. 'The young kids, such as Koki Mizuno who has signed for Celtic, have come through an infrastructure in which they get intense coaching in the right sense from a very young age. The Japanese are great admirers of Dutch football and have looked to their model to produce young players. I think we will begin to see a steady stream of young players coming out of Japan. If they leave Japan early enough, there is a chance that one of them will become world-class. I think Nakamura and Nakata left it a little too late. Mizuno is only twenty-two and will benefit from five or six years at Celtic. Real Madrid were interested in Nakamura before the World Cup in 2002, but Philippe Troussier didn't pick him, and Madrid seemed to drop their interest because of that. If Nakamura had made it to Madrid at that point, he could have been even further on than he is just now.'

After a nine-year absence, Baxter returned for a second spell in Japan in 2006 with Vissel Kobe and noticed a marked improvement in standards. He believes that they are inching ever closer to producing a genuine world-class talent. 'I thought they had moved on considerably. They had a greater breadth about their play. A lot of work had gone on with the youth players, and they were also tactically more astute. World-class players are a product of their environment. India has a bigger population than anyone apart from China, but the environment and culture is not conducive to football, so they don't produce many footballers. Japan is becoming more and more conducive to football. Their diet is very good, and they are moving forward in all aspects. Five to ten years ago, there were hardly any track-and-field athletes in Japan, but now they are starting to produce them. If you think of top European-class players such as Kaká, Nakata and Nakamura are probably just below them, but it will not be long before they produce one or two world-class players. They too are going to have to move out of Japan pretty early and develop themselves elsewhere, but, at that point, they will have a lot in their locker.'

Troussier is also convinced of Japan's credentials as an emerging force in world football. 'They have played in three World Cups, and 90 per cent of the players are playing in Japan, which shows that the league is strong. Also, Urawa Red Diamonds were Asian champions in 2007. For me, their level is maybe top fifteen in the world, and I'm sure they can get into the top ten in the next ten years. They have the infrastructure, collectively they know how to play together, individually they are starting to fulfil their potential, some of them are stronger and some are starting to play in Europe. It is a very strong football country. They are improving every year.'

The J. League has been a typical triumph of Japanese planning mixed with shrewdness and vision. It is reasonable to conclude that, given continued development over the next decade, they will produce their share of superstars. Allied to a superb work ethic, their emergence could finally establish Japan as a global force in world football.

EIGHT

·············

An International Incident

PHILIPPE TROUSSIER HAS WAITED SIX YEARS TO EXPLAIN why he dropped Shunsuke Nakamura from the 2002 World Cup in Japan. At the time, he refused to justify himself to a dumbfounded national media. He had made the decision and insisted that his squad, the host nation, would move forward with confidence. End of story.

Japan's subsequent qualification for the first knockout stage of the finals vindicated the omission of the Yokohama F. Marinos midfielder from the 23-man pool. It was widely speculated that Troussier felt he lacked the physical presence and defensive discipline to fit into his dogmatic team vision, but in the six years since he has kept his counsel.

It remains one of the defining moments of the midfielder's career. Missing out on a World Cup finals is tough enough but even more so when it is being staged in your home country. Six years later, and even after representing his country at the 2006 finals, Nakamura continues to be asked about the disappointment of 2002.

Now it was Troussier's turn to answer the questions. The problem was I had to find him first. 'Itinerant' is the most common adjective applied to the larger-than-life Frenchman. 'Top coach, will travel' could be the motto of the man who has managed everywhere from Marseilles to Morocco. The trail went cold in 2006 when he left his post as manager of the Morocco national team after two weeks following a difference of opinion with the football association. Troussier does not have an agent or management company. Without his phone number, there is no way of contacting him. And I didn't have his phone number.

Then, one day, the tentacles of Google finally tracked him down. Typically, he had turned up in the most unlikely of locations. He had taken a job as general manager of FC Ryūkyū, a team plying their trade in the Japan Football League, the semi-professional division below J. League One and Two. They are a tiny outfit, established in 1993 and based on the Pacific island of Okinawa, a two-and-half-hour flight from the mainland. In a list of football's most obscure outposts, FC Ryūkyū would be near the top. It was more in hope than expectation that I dispatched an email to the club's press office. Again, the trail went cold. Weeks later, I finally received a reply. 'We will be delighted to welcome you in Okinawa for an interview with Mr Troussier,' it read.

Two weeks later and I was on a flight to Okinawa, via Tokyo, for an audience with the godfather of Japanese football. Troussier is a national hero in Japan, where he spent four years as national team manager between 1998 and 2002. It is no exaggeration to say that he single-handedly revolutionised the country's approach to football. At the 1998 World Cup, Japan had failed to win a game and proved that they could not cope with the physical demands of top-class European football. The Japanese Football Association decided that they needed to hire a European coach, so Arsène Wenger recommended his countryman Troussier.

In September 1998, he took control of three different categories: the A group for the 2002 World Cup, the B group for the 2000 Olympics and the C group for the World Youth Championships in 1999. Nakamura was in the B group and central to Troussier's plans.

He played a key role in the team that reached the quarter-finals of the Sydney Olympics in 2000 and also the victorious Asian Cup side the same year. 'He was a star in Japan, a very talented, skilful player on his left foot,' recalls Troussier. 'But when you see him for the first time with his hair brushed down, you think, "He is not strong." He was fragile, very shy and in his own world. He was already a big star at his own club and also with the national team, but he was at the beginning of his career and everybody expected many things from him. Having said that, he played a lot of games in the B category and did well.'

It was in 2001 that things started to go wrong. At that point, Troussier had started to build his team for the finals. He cherry-picked the best players from the three levels and began to think seriously about who would make his final squad. The team suffered a setback in 2001 with a crushing 5–0 friendly defeat by France in the Stade de France, a match in which Nakamura, like the majority of his teammates, performed poorly.

Troussier already harboured misgivings about the player's mental and physical strength, and the seeds of doubt continued to grow in the lead-up to the finals. 'In 2002, before going to Spain for the last camp, Nakamura was injured. I said, "Come with me. We will do preparation in Madrid and play some matches." He came along, and during three weeks' preparation he stayed with the doctor all the time. I never felt the motivation from him to say, "I want to come back." In the last three matches before the finals, he didn't play, so I had to take a decision.'

It was not one he took lightly. His friend was the head of Adidas, so Troussier was fully aware that their marketing in Japan was focused on Nakamura's appearance. 'Imagine the pressure I was under,' he says, shaking his head at the memory. He knew that the decision on Nakamura must be a robust one, so he drew up criteria which every player had to fulfil to be part of his squad. 'I had three separate groups in my squad,' he explains. 'The first group was made up of 14 or 15 players who would come into my thinking for the starting line-up. Nakamura was not in the first category, so would he fit into my second category? The second was the nine players on the bench. Those were the players whom I could ask to come on for five minutes and make an impact. I looked at Nakamura and thought, "No, he doesn't fit into that category either." When I was making my final list, I considered that this would be a final squad of players who would be together for four, five or six weeks. I wanted good squad men who would share good times and bad times, eat together and sleep together. So, for the third category, I decided to call up two veterans who, for me, were the symbol of Japan. They hadn't participated in the four years under me, but they were like assistant coaches to help me wake up the dressing-room. My choices were Masashi Nakayama and Yutaka Akita, one striker and one defender, both with strong dressing-room personalities, something Nakamura couldn't give me. So, when we got together for the first match, the atmosphere was very strong.'

Troussier knew that Japan, despite having home advantage, were serious underdogs. His players had not yet proved themselves at the highest level and would have to dig deep into their mental and physical reserves to cope with the top teams they would come up against. Talent alone was not going to be enough. 'If you play against Spain, then for 70 per cent of the game you have no ball. If you play France, you have next to no ball. You have to fight and fight, and when you get the ball you have only five seconds to try and make forty-five metres. You don't have time to make ten passes. You only have time to make three passes maximum when you play against these kind of teams. With that realisation, I decided that I couldn't play with Nakamura. For the type of football I wanted to play, he was not enough physically or mentally. When I announced my final list, I was not in Japan. I took a cold decision. I didn't feel I had to go to Japan and talk about it.

'If I had to take another decision in two weeks' or two months' time, then it might have been different. Some people were happy and some weren't, but I had to take responsibility. That is the life of a coach. Maybe Nakamura deserved to be in the last twenty-three because of his time with me over the course of the previous four years. But in terms of the five or six weeks of the World Cup, I felt that he was not enough for me. I took Alessandro dos Santos instead. Six months before, he was naturalised from Brazil. He played the same position. Nakamura had been injured, and Santos was fresh and could come into that second category. I could say, "Santos, give me five minutes," and he would say, "OK, coach." I don't regret my vision of the group and the decision not to include Nakamura.'

Mental and physical strength were the two attributes that Troussier had been working on with his players and the areas in which he deemed Nakamura to have fallen short. It is a familiar complaint about Japanese footballers, although less so now. It was widely acknowledged at that stage that Japanese footballers were technically accomplished but their lack of presence held them back.

The Frenchman, on taking the job, quickly identified an endemic problem in their game that had its roots in society and could be traced back to the start of the J. League in 1993. Teams were 'respectful' of their opponents, and there was a lack of the mental toughness, professionalism or gamesmanship that can win you a game.

There is a saying that when a player has enjoyed an easy game he has 'got the cigar out'. Les Mottram must have puffed through hundreds of packets of Hamlets in his first couple of years in the J. League. He had arrived in Japan with the brief of trying to raise the standard of refereeing in the country. He soon realised that he was hardly needed. He would watch in disbelief as attackers waltzed by defenders who jumped out of the way like matadors avoiding a bull. The Scot had spent his career refereeing European football and had grown used to its physicality. Some players practised the dark arts more than others but all were acquainted with the need to put their foot in where it hurts. Even the nice guys could reveal a brutal streak in the heat of battle. Football the way it was played in Europe was not necessarily an extension of a player's off-field personality. In Japan, it was.

'Their whole culture is built on discipline, hard work and respect,' explains Mottram. 'They respect each other off the park, and that carried onto the park as well, perhaps too much. There were very few red cards. The skill and technical ability is as good now as it was then, but if a player went past another, they would give up. As a referee used to European football, you would prepare yourself for a tackle from behind as the defender tried to get back at the attacker, but it never came. The defender would just let him go.'

An almost unnaturally happy atmosphere accompanied the start of the J. League. At the end of matches, it was a familiar ritual for the opposing teams to line up side by side in the middle of the pitch and wave towards the main stand. The players would then trot over to the goal-line and bow in unison. Supporters reciprocated by cheering and singing songs, regardless of whether their team had won or lost. The great Kazu once reflected on the unwavering good nature of the supporters. 'Playing football in Brazil, with the spectators booing, was really frightening,' he said. 'But in the J. League, you get applauded even when you make a mistake. I always think, "Is this really good enough?"'

J. League fans are so polite that they have been known to clear their litter up and take it home. Clubs had to work extremely hard to generate match-day atmosphere, as supporters were often too embarrassed to cheer their team. The introduction of crowd leaders, whose job it was to coordinate and motivate the crowd, eventually drew Japanese fans out of their shells.

On the field, it became clear that there was something seriously lacking in the Japanese players' competitive instinct. No one wished for a league full of cloggers, but something had to be done. Once again, the J. League's ability to attract the right kind of foreigner would hold the key to adding bite to their game. They were already acquainted with the thrilling wing play of Pierre Littbarski, the sublime gifts of Zico and the poaching instincts of Gary Lineker. Dunga, the Brazilian midfielder, soon became the snarling face of the J. League.

Dunga was as far from the stereotypical Brazilian player as it was possible to be. Although in possession of adequate technical abilities, Dunga was essentially a ball-winner, the team's 'water carrier', the famous term coined by Eric Cantona about Didier Deschamps. Dunga's iron will saw him carve out a distinguished career with teams such as Fiorentina and VFB Stuttgart, as well as the Brazilian national team, who he captained to victory in the 1994 World Cup. Dunga had first visited Japan with Internacional to play in the 1984 Kirin Cup, an annual mini-tournament, and had been taken with the culture. When he got the chance to move to J. League side Júbilo Iwata 11 years later, he jumped at it. However, Dunga was taken aback by the reaction of his teammates to his arrival, some of whom were so in awe that they refrained from tackling him in training. He began a personal crusade to add some guile and gamesmanship into the Japanese mindset. He taught his teammates techniques designed to help them win, but ones that also pushed the rules to the limit. Under his influence, Júbilo became the craftiest team in the league, constantly diving for penalties and faking injuries, but also one of the most successful. He was given the nickname 'Daddy Thunder', and clips of him verbally abusing his teammates were regularly shown on television.

'Dunga arrived in Japan and was a very aggressive player, not so much towards opponents but more so his own teammates,' recalls Mottram. 'He gave them a hell of a time. If they made a mistake, he would go through them like a dose of salts. Because of him, Júbilo were the most successful team for a few years and won the championship. Japanese players were all nice and skilful but not really competitive.'

Dragan Stojković was another whose all-consuming passion for the game rubbed off on those around him. The hugely talented

Yugoslavia international joined Nagoya Grampus Eight in 1994 and was shocked at his teammates' lackadaisical attitude towards winning or losing. Stojković swept through the J. League like a Tasmanian Devil, picking up an incredible total of 13 red and 72 yellow cards. He stayed for seven years, though, so clearly felt that his attempts to put more fire in Japanese bellies were working.

Stuart Baxter believes Japanese players were more guilty of tactical naivety than physical frailty. 'The physicality thing wasn't a big issue for me,' he argues. 'The goalkeeper I had was six feet two inches and built like a brick shithouse. My centre-forward was also a big lad. But I found a lot of players to be naive. Rather than being timid, they would get caught in possession very easily and would not know how to use their bodies to get the ball back. When we played against the Koreans, they were always more aggressive. So, we had to move the ball around quicker and be better tactically. I did find that physically they were badly lacking at set-plays, at both ends of the pitch. I saw the national team during that period, and they were beaten by Bulgaria on two set-plays. But again it was more that their defending was very naive. They would dive into stupid challenges. Around their own or the opposition's box, they were not good at taking individual responsibility. They would make rash tackles and lose composure when they had a goal-scoring chance. It is no surprise that the Japanese have not produced any really good defenders or strikers.

'Box to box, they have had lots of good players. Many of them are two-footed as well. They are very mobile and flexible. A lot of them get their flexibility from martial arts, which they practise when they are younger. Nakata and Nakamura would both have had an excellent schooling in the technical aspects of the game. When I first got to Japan, I found that because of the lack of tactical knowledge they would spend longer on technical drills. Both Nakata and Nakamura became very proficient in those aspects. But I am in no doubt that it was at Celtic, not in Japan, where Nakamura became more streetwise and tactically aware.'

Structural change was responsible for the next major shift in attitudes. When Mottram arrived in 1996, there was only one league. Three or four teams competed at the top every year, and the rest bobbed along, knowing that they would never realistically challenge for the title but equally content that there was no relegation. 'I remember refereeing a game between the two bottom teams in the division, and there was no bite to it,' says Mottram. 'Japanese players didn't have real aggression anyway, so refereeing them was very easy.'

Then, in 1998, the J. League introduced the Second Division, and suddenly players' mindsets were transformed. 'The Japanese players changed their attitudes at that point, because they were playing for their contracts and their livelihoods. It meant they had to fight for survival. Some people will kick their granny if they think they are going to lose their pay cheque. I wouldn't say that they are overly physical now, but they are certainly competitive. That was when referees really started to earn their money, because there was an edge to the games. I liken it to when Ally McCoist became known as super-sub during the Graeme Souness years. Before that, he had been a great character for referees, but when he came off the substitutes' bench he was a different player because he knew he had to make an impact.'

Nakamura began to make ripples in the Yokohama Marinos first team during the years when most Japanese players would not have said boo to a goose. Nakamura was also physically slight and not suited to, or interested in, the physical side of football. By the time the Second Divison was set up, though, he had learned a few tricks. 'He was a regular in the Marinos team,' says Mottram. 'I remember giving him some yellow cards. Not for being overly physical, but for committing a lot of wee fouls.'

Baxter recalls watching Nakamura at that time. 'He had started to emerge during my time in Japan. Marinos were a good side. I remember him as a talented player breaking through. I watched him in a couple of games and thought, "This is an interesting kid." He has developed from there and gone on to achieve great success. I have been a bit surprised that he has gone to Scotland and done it. If you had asked me in Japan where I would have placed Japanese players in Europe, I would have perhaps said France, or maybe Serie B in Italy. I have great admiration for the way he has learned to cope with the physical side of the game.'

So, a fusion of South American and European passion, combined with the creation of a second tier, had given the J. League an edge. However, they still lacked the required physicality for the very top level. That had been proven at the 1998 World Cup. Enter Troussier. The brash Frenchman had spent the previous decade coaching in Africa. He had been a journeyman player who'd spent most of his career with smaller clubs in France. Towards the end of the 1980s, he entered management for the first time and headed to the Ivory Coast to take over First Division side ASEC Abidjan. After leading them to success in the West African Club Championship, he moved on to manage Burkino Faso to an African Nations Cup semi-final. He then helped Nigeria qualify for the 1998 World Cup and took charge of South Africa at the finals themselves.

He later declared, 'It is in Africa that I earned my stripes of recognition. I have not needed to coach Arsenal or Manchester United or England or Germany to be one of the top coaches in the world today.'

On arrival in Japan, he identified Japanese players' tactical naivety as a major flaw. 'My first image of Japan when I came to the country was of the national team at the 1998 World Cup. The image that I got was that the teamwork was not so bad – they played together with a very strong fighting spirit – but the football was very naive. They shot from anywhere. They used the first idea in their minds. It was difficult for them to manage a match. In the J. League, if a team led 3–0, you were still not sure if they would win, because they only played to score goals.

'In the J. League at that time, there was three points for a win.

It was impossible to draw. If it was equal at full-time, you went to extra time, then if it was still a draw, you went to penalties. For them, defeat was dishonour. When they lost a match, you would have thought they had lost their family. In Europe, we teach players to win, but before that we teach them to protect their goal. Their culture was winning and scoring goals, so it was difficult for them to consider the defensive culture. My job was to say, "OK, now we have to play differently.'"

Troussier had been dubbed the 'White Witchdoctor' in Africa, but the moniker 'Red Devil' was given to him in Japan in reference to the colour his face turned when he was angry. He was angry a lot. It is no exaggeration to say that Troussier fell out with or challenged almost everyone he came across in Japan. An abrasive, headstrong character, his unconventional approach shocked the Japanese to the core. In a country built on respect and politeness, he broke social protocol by screaming and shouting at his players and even man-handling them on occasion. Causing others to lose face in public is a major taboo in Japan, but Troussier violated such conventions wilfully. He accused the J. League of fostering a culture of complacency among Japanese players, thereby blunting their competitive instinct, and laid out his game plan for making them more aggressive. He brought in sports-conditioning analysts from France and was surprised at the findings. In his book, *Passion*, he wrote:

> The first round of tests produced a surprising result: the Japanese players' muscle strength was superior to that of the French and Italians. But when muscle strength was translated into speed, the Japanese lagged behind the Europeans. The Japanese were weak at short-distance sprints, the sudden movement required to fool an opponent, execute a header or make a sliding tackle. Players rarely went in for hard sliding tackles, they hardly ever used their elbows and they didn't pull opposition players' jerseys – at least not to excess.

Troussier's conclusion was that Japanese players needed to start exploiting their natural physicality. 'Their respect for the rules meant that they didn't tackle from behind. Football in Japan is a nice experience, the whole family goes along, everyone is happy, the pitch is nice – I like football in Japan. They could do football with their own rules, and it would be a good experience. The problem is that they want to be involved in European football, so they needed a new vision. My challenge was to get them to impose themselves, to use their shoulders, to walk on people's toes. This kind of play is necessary to play against European teams in the World Cup.'

So, Troussier's training sessions placed an emphasis on physicality, and he would frequently push and shove players around the training pitch to convey his message. One of his drills involved an attacking player pushing the ball between two defenders standing close together and then barging through the middle of them. 'I had to get rid of the inferiority complex that made the players act like little children when playing the best teams,' he explains. 'At a training camp, I made them practise pulling jerseys and got them acquainted with contact play using elbows, shoulders and tough tackles. Players who weren't keen on the rough side had to get used to the reality. I didn't want them to get trampled into the dirt. When I arrived, I appeared like a member of a guerrilla group to the Japanese. But coaching Japan was like discovering raw diamonds and cleaning and carving them.'

Troussier believed that Japanese players lacked initiative. When they were given a plan, they carried it out to a tee But when they were asked to make individual decisions, they either froze or buried their heads in the sand. Once again, their inability to express themselves on the pitch reflected societal mores. 'In Japan, you have a green light to cross the road, and the red light tells you to wait on the pavement. I once said to the players, "If it is 5 a.m., you are alone, the red light is showing but you see nothing on the right or left, you can go." That was not acceptable to them. They said, "No, we have to wait for the decision to be made for us." I said, "No, you have to take an individual decision. Sometimes the decision is wrong, but you have to take responsibility for it." In four years, I tried to change their mentality.

'My belief is that 60 per cent of the result in football comes from teamwork and tactics, the relationship between the manager and players. Sometimes that is enough to win a match and sometimes it isn't. I had good players who respected the coaches and worked well collectively, but my aim was to try and improve their individual potential. Sometimes you need players who can beat one, two players, who take a risk and from that open a game up. Initially, that was impossible for Japanese players. They played football according to the rules of society. They couldn't play with an individual attitude, because it was not acceptable in their country. Doing well at the World Cup meant it had to come from our personality as well as our teamwork. I don't want to say their way is bad, because it is the collective way and allows them to concentrate very hard, but we needed more individuality. I broke many barriers in trying to get them to do that.'

Troussier purposely did not learn Japanese or immerse himself in the culture. He was there to impose his culture and identity on them, not the other way around. Indeed, he regarded himself as a cultural missionary. He employed a French assistant, Florent Dabadie, who spoke Japanese, and he frequently wrote books and newspaper columns instructing the Japanese on how to be more cosmopolitan.

'We went to a friendly match in England, and I had to go with a chef with Japanese food. I had to move a small Japan with me. If I presented them with English food, they said they couldn't eat it. If you said to the players, "Your night is free," they would ask me, "What time do we meet in the lobby to get on the bus and go to the Japanese restaurant?" That is freedom for them. Imagine if you gave a free night to French, English or Scottish footballers – they would go to the pub and end up I don't know where. So I said to them, "If you go to England, you eat English food. If you go to Italy, you eat Italian. Same with France." For the federation, its members and the players, that seemed impossible. But my first job was to open their eyes.'

In a bid to encourage his players to think for themselves and become more worldly wise, he organised as many matches as possible outside of Asia, employing his own brand of shock tactics. He took them to some of the world's most inhospitable locations. Once, at a training camp in Burkino Faso, the world's third-poorest country, he ordered his players to take a bush taxi 300 miles across dirt roads to get to a friendly game in Bobo-Dioulasso. He described his management style as 'guerrilla tactics' and took his unconventional approach one stage further during a trip to Lebanon for the Asian Cup. 'We played Qatar in a group match, and two days before I gave the players the night off. Then I went to the hotel and had them close all their restaurants. I banned the players from using the team bus. I wanted them to experience Beirut, eat wherever they liked, act freely and wander around the streets not as a team, but as individuals. It helped open their eyes. Afterwards, they all had a bit more confidence in themselves. We went to places such as Africa without any chefs or Japanese food and stayed in hotels with big cockroaches. We visited many, many countries. I brought in foreign coaches, doctors and physios to open their minds and exchange ideas. It would be impossible for a Japanese coach to have acted like me. Japanese people must respect social conventions. But I had not been influenced by things in Japan, and it was a great advantage.'

Troussier also dismissed traditional ideas of hierarchy – football had the same system as the workplace – by dropping senior players in favour of youngsters. When appointed, he quickly realised that younger players thought it disrespectful not to pass to their elders. He encouraged them to challenge the senior players' supposed superiority and change the order of things. In doing this, his aim was to create a competitive spirit and send out the message that no player, regardless of their age or experience, would be able to walk into his squad. His approach would take on greater significance for Nakamura, who became his highest-profile victim with his omission in 2002.

Troussier took responsibility for every level of the national team, from Under-20 to seniors, and quickly identified a core of promising youngsters from the Japan side that had finished runners-up in the World Youth Championships in 1999. 'Eighty-nine per cent of the national team in 2002 came from the Under-20 group or the Under-23 Olympic squad, players such as Shinji Ono, Naohiro Takahara, Koji Nakata, Hitoshi Sogahata, Junichi Inamoto. The rest, such as Nakamura and Mitsuo Igasawara, came from the Olympic group. After one training session, I realised that the Under-20 group was more flexible and skilful. They grew up with the J. League, and they were educated with new coaches and new players from abroad. The first ten years of the J. League was very important. I was very lucky to find players of great quality. We were runners-up at the World Youth Championships, where we eliminated England, Cameroon, United States and Uruguay then lost the final to Spain.'

Team spirit was central to Troussier's philosophy, and he encouraged his players to be more tactile when celebrating goals. He joined in too and, in typically Gallic fashion, would plant kisses on players or pat them on the rear when they pleased him. 'When I arrived in Japan, I had the impression that people didn't ever look at each other,' he reflects. 'I couldn't understand how crowds functioned. No one bumped into anyone else, even though people's eyes never met. Sometimes I would ride the subway and think that people never communicated with each other. But that is completely false. Though I still might not have earned my licence for walking in crowds, I've learned that this society has its own rules for communication.'

Troussier's confrontational style, perhaps inevitably, brought him into conflict with the team's biggest star, Hidetoshi Nakata. Prior to the Frenchman's arrival, Nakata was the focal point off the field and on it, where he was given freedom to roam around the midfield. But Troussier did not want a focal point. He did not want younger teammates to be intimidated by Nakata's presence, which they clearly were. He had a more democratic ideal of how a team should function. He wanted all his players to be equal and totally committed to the national cause. He felt Nakata was not. By that point, Nakata's career had taken off in Italy, and the Frenchman accused Nakata of putting club before country when he failed to turn up for the 2001 Confederations Cup final, which Japan lost to France by a single goal.

By then, Troussier had already achieved considerable success. The year before that, Japan had been crowned Asian champions and reached the quarter-finals of the football competition at the Sydney Olympics, where they were knocked out by the USA in a penalty shoot-out. Troussier and Nakata's relationship became so fractured that at one stage it seemed possible that he too would not make the 2002 World Cup squad. The team's success in his absence had proved he was not indispensable. Much of the problem stemmed from the fact that, unlike the rest of the squad, Nakata did not play in Japan. 'He only came when the FIFA rules allowed him to, that was the problem,' says Troussier. 'He would come just 30 days, but the other players would be able to attend 110 days of the year.'

Ultimately, Nakata was offered a reprieve and edged his way back into contention with an excellent performance in Japan's 2–0 win over Poland in March 2002. At the time, Troussier reflected on the change in the player's attitude. 'Nakata's attitude has been completely different. Before he came with five managers, two doctors and a helicopter, and now he comes with his bicycle,' he said, with just a hint of overstatement.

When asked to reflect on his relationship with Nakata back then, Troussier says, 'That is a normal situation for a coach. It is the same for Zinedine Zidane in France, David Beckham and Steven Gerrard in England, and Kaká in Brazil. Each country needs a symbol for the young generation. Who decides that these players are stars? Is it me? No. It is the press. For me, the star is the team and teamwork. I look at things collectively, but the media view things individually. When I first arrived in Japan, I discovered a star system. Being coach of Japan meant I was given the status of a rock star. To be a coach is more like being a politician. People want to recognise themselves in the team. You have to have a balance between your tactical approach and the expectations of the people. People must love the team, and for that you need a figurehead. That is Zidane, Beckham, Nakata. Nakata was strong, never injured and had a strong image in Japan, so when he played the team felt better.'

The up-and-down relationship between Nakata and Troussier is crucial to understanding the decision to drop Nakamura. The Frenchman was no respecter of reputations, and given his boldness in taking on the country's biggest football icon it should be regarded with little surprise that he had the guts to leave the Marinos midfielder out.

Troussier continued to bang the drum of teamwork and democracy in a portentous message to the media before the World Cup. 'Liberty, equality, fraternity,' he wrote. 'Four years ago, those were the values of the champions, France. Now they are the colours of Japan. Have faith in your values. From there success will come.'

And so it did. The co-hosts, in front of a home audience, were under major pressure to deliver. In their opening match against Belgium, the fruits of the Troussier revolution showed. Marc Wilmots gave Belgium an early lead in the second half, but suddenly Japan flickered to life, equalising through Takayuki Suzuki before a great individual strike from Inamoto. Belgium defender Peter van der Heyden denied Japan a famous victory late in the game, but the hosts had proved that they could compete at the top level. A 1–0 victory over Russia in their second group match, with another Inamoto goal doing the damage, was further evidence of their progress under Troussier and gave them their first-ever win at a World Cup. When they followed that up with a 2–0 win over Tunisia, Japan had reached the last 16, where they played Turkey.

A 1–0 defeat to an impressive Turkey side burst the bubble of an expectant nation, but the tournament had been a huge success for the co-hosts. 'Our great adventure is over,' said a tearful Troussier. 'Today, I was very proud to be their trainer and to have worn the Japanese shirt for four years. I say bravo to this Japanese team. I would tell the Japanese players to believe in their potential and their capacity to succeed.' Content his revolution was complete, he announced his decision to step down shortly after the finals.

Nakamura had watched all this unfold from his sofa. It must have been a torturous experience for a player who was no stranger to rejection. Troussier had shattered his dreams but also challenged him in a way that would prove the making of him. On reflection, he harboured no bitterness over the decision. 'People were saying all kinds of stuff about me,' says Nakamura. 'I was a little shocked, but not depressed, because my teammates from Marinos were a really good help to me, and I had prepared myself by thinking of it both ways, whether I was selected or not. I just wanted to play football, and when you can't do that it's frustrating. There were a few left out, and I think they had a chance of getting mentally strong compared to the guys who played in the World Cup. Maybe I wasn't good enough at the time, so I don't have a problem with that.'

Aged 24, he now faced the biggest test of character of his career. He could stay in the comfort zone of the J. League or move to Europe and start working on the deficiencies that had prevented him from making Troussier's squad. Just a few days after the Frenchman resigned as national coach in 2002, Nakamura signed a three-year contract at Reggina. Initially, it seemed a strange choice of club, but he knew that playing for a relegation-threatened Serie A side would develop the areas of his game that Troussier felt were lacking. Once again, it was a bold decision that reinforced a willingness to confront his limitations. Baxter noticed a change in Nakamura after the World Cup. 'He is one of many Japanese players who have come on leaps and bounds since the World Cup in 2002.'

Troussier's successor would also prompt an astonishing change in Nakamura's international fortunes. Zico, the Brazilian legend, immediately handed Nakamura the number 10 shirt. 'Great players such as Maradona wore this number,' said the midfielder. 'It is the number special players wear, players who if they weren't there, the team wouldn't win. I'm not yet at that level, but I will keep looking to improve and aim to keep the number 10 shirt.' From reject to key player in one change of coach.

Zico proceeded to build his team around him. 'Nakamura has great talent and technique,' gushed the Brazilian. 'He is one of the most accomplished players Japan has produced. He is an essential part of our Japanese team and has great sense in terms of passing and free-kicks, which makes him special. He is sure to succeed wherever he plays. I highly appreciate Nakamura's talent, and he is one of the best players in Japan right now. He is a very dedicated player and always gives 100 per cent for the team, which I really appreciate. He is good at defensive chores, but he performs best when he looks towards goal, as he has great command of the ball and can change the rhythm of the game.'

Nakamura responded to being given greater creative licence with some impressive performances. In 2004, his goals led Japan to Asian Cup triumph, beating China in the final. At the Confederations Cup the following year, he produced a Man of the Match performance against Brazil in a 2–2 draw. The result marked one of the most memorable moments in Japanese football. As a nation, Japan have always revered Brazil's football abilities, and they could even have beaten the South Americans that day had they not had a goal disallowed.

The game also had wider implications, because it was the first time Gordon Strachan had seen Nakamura play. In his autobiography, *Strachan: My Life in Football*, the Celtic manager wrote:

When I watched him on TV, in his Confederations Cup matches for Japan against teams such as Brazil, I actually thought my eyes were deceiving me. I kept asking people, 'Is he really as good as I think he is?' At Celtic, it quickly became clear that he was.

In the years since Troussier's controversial decision, Nakamura has established himself as Japan's creative fulcrum. He has become indispensable and played in every minute of their three group games at the 2006 finals. He admitted at that time that the disappointment of 2002 was his driving force. 'I was so determined not to miss out on the World Cup like four years ago. I have been working really hard over these last four years to try and take my game to the next level. It hasn't been easy, but I think my time abroad has made me a better player, and my experiences off the pitch have made me a stronger person, too. Troussier had his reasons for not picking me, but I have just tried to work hard and become the kind of player that no coach could leave out.'

It did not prevent him from experiencing a heart-stopping moment, however, when Zico read out his squad for the 2006 finals live on Japanese TV. Nakamura's name was 18th to be read. 'It was called late, so my heart was pounding, and I was thinking, "Not again." Four years ago, the worst happened to me. So, now I am just really happy to have been chosen. The hard work I've put in over the past four years has paid off. I felt at that time I had to become the kind of player that any manager would want in his team. I have become more mentally strong, too.'

After their strong showing in 2002 and their form under Zico, expectations in Japan were high going into the finals in Germany. Their chances were not helped, however, when they were drawn in a tough group that included Brazil, Croatia and Australia. Japan faced Australia in the opening game and were handed the perfect start when Aussie keeper Mark Schwarzer got caught under Nakamura's 26th-minute cross, the ball floating over him and into the net. With six minutes to go, Japan looked on course for a historic win, but things then took a turn for the worse. Tim Cahill equalised in the 84th minute and added a second in the 89th before John Aloisi completed the scoring in injury time. Australia had snatched victory from the jaws of defeat. An uninspired 0–0 draw against Croatia in the second game, after which Zico complained that his side had been unfairly scheduled to play in blazing mid-afternoon temperatures again, left their qualification hopes depending on victory against Brazil. Japan failed to repeat their performance of the Confederations Cup the year before and lost 4–1, with two goals from Ronaldo. Nakamura had failed to impose himself on the game, though the whole team were comprehensively outclassed.

After 2002, their elimination was a massive anticlimax, and Nakamura and his teammates attracted criticism. But Nakamura had barely had a break between international duty the previous summer then a full season with Celtic, and it showed in his performances.

Shuhei Takahashi, the former Japanese consul general and a seasoned Nakamura-watcher, believes that the midfielder's failure to hit the heights in Germany marked another pivotal moment in his career. 'He was so exhausted during the World Cup, and it showed in his performances, but after that he knew that he had to improve himself. He worked harder on his physical training. I think that was one of the reasons he was so successful in the 2006–07 season for Celtic and won both the Player of the Year awards.'

Troussier leans back in his seat, exuding a satisfied glow. He has followed Nakamura's career since 2002 and is genuinely pleased to see how the midfielder has developed his game. That is one of the reasons he finally agreed to speak in-depth about the subject. The Frenchman, as he showed in some of his dealings with Nakata, knows the importance of icons to supporters. He is delighted that Nakamura has become the country's number-one football hero and believes Japan need even more of his kind to further inspire the new generation and continue their remarkable development as a football nation.

In 2002, Troussier needed his players to have a bit of everything. He needed them to be able to pass, run and tackle. Nakamura was an unashamed specialist, a playmaker with a wonderful left foot but who was limited in other areas. He believes Nakamura's subsequent success has been built on playing in teams that allow him to concentrate on his strengths. 'Initially, I was surprised when he went to Scotland, and also Italy, because in those places you have to fight before you can play football. But now I think if you play him in the right position to complement the Scottish fighting spirit, then he is a very important player. If you have good players for running and heading, then he can concentrate on what he does. If you ask him to fight all the time, he is no good, but if you ask Nakamura to give good service to the fighters, he is one of the best in the world. Football is not only fighting. Corner-kicks and free-kicks are very important at this level, and maybe he can help win a match. I understand that he can add a good balance for this kind of football. Now he is married, has a family, he is 30 and is playing at a high level in Europe. The national team without Nakamura is not the same national team. He is a key player, particularly from set-pieces. I'm pleased to see the success he has gone on to achieve.'

NINE

···········

The Toe of the Boot

'Non e' brasiliano, pero', che gol, che fa. A Reggio, e' un idolo gia',
Nakamura' ('He's not Brazilian, but what goals he scores. He's
already an idol in Reggio, Nakamura')

The Reggina Ultras' song
for Shunsuke Nakamura

REGGIO CALABRIA ON A QUIET DECEMBER EVENING.
Winter sunshine streams down on the immaculate lawns of
Sant'Agata, the training centre of Reggina FC. The smell of sea
air fills the nostrils. In the distance, across the Strait of Messina,
the lights of the island of Sicily glint invitingly. Young players
fresh from a training session drift across the small courtyard:
Africans, Asians, Europeans, even one Brit, an aspiring centre-half
from Newcastle. They chat animatedly as they make their way
into the residential quarters, an impressive white stone building
they call home as they pursue their Serie A dreams. I have come
in search of Shunsuke Nakamura's legacy. It soon becomes clear
that it is all around me.

Nakamura played for Reggina for three seasons between 2002 and 2005. To say Nakamura made an impression on the tranquil seaside city is like saying Tiger Woods has made a ripple or two in the world of golf. The Japanese midfielder almost single-handedly revolutionised the club and the city. He opened up new horizons, he generated the finance that helped fund new facilities, he scored goals, he helped keep them in Serie A, he inspired devotion. The last aspect is apparent everywhere you turn. Inquisitive looks from the locals melt into beatific smiles at the mention of his name. 'Ah, Shunsuke . . .' they say, eyes gazing into the middle distance as if they are watching a slideshow of the Japanese midfielder in their minds. If football is like a religion in Italy, then Nakamura is revered as a saint in this small city on the toe of the country's boot.

Mention his name in the local pizzerias and they will talk you through the 'Shunsuke Special', a pizza with the Japanese flag in the middle, made out of slices of mozzarella and one of tomato, representing the red sun. In the *gelaterias*, they will tell you that his favourite flavour of ice cream is lemon and present you with a tub on the house. If you are brave enough to knock on the shop door of the menacing Ultras in the main street, then they will, at first, peer threateningly from behind pairs of shades before beckoning you into their darkened premises with hearty laughs when you namedrop their Japanese hero. Reggio Calabria has not forgotten Shunsuke Nakamura. In so many ways, he has never left.

Pasquale Foti taps his cigar on the edge of the ashtray and flashes the kind of proud smile that a father reserves for his favourite son. The president of Reggina was the man responsible for first enticing Nakamura to the south of Italy back in 2002, which in itself was an astonishing achievement. Reggina are Serie A's perennial bottom-feeders, the tadpoles in the shark-infested waters of the Italian top flight. In Scotland, their equivalent would be St Mirren or Inverness Caledonian Thistle: well-run, proud clubs but with limited financial resources and no chance of competing with the big boys. Reggina, and Foti, are under no illusions as to their status, but they remain laudably ambitious. They have, after all, accomplished much in the last decade. 'Reggina are a small provincial club who had always been confined to Serie B and C until we were promoted to the top division for the first time in 1999,' explains Foti. 'From that point, a whole series of initiatives and a whole ethos of growth have been put in place that have allowed us to stay there for eight of the last nine years. I would say that we're a typical "southern" club. The culture of the place has all the elements you associate with teams from Mediterranean countries: huge passion, huge enthusiasm, huge appetite for detail and knowledge about what's happening in every nook and cranny of the club. The people of Reggio are absolutely involved with their club. They are effectively one and the same thing. We've been the launch pad for a number of very successful playing careers. Players like Andrea Pirlo, Simone Barone and Bruno Cirillo all started out here and have gone on to bigger and better things. That tells you something about the environment we have created here – these players help us to grow, but we help them develop as well.'

The south of Italy is viewed differently from the rest of the country. With much of their economy rural-based, southerners are dismissed as country bumpkins by denizens of the more urban and sophisticated north. They are also viewed as insular people, with a deep suspicion of outsiders. It is a stereotype that Foti has always railed against. The Reggina president grew up in the south and has made his home and his fortune amid the resplendent natural beauty of the Calabria region. He rejoices in the community values that have effortlessly survived the passing years and believes the warmth of the people and the beauty of the countryside have either been overlooked or obscured by casual stereotyping. His involvement with Reggina has allowed him to use football as the vehicle with which to change people's perceptions of the south.

For years, Foti had been searching for a way to showcase the region and explode the myth of parochialism. In 2002, he found

Nakamura. 'It had been a tumultuous couple of years for the club,' he reflects. 'We'd gone down to Serie B, then come back up again, and we decided to re-examine what we were doing to try to make sure we got more stability about the place. One of the things that came from that was a desire to open up the reality of Reggio and of Reggina to the whole world. When we came to know about Nakamura, he ticked all of the right boxes on that front.'

Nakamura had first come to Reggina's attention while playing for Japan in a friendly against Honduras in which he had scored twice and had an outstanding game. The wheels were soon set in motion, though it was not the first audacious transfer move they had attempted. Reggina had been looking to attract a marquee signing for some time and two years before had come very close to signing Roberto Baggio. That Nakamura was considered to be a fitting alternative to the legendary Italian striker conveys an idea of how highly they regarded the Japanese midfielder. After establishing a link with Yokohama F. Marinos, Foti and Gabriele Martino, Reggina's then director of football, were invited to Japan for Nakamura's farewell game against Tokyo Verdy. It was then that they realised the level of his popularity. His lap of honour took twenty minutes, and everybody in the stand behind one of the goals was wearing a top with 'Shunsuke' on its back.

'I was bowled over by the reception he got from the fans there as he prepared to leave and the hundreds of photographers who snapped away at him all night,' recalls Foti. 'All that brought it home to me what a big deal we would be buying into. I met Shunsuke and his agent, with various officials from Marinos also flitting about. The talks were very long and very difficult, with hundreds of journalists waiting around for any scrap of information. It was a completely new experience in so many ways for this club.'

With perfect timing, Reggina had just been promoted to Serie A, and it was reported that as the players were still on the pitch celebrating their return to the top flight on the last day of the season Martino was already on the phone to Marinos to get the deal moving. After making contact with the club and meeting with the player's agents, Reggina had the most difficult part to come. They had to persuade Nakamura to sign. At that point, he was the rising star of Japanese football. He had other offers, more lucrative ones. As well as Reggina, Chievo, Perugia, Napoli, Lecce and Atalanta were all interested in acquiring his services.

Nakamura was already well acquainted with Italian football. He had fallen in love with the Italian style in the late 1990s when the great AC Milan side that included Marco van Basten, Ruud Gullit and Frank Rijkaard had won the Intercontinental Cup, then staged in Tokyo, twice in a row. But would Reggina really be the right club to move his career forward? On paper, probably not, but Foti was not a man to give up without a fight. He was a salesman, after all. Selling ice cream to the Eskimos and sand to the Arabs was one thing, but could he really convince this Japanese genius to sign for lowly Reggina?

Foti's trump card was to emphasise the passion of the supporters and the hospitality of the local people. Reggio may be a relative backwater, but the zeal of the fan base is not in question, as Foti will testify. The Reggina president has been attacked on several occasions by supporters and on one occasion received a severed calf's head in the post. The flipside to such fanaticism is the devotion that can be heaped on a player who the supporters take to their hearts. After momentous away wins, it is not uncommon for a crowd of 10,000 to be waiting at the airport to welcome the team back.

Simply, Foti told Nakamura that he could become a legend. 'Reggina is not a place that automatically sells itself. We had to actively convince Shunsuke to come here,' he says, smiling. 'The discussions had gone on hours and hours without us really getting anywhere, so at a certain point I asked to speak to him myself. He couldn't speak Italian, and I couldn't speak Japanese, but I somehow made myself understood and got across to him everything that was waiting for him here if he agreed to come and take it.' Foti then mimics how he grabbed Nakamura playfully by the cheeks in a desperate attempt to convey his desire to sign him. 'I said, "Come on, Shunsuke. Tell your directors that it wouldn't be good to wait. Who knows when a chance like this will come round again?" I think he fell in love with me!' he says, chuckling. 'I expressed something of the passion and warmth that Calabrian people have, the adoration that this club and this city could give him, and eventually we got our "yes".'

With Nakamura's signing sealed, the club wanted to make a statement both about their own upwardly mobile intentions and people's perceptions of the Italian south. 'The choice of venue for Nakamura's introductory press conference was quite deliberate. We took it to The Four Seasons Hotel in Milan, one of the most cosmopolitan cities in the world, to emphasise that Reggina and Reggio were opening their doors to the world. There were more than 100 journalists there from all over the world, and we had many of the Calabrian institutions and authorities send representatives to again fit in with the theme of opening new horizons and exploring new realities,' recalls Foti, who also gave out Reggina tops with Nakamura's name on the back to all the journalists in attendance. 'That press conference gave a very powerful new image of this city and this club. Through Nakamura, we were offering up to the world all that is good about the south, while at the same time showing that we ourselves were open to what the rest of the world had to offer us.'

The process of expanding their horizons also had lucrative financial advantages, and the club sold 25,000 Nakamura shirts in his first five months at the club. 'Nakamura was, in part, a commercial investment on the club's behalf,' adds Foti. 'I should make it clear, however, that it was Nakamura's technical appeal that attracted us in the first place. The commercial aspect was a happy by-product, something that came along later. I will always remember the friendly we played in Yokohama soon after the World Cup final in 2002. We were granted an official reception by the Italian embassy, and a lot of Japanese businessmen were there. Again, we were able to show just what the club and the city had to offer, and a lot of them realised there was a real opportunity to establish new and profitable links. Many of these companies went on to get involved with us as sponsors, and there started to be a real wave of tourism from Japan into Reggio and the rest of Calabria as well. At the game itself, there were 67,000 fans, many of whom bought Reggina shirts, and the homage they paid to Nakamura was extraordinary. The whole ground was on its feet applauding him for the whole game, and it brought home just what an idol the man is.'

One story encapsulates how Reggina regarded Nakamura as a cultural ambassador. Reggina travelled to the San Siro to face AC Milan a couple of months into his first season. It was a huge day for the club on their return to the top flight. It was also a big chance to showcase the abilities of their star Japanese signing in the city where they had unveiled him to the world only a couple of months previously. The huge San Siro press box was heaving with Japanese journalists. The stage was set and anticipation was huge but, as is typical in football, things backfired spectacularly. After 20 minutes, the visitors had Jorge Vargas sent off and Bortolo Mutti, the Reggina head coach, was forced into a hasty tactical rethink. His next move would have far-reaching consequences. Mutti substituted Nakamura and brought on a defender. As the legions of Japanese journalists hung their heads in despair, it is rumoured that Martino and Foti were so angry that they immediately stood up and left the directors' box. When Reggina were thrashed at home by Lazio a few weeks later, it was no surprise that Mutti was relieved of his duties.

Soon after Nakamura's arrival, the local tourist board for the first time began to publish its brochures in three languages: Italian, Japanese and English. The club were also actively involved in attracting Japanese tourists and set up a package whereby groups of around 30 fans could fly from Tokyo to Reggio Calabria, attend a couple of training sessions, go to the game and then go out for dinner with Nakamura himself. Japanese television crews were regular visitors, and as well as recording Nakamura's progress they made documentaries about the history of the Calabria region.

'Nakamura effectively became a bridge between Calabria and Japan in a number of ways, to do with football and in everyday life,' says Foti. 'If you look at the club now, we have so many different nationalities, and so many different influences, particularly in our youth sector. Nakamura was undoubtedly responsible for opening a number of those doors. Reggina is now an international club; Reggio is now an international city. There are no longer any boundaries for us.'

We are standing outside an apartment block near the seafront in Reggio Calabria. It is an unremarkable building, freshly painted and with great views over the water to Sicily, but not the kind of luxury quarters commonly associated with the glamorous lifestyle of professional footballers. However, the small apartment on the third floor is probably the most famous flat in Italian football. For three years, it was the home of Shunsuke Nakamura. Before that, it housed the World Cup-winning Italian midfielder Simone Perrotta, who came through the ranks at Reggina. It was also home for Andrea Pirlo, who spent a season on loan at Reggina early in his career and won the World Cup with Italy in 2006. It is currently occupied by an Icelandic centre-half.

At the foot of the building is the local post office, whose owner doubles as landlady to the stars. Mention of Nakamura produces a fit of girlish giggles, and she shuffles into the backroom to look for photographs of her former tenant. She remembers him fondly and recalls how she used to cook him food to ensure he felt at home. Significantly, she declines to do a formal interview because of the publicity that a previous mention in print generated. She describes how hordes of Japanese girls used to come into the shop, desperate to find out what apartment their hero stayed in. 'I used to tell them he stayed on the other side of town,' she says with a wicked grin. Nakamura, she recalls, used to park his car outside the front door of the shop but remove all of the sponsors' stickers from the windscreen so that no one would realise he stayed in the adjacent building. Nakamura also insisted that his interpreter, Goro Kawano, stay close to him, so he rented an apartment 50 metres away in the same street.

Foti claims that the 200,000 residents of the small seaside city were in thrall to the Japanese midfielder. 'The public were utterly fascinated by and in love with Nakamura, but they knew how to be discreet. They showed him a sort of contained love, expressing their affection in practical ways, like helping him adapt to life in a very different reality, showing him where to eat, where to relax. And he always had a special smile for his president, let me tell you.

'He led a pretty reserved life. The people he mixed with most often were the Japanese journalists who had come here with him and a few people involved at various levels with the club. He used to like walking by the sea, I think, and going out to some of the fish restaurants that you find around Reggio. Nothing spectacular, just a quiet, peaceful life that let him focus on his football. He spent so much time on the training field, it was absolutely incredible. Nakamura endeared himself to the public with what he did on the park, but they took him to their hearts for how he conducted himself away from it as well. There is no other word than "perfect" to describe his behaviour and attitude in everyday life.'

One of the key reasons for Nakamura's ability to adapt to changes in environment and culture are the ever-present Japanese journalists. Wherever he has gone, they have followed. As such, he has always had a band of young countrymen and women, all of a roughly similar age to him, with whom to share his leisure time. In Italy, around 20 journalists set up camp to follow his progress. Their interest bordered on the obsessive. One Italian journalist tells of covering a Reggina game in the cup away from home. Nakamura came on as a substitute but had forgotten to put on his shinguards. The referee sent him back to the bench to retrieve a pair before he re-entered the field of play. After the game, the Italian journalist was besieged with calls from Japanese journalists who, used to feeding on Nakamura minutiae, were desperately trying to establish whose shinguards he had borrowed. The sizeable press room beside the training pitch at Sant'Agata was built specifically to accommodate his legion of scribes, and the press box at the club's stadium also doubled in size after their arrival.

In Reggio Calabria, Nakamura's legacy endures in the shape of his faithful press pack. Of the twenty or so dispatched to follow him in Italy back in 2002, two still remain. One is engaged to an Italian and the other, Takashi Yuge, still happily resides in the city. He now works as the Italian football correspondent for a Japanese magazine, reports on Serie A and follows two Japanese footballers at Catania and Torino. He has gained a unique insight into the residual impact of Nakamura. 'It's no exaggeration to say that Nakamura wove himself into the very fabric of this place,' reflects Yuge, sitting on a bench on Reggio's impressive promenade. 'You can see that from the fact that three years after he left they're still talking about him as if he were still here. And remember, it's much easier to win your own countrymen's hearts than those of foreigners. For a Japanese player to be so loved in the deep south of Italy is phenomenal, when you really think about it. The fans fell in love with him straight away for a mix of how impressive he was on and off the field. There's a great picture of the Ultras carrying a banner with his face on it and "one of us" written underneath in Japanese. They used to sing a song in his honour, too: *"Non e' brasiliano, pero', che gol, che fa. A Reggio, e' un idolo gia', Nakamura."* By the end of his first month in Reggio, the whole city was singing that. Even Nonna Maria, the most famous fan the club has, who is in her 90s, wanted to have her picture taken with Shunsuke.' The city's football-mad mayor, Giuseppe Scopelliti, was regularly seen walking around the streets with a Nakamura top on, and it was little surprise that after just a few months the player was given the prestigious San Giorgino d'oro, the equivalent of the keys to the city in Britain.

It is hard to imagine Nakamura, the most reticent of footballers, thriving amid the larger-than-life locals of Reggio Calabria, but that is what happened. Maybe it was a case of opposites attract. Nakamura did not kiss badges or indulge in over-the-top celebrations. He did not display emotions; he kept himself to himself. More than anything, though, he treated people well and worked like a demon. 'People loved him because they could see that he was a good person as well as an excellent footballer,' adds Yuge. 'His mannerisms, the way he conducted himself, were enough to form that impression. The public knew it wasn't aloofness that kept him away from socialising with his teammates or going to the discos in the city – he just didn't go in for that sort of thing. He would much rather be out on the training field. In that regard, he is like a child. He can never be parted from his football. He's never happy with his performance. He never stops tying to improve.'

In Italian football, there has generally been a greater emphasis on physical conditioning than in Britain. Italian players, as a rule, train harder and longer than their British counterparts and adapt their lifestyles to better maximise their talents. It is, therefore, testament to Nakamura's work ethic that even the Italians were impressed by him. Luigi De Canio, his second manager at Reggina who had a seven-month spell in charge of Queens Park Rangers between October 2007 and May 2008, gives a fascinating insight into the midfielder's meticulous approach. 'A couple of days before he was going off to play for Japan, I noticed he was speaking animatedly with Goro, his interpreter, and I couldn't understand why,' he explains. 'I asked what the problem was and was told that Naka had asked for notes to be taken from all the training sessions he was going to miss while away. He had given the interpreter a block of Post-it notes and told him to record with maximum precision what he had missed. Normally, when a player goes away with the national team, he doesn't have to justify himself, but Nakamura was a very scrupulous individual and very fearful of falling behind. When he got back, the interpreter gave him the notes session for session, and Nakamura studied them in the most minute detail. These are unforgettable moments in the life of a coach.'

Yuge explains the extent to which Nakamura's popularity in Reggio Calabria endures to this day. 'I know a lot of Italians who have made the journey from Reggio to Glasgow to go to see him play for Celtic. That's not an easy thing, with the distances involved and the lack of flights from Calabria, but it tells you everything you need to know about the regard Nakamura is still held in here. Every time I go to Scotland for work, I'm asked to bring back Celtic tops with his name on the back. Nakamura and Hidetoshi Nakata created a lot of interest in Japan for Serie A, so I've stayed behind as a kind of Italy correspondent for my magazine. It's generally accepted that Japanese fans follow players instead of teams, but I don't think that is entirely true in Nakamura's case. Before he arrived, nobody in Japan had any reason to know that Reggio Calabria even existed, but it quickly became quite a popular tourist destination, and that hasn't disappeared with Nakamura. As president Foti says, Nakamura was a bridge between Reggio and Japan, and it is still standing. I think the same will go for the link he has helped create between Celtic, Glasgow and Japan.'

In the summer of 2002, Nakamura was looking for a refuge after the devastating blow of missing out on the World Cup. Yuge explains how the switch to Reggina helped Nakamura regain confidence in his own abilities. 'I think the timing of his arrival here was absolutely perfect, even if none of us maybe realised it at the time. Being left out of the 2002 World Cup was a horrible open wound for Nakamura, and he needed a very special sort of club and city to help him recover. Reggina and Reggio provided both, I think, with the affection they showed him right from the start and the space they gave him to develop. The fans' love grew with every good thing he did for the team, and it became a very special, very healthy relationship. They knew how to make each other happy. This was the perfect place for Nakamura to prove to himself that he was good enough to make it in European football.'

Troussier's rejection also prompted some soul-searching on Nakamura's behalf. His omission was a stark reminder that he was not the finished article. His technical abilities were never in question, but he needed to play somewhere that would toughen him up mentally and physically. Reggina, perennial relegation candidates, would provide all that and more. 'It was so hard for him. Reggina are a team fighting relegation all the time,' says Shin Toyofuku. 'You have to defend and you have to run. Those were not Nakamura's favourite jobs. Having had the experience of playing several positions at Reggina – behind the centre-forward, defensive midfield, right side, left side, middle – he now had options. At Celtic, he plays on the right in a 4–4–2. It is not his position, but he can play it because he is versatile. That's what he learned in those three years.'

Most presidents or chairmen of football clubs are more intimately acquainted with the financial, rather than the football, side of the club. Not Foti. When we first meet, he is standing at the side of the training pitch, wreathed in plumes of cigar smoke, as he takes in the first-team squad's latest training session. He never misses one. As such, he is well versed in the strengths and weaknesses of every squad member, past and present. It is clear that Foti was just as seduced by the technical gifts of Nakamura as his personality. 'I'm what you'd call a "pavement president". I involve myself in every aspect of the club, every age group. I've been going to watch every training session for years now, so I think I've got a fair degree of knowledge on which to base my judgements, and to my mind Nakamura was simply a champion. There is no other word to describe the mix of attributes he had. He was so dedicated, so professional, so skilful. Every day after training, he would stay behind for an hour, sometimes more, to hit free-kicks. We got one of our sponsors to source different types of defensive walls for him to use. Just like at Celtic, those free-kicks were worth a large number of points to Reggina over the course of a season. I just loved watching him, and I still do, with what I see of him at Celtic. I love the way he's developed there, too, the way he has adapted his game. I know he had real difficulties at the start, because he preferred the Latin-style game to the physicality of British football, but he's shown that he is resourceful as well as naturally talented. Reggina brought out the heart and soul you now see him putting into games. We're the sort of club that has to fight and earn everything we get in Serie A, and Shunsuke bought into that culture massively.'

In his first season, he was deployed as a second striker or in the 'hole'. As such, the number 10 shirt, which holds particular prestige in Italy, was taken off Reggina stalwart Francesco Cozza and handed to Nakamura. Mutti only worked with Nakamura for a brief spell but remains a huge admirer of what he brought to Italian football. 'Even in the short time I worked with him, it became clear to me that of all the players I have managed only Roberto Baggio was on the same level. If you asked me to choose between the pair of them, I wouldn't be convinced that I'd end up choosing Baggio. The differences are minimal.' Martino, meanwhile, sums up Nakamura's style succinctly. 'Nakamura is spontaneity and class. He loves risk, but calculated risk.'

Nakamura's influence declined with Mutti's abrupt departure and De Canio's subsequent arrival at the club. In the latter part of his first season, he was used more as an impact player, coming off the bench, charged with changing games. In the longer term, De Canio also switched him to the deep-lying playmaker position, the role that AC Milan midfielder Andrea Pirlo performs with such aplomb. The coach, uniquely during Nakamura's Reggina years, had a very unflattering view of his ability. He insisted the move to a deeper position was because he felt Nakamura lacked the pace or physicality to make a serious impact in the final third. Nevertheless, after De Canio's departure Nakamura started to acclimatise more to the physical demands of the Serie A, and his adaptability was the making of him.

* * *

In 2008, Reggina is an impressively run club. The stadium, while hardly state of the art, exudes a gone-to-seed glamour. On one side, the craggy peaks of the Aspromonte mountain range are visible. On the other, there are impressive views over to Sicily. The huge netting behind the goals and the plastic wall that skirts the perimeter of the pitch are tell-tale signs of the occasionally overzealous atmosphere that can be generated on match days. In recent years, the club have been diligently upgrading the stadium's facilities, and a lick of fresh paint is being applied on the day I arrive.

It is their training centre, however, that is the jewel in the crown. Training pitches, elegantly framed by the surrounding mountains, stretch out as far as the eye can see. The three-storey residential facility, which houses the academy acolytes, is a direct result of the money earned from Nakamura. Yuge is amazed by the difference in the club from Nakamura's arrival in 2002 to now. 'When we first arrived, I think it's fair to say we were all shocked by the state of the facilities, particularly at the training ground – it wasn't at all what you expect from European football. But very quickly, as the profile of the club went ever higher with Nakamura's presence, the whole place was transformed, the Sant'Agata centre became the first-class place it is today and Reggina began to register with more people on a global scale. That is part of Nakamura's legacy here, but I think even he would be completely surprised to see just how impressive Sant'Agata and its youth academy have become.'

As a result of Nakamura's signing, Reggina started to think bigger and bigger. They extended their scouting networks and began to bring in players from all over the world. They now have youngsters from as far away as the Congo, Brazil and Spain. Kris Thackray was playing for the English Colleges national team in a tournament in Italy when he was spotted by a Reggina scout. Initially, Thackray hoped to break through at his home-town club of Newcastle United, but after eight years on their books his dream of turning out at St James' Park were shattered when they released him, aged sixteen. He did the rounds of other

English clubs – Scunthorpe, Darlington, Scarborough, Derby and Rochdale – without success. 'There aren't many players who escape the attentions of Premiership clubs and get back in,' he reflects. 'When you're 17 or 18 and not at a club, your chances are slim, and that's when people fall off the wagon.'

With a career in football looking increasingly unlikely, Thackray enrolled in a sports diploma course at Gateshead College and was subsequently selected for the English Colleges team. In a tournament in Italy, he was named England's Player of the Tournament and returned for another there a few months later, where he was then spotted by Reggina scouts. 'In the semi-final, I was 30 yards out and hit a shot with my left foot, and it flew into the top corner,' he recalls. 'Afterwards, a Reggina scout came up and asked me to come down for a week's trial. I did well, and they offered me a two-year contract.

'I've been here for a year now. I've learned the language, and I've changed position. I came as a central midfielder, and I'm a centre-half now. It's a big risk. I'm engaged to a girl in Newcastle, I left my family and friends behind, but you've got to make sacrifices when you are in my situation. If I manage to get into the first team, I'll have got there. I'm 19, and I've got to move onto the next stage now.'

Reggio Calabria sleeps by day and barely opens its eyes by night. The pace of life is slow, and there are few of the leisure attractions that often help occupy the free time of professional footballers. Pubs are few, restaurants are also thin on the ground, and as for Japanese cuisine? No chance. It is a simple, tranquil existence, uncomplicated by many of the trappings of modern society. To move from the port city of Yokohama, with a population of over 3 million, to Reggio Calabria would have been a major culture shock for Nakamura. The majority of foreign players would have taken one look around and set about planning their escape route, but there is more to Nakamura and more to the life of a Japanese footballer abroad. There is a fierce pride in furthering the cause of their nation in foreign lands. Returning home too soon would be to let their country down. So, Nakamura stayed for three years. He diligently rebuilt his career after the shattering blow of missing the World Cup and became a better player tactically. It was an essential learning curve that would prove crucial in his next career move.

Reggina were under no illusions that Nakamura would stay for ever. Spanish clubs were already sniffing around him, and, with his learning curve levelling off, his departure became inevitable. 'Every road comes to an end at some point,' says Foti. 'Nakamura felt he had given as much to and got as much from Reggina as he could, and he wanted to broaden his knowledge of European football. He was always going to leave that summer, whether it was Celtic or someone else. There was a lot of attention coming from Spanish clubs, but Celtic acted quickly and got the deal done. When Celtic discovered he was available, they declared a very strong interest straight away, and Peter Lawwell came to meet me in Milan.'

Nakamura had a long-stated desire to play in Spain's Primera Liga. The pace of the game and the emphasis on technique would have allowed him to flourish. The climate would have been to his liking, and, depending on where he chose, he would surely have ended up in a more densely populated environment than Reggio Calabria. He was 27, the perfect age to fulfil his dream. So, how did he end up playing for Celtic in the Scottish Premier League? 'It's funny – I think Peter Lawwell had to do a similar sort of selling operation as I did to get Nakamura to go to Glasgow as opposed to some of the other more obvious destinations,' says Foti. 'He talked about the passion, the warmth of football in Glasgow, the sell-out crowds, the atmosphere in the ground. All the same sort of things I had said about Reggina.'

And so Nakamura's three-year odyssey in Italy drew to a close. It had been a mutually beneficial relationship, and Foti's heart swells with pride at his former player's subsequent achievements. 'I've not been to see him play in Glasgow, but I catch him on satellite TV and still love to hear from him in person. He phones me when he feels the need and manages, in the few simple words of Italian he picked up, to get across his appreciation of the role Reggina played in everything he's enjoying now: the status, the attention, the professional satisfaction.'

Yuge developed a strong relationship with his countryman in Italy and visits him a couple of times a season in Scotland. When we meet, he brings along a Celtic strip he picked up on his last visit along with a scarf from Baird's Bar, the famous Celtic pub in the Gallowgate in Glasgow's city centre. He believes that Nakamura's stint in Italy, where he was away from his homeland for the first time, led to a sharper appreciation of his commercial value. Yuge believes he grew to embrace the media hoopla that built up around him in Italy and was more able to handle the off-field pressures when he moved to Celtic.

'I think he's matured massively over there. Not so much from a technical point of view, even though his free-kicks are definitely better, but internally. He seems a lot stronger, much more of a man. There's a lot of class and intelligence about him. For example, think of all the interview requests he gets and meets. He won't just rattle off any old thing to them all. He adapts his speech and his style for each: a quick, simple soundbite for TV; something more in-depth for a newspaper or magazine interview. He's very quick at summing up a situation and acting appropriately, and that's a sure sign of intelligence.

'You can tell he loves it. I watch his face closely when I'm there, and there's a real joy displayed there. The passion of the environment has done a lot for him and his game. And then there's the state of the pitch, too – much better than the potato field they used to ask him to play on at the Granillo [Reggina's pitch]. The pitch at Parkhead is a magic carpet compared to that.'

Nakamura's impact in Italy has led other Italian clubs to enter the Japanese market. Takayuki Miramoto, who holds the record for the youngest player to make his debut and the youngest scorer in the J. League, is currently with Catania. Masashi Oguro, meanwhile, is a 27-year-old striker with Torino. Despite the club's success with Nakamura, Foti admits that he has never been tempted to bring in another Japanese player. 'We've had the chance, several times, to sign more Japanese players, but there was always a real fear in my mind that the experience just couldn't live up to what we had with Nakamura. In a way, we were spoiled by what he brought – he was such a great player, and such a great person, nobody else could really compete. We've decided to keep our memories of him intact, and we cherish them religiously, like precious artefacts.'

Asked to describe Nakamura's legacy to Reggina, Foti leans back in his seat and draws deeply on his cigar. 'Memories. Great, warm, loving memories. The knowledge that we had a real champion, a real great, for a few years here, who also had the gift of being a champion human being as well. As I've said, he's also there in the international image the club and the city now have. He gave us that. That is his legacy.'

TEN

·········

Naka Sells the Jerseys

THE WINTER SUN STREAMED DOWN ON BROADWOOD Stadium, home of Clyde FC. An 8,000 capacity crowd was shoehorned into their small three-sided stadium on the outskirts of Glasgow, and the atmosphere was at fever pitch. Media interest was huge. Clyde had received accreditation requests from America, Canada, Australia, Japan, Sweden, Belgium and the Netherlands. Then there was the English press, some of whom had hired out corporate boxes, as there was no room for them in the bulging press area. The game was to be screened live on Sky television, with pictures being beamed beyond the UK and Ireland to the Far East, USA, Canada, Australia and Europe. An estimated TV audience of 20 million was expected to tune in. This was the biggest game in Britain. This was Clyde v. Celtic in the third round of the Scottish Cup. What on earth was going on? The answer was simple: Roy Keane. One of the greatest midfielders of his generation was about to take his bow for Celtic, the club for which he had a long-held affinity. From Cumbernauld to Cork and beyond, the anticipation was huge. Chants of 'Keanoooo' rang around the stadium. The stage was set.

Keane was not the only Celtic player making his debut that afternoon in January 2006. With Bobo Baldé's departure to the African Nations Cup, Gordon Strachan had decided to hand a first start to the China captain Du Wei. In late August, Du had agreed a four-year contract that, crucially, would be activated after a five-month probationary period, allowing him to move permanently from Shanghai Shenhua. The Clyde game was seven days before the break in the deal that would allow either party to pull out. Strachan had been sensitive enough to allow the 23-year-old defender as much time as possible to acclimatise to Scottish football. He had broken him in gently to reserve-team football and worked diligently with him on the training ground.

Keane had already proved a commercial asset to Celtic, with replica tops bearing his name flying off the shelves, but Du Wei was part of a much broader attempt by Celtic to establish themselves as a global brand. Celtic's market on either side of the Irish Sea was nearing saturation point, and they had made inroads into North America, so they were now looking to expand their outreach programme into the Far East. The combined population of China and Japan represented a potential market increase of 1.5 billion. Shunsuke Nakamura's signing had already given them a foothold in Asia, and Du Wei represented the next stage in their master plan. At the age of 19, he became the most popular footballer in his homeland after replacing the injured Fan Zhiyi at the 2002 World Cup, where he man-marked Brazilian striker Ronaldo. He had acclimatised well to Scotland and, aged 23, felt he was the right age to make an impact in European football. The contract was drawn up. Then came that sunny afternoon at Broadwood.

On paper at least, there could have been worse baptisms for Keane and Du Wei than a third-round Scottish Cup tie against an average First Division outfit. For a team such as Celtic, they were cannon fodder. So, the eyes of the football world had tuned in to witness another special moment in Keane's illustrious career.

The script had been written, but, famously, Clyde popped up with a few plot suggestions of their own.

The joke goes that Du Wei made his only two appearances for Celtic that afternoon: his first and last. Rarely has a player looked so out of synch with his surroundings. Celtic fell a goal behind after thirty-two minutes, and Du Wei conceded a penalty four minutes after the opener, a foul for which he could have been sent off. Stephen O'Donnell's spot-kick was saved by Artur Boruc, but Clyde scored from the resultant corner-kick when Eddie Malone's thundering half-volley nestled in the net. Żurawski's goal seven minutes from time was scant consolation. The damage had been done, in Du Wei's case irreparably. The 23 year old had been replaced at half-time by Adam Virgo and would never wear a Celtic shirt again. Clyde's victory would mark an ignominious entry in Celtic's history, but it was also the day that their Chinese dream died. Strachan was sympathetic towards the defender's plight. 'It was hard to make debuts on a day like that – it wasn't a great day.'

Du Wei's agent then claimed that Celtic had asked for more time to assess the player to see if he could successfully adapt to Scottish football, but Shenhua refused to change the original terms of the deal and ordered him to come home. Either way, he had no future at Celtic, and the proposed four-year contract went up in smoke as Strachan picked over the embers of the defeat. The Du Wei episode proved that unlocking the treasure chest of the Far East market required the right player. Celtic were not the first to have tried and failed.

Five years before, Dundee signed Fan Zhiyi, the former China captain, but he failed to make a sufficient impact on the park to be an asset off it. In contrast, Sun Jihai, who arrived in Britain around the same time as Fan Zhiyi, earned a £2-million move from Crystal Palace to Manchester City. He has become a commercial asset for the club, because he has made an impression in the first team. The profile for the ideal Far East footballer involves aspects such as marketability, but at its core is talent. Fan Zhiyi and Du

Wei were not marketable because they were not good enough. It proved that Far East football enthusiasts could not be fooled. They would not buy into just anyone.

Hidetoshi Nakata was a major commercial asset to clubs throughout his career but only because he backed up his marketability with talent. When he moved to Perugia in 1998, the club sold 100,000 'Nakata' shirts back in Japan, and Japanese TV rights in Italy rocketed in value from £5 million to £12 million. Over 1,000 Japanese tourists would also descend on Umbria for Perugia's home games. Crucially, Nakata was also a good player and helped keep them in Serie A with ten goals in his first season. When he moved to Roma, they sold 70,000 of his number 8 shirt. Again, though, he contributed to their winning a *scudetto*.

The phenomenon is not confined to football. Hideki Matsui, the baseball player known as 'Godzilla' in Japan, became New York's Japanese tourism ambassador when he joined the Yankees in January 2003. When Ichiro Suzuki joined Seattle Mariners three years earlier, most of the club's games were televised back in Japan. Both Matsui and Suzuki were exceptional talents, the essential ingredient for any commercial enterprise.

As Peter Lawwell explains, the correlation between on-field impact and off-field profits is a very real one. 'You need the player to be playing. If we bought a Chinese player and he was in the reserves or on the bench, then there would be no spin-offs because there is no recognition and no exposure. He needs to be an active, and if possible high-profile, member of the team. We identified Du Wei, who was a great lad. He came over, but it didn't work out on the playing side. We felt pretty bad that it didn't work out, but we had to say, "This time it's not going to happen." We've got a scouting network in China, and should there be a player for the right value who we believe would add value to our team I'm sure Gordon would want him. But they have to play.'

David Thomson, Celtic's commercial director until August 2008, was heavily involved in setting up the Du episode and was particularly disappointed that his best-laid plans foundered on a frosty surface, despite the glorious sunshine, at Broadwood. 'There were loads of commercial deals set up for him, but, at the end of the day, if he's not good enough to play regularly in the first team, then the deals are worthless. It was a real disappointment. Everyone wanted him to succeed. He was a really, really nice guy. The players liked him, but the SPL is a certain type of league, and you have to be a certain type of player. Fitness levels and physique all come into it. Sometimes you need players with a bit more weight for the type of football we play.'

In financial terms, Celtic continues to be a big fish inhabiting a tiny pond, their ambitions hamstrung by their environment. In February 2008, they announced an impressive set of financial results for six months to 31 December 2007. Debt was reduced from £15 million to £6.8 million and pre-tax profits stood at £10.07 million. Around the same time, they made the list of the 20 richest clubs in the world. The Deloitte Football Money League placed them in 17th position, the only club in the top twenty not to come from the big five European leagues of England, Italy, Spain, Germany and France.

The question was: how could Celtic make further progress up the league? With great difficulty was the answer. It all centred around television revenue. In 2007, Barcelona made £75 million from TV revenue. Manchester United made £69 million. Celtic made just £2 million. 'If you added even the minimum amount of money that a Premiership club is guaranteed from television, which is £35 million, then we would be in the top ten of the richest clubs in the world,' says Dr John Reid, the Celtic chairman. 'We would not even have to sell one more ticket for a match or another strip. The financial figures are fantastic, and to do all that from a restricted base, such as the Scottish Premier League, simply shows what a great job everyone at the club, from Gordon Strachan to Peter Lawwell, is doing.'

With a switch to the Premiership an unrealistic ambition in the short term, Celtic have had to reconcile themselves to working within their boundaries. That has involved a concerted effort to open up new revenue streams. Lawwell explains the strategy. 'The financial and emotional commitment of the Celtic supporters are second to none, but playing in Scotland, which we will be doing for the foreseeable future, means that the disadvantage lies in much smaller media rights. There is also the fact that we are almost at saturation point in terms of the disposable income of our fan base. However, the expectations of all the fans and stakeholders correctly remain to compete at the highest level. So, you have that dilemma – how can we improve the finances to allow us to compete in the Champions League regularly and try to progress as far as we can? At that point, we realised that it is a big world out there. We had America, Australia, even Africa in terms of the Irish–Scots diaspora – so we started trying to generate revenues from there.'

Regular pre-season trips to North America have allowed Celtic to tap into that market over the past decade, but more recent times have seen an even greater widening of the net. Celtic's current first team is a hotchpotch of nationalities, and the club have not been slow to capitalise on the markets that the profile of their foreign players have allowed them to penetrate. 'The Polish players Artur Boruc and Maciej Żurawski did phenomenally well in their first season [2005–06],' says Thomson. 'We went to Poland and played Legia Warsaw and Wisła Kraków that pre-season. One was Żurawski's old club, and the other was Boruc's. On the back of that we did a deal with a Polish airline. There was a large number of Poles coming over for the games, and it brought together the large Polish community in Glasgow, which also helped ticket sales. The games are broadcast in Poland, and we have had a Polish vodka company taking sponsorship with us for the last two seasons. If we didn't have the players, that wouldn't have come off. It's just joined-up thinking around the club.

'We've always known we've had a good fan base in Australia. Although it's been years since we've been out there, it's something we would look to do. The easiest measure is the number of hits on Channel 67, and the number of subscribers to the games is a clear indication of where the pockets of supporters are in these countries. It has been very good in Australia, but interest has doubled since Scott McDonald has come on board. There are other areas that you wouldn't expect. Holland is very good on the back of Jan Vennegoor of Hesselink and Evander Sno.

'We could never be like Manchester United, who have a huge amount of TV money from the Premier League and whose games are shown in every country around the world. Everyone perceives India and China as the fastest-growing markets. Well, they don't broadcast the Scottish Premier League in those two countries. They would have done in China if we had signed Du Wei. Rather than take on the whole of the world, we have some very strong markets, whether it is Australia, Japan or North America, and we know where the supporters are. We communicate with the supporters' clubs regularly, and they are always great for ringing us up and saying, "You should be doing this," or, "Can you talk to Setanta about X, Y and Z?"'

The summer of 2005 was a big one for Celtic on and off the field. At the end of the previous season, Martin O'Neill had left the club after a highly successful five-year reign to be replaced by Gordon Strachan. Investment in the team was needed, and it was a welcome by-product that several of the players Strachan had identified for his new side, such as Boruc and Żurawski, would also prove to be commercial assets. However, it was the emergence of Nakamura on Strachan's scouting radar that had the commercial department rubbing their hands in glee. There is no doubt that Nakamura was a football rather than a commercial signing. He fits the mould of a Strachan player – he is skilful, has good vision and is an excellent passer. His on-field contributions are also a firm rebuke to any suggestions that the club just had pound signs in their eyes when they took him from Reggina in 2005.

'It became clear that the world was not going to come to Scotland, so we had to go out and get it,' says Lawwell. 'In the States and the Far East, for example, supporters follow personalities. We thought, "Wouldn't it be good if we could get the world to come here by bringing personalities from the world's growth areas in soccer terms, such as the States and the Far East?" That was part of the strategy, and in terms of the achievement of that whoever we bring in has to be able, first and foremost, to play football in the first team. The decision to bring Nakamura was not us saying to Gordon, "Go out and see if you can find a Far Eastern player." It was Gordon saying, "I've found this gem, and it fits nicely, so thanks very much." The effect of that has been that Celtic in terms of awareness in the Far East has grown to a great extent.

'The strategy then was to get a global distributor. Umbro were fantastic, but we needed someone who could feed the world. Nike came along and followed that up. They've been first class in terms of distribution to these areas. First of all, it is about exposure. Playing in the Champions League is short-term revenue, but the long-term investment is brand awareness and exposure around the world. China, Korea, India, the States, Japan, they're avaricious for football. We'll continue to invest resources in those areas to understand what is going on there.'

If off-field returns pivot around on-field success, then it follows that the 'football department' is the most important area in the creation of a global brand. The success of the club's commercial department is due in no small part to the success enjoyed by Strachan and his side over the past three seasons. Domestic dominance has been key, but the worldwide exposure that progression in the Champions League has given them has been invaluable.

Most importantly, Strachan has bought into the club's attempts to penetrate new markets. In the past few years, Celtic have travelled to North America on pre-season trips. They also played a one-off friendly against Yokohama F. Marinos in August 2006, which they lost 3–0. The latter trip attracted criticism, because it was scheduled during the football season and on their return

Celtic lost in the league to Hearts. However, the inconvenience of the twelve-thousand-mile round-the-world trip was eased by the six-figure sum, estimated to be just under £1 million, that they received in return. 'Gordon's great because he's got the vision to see that by going to Japan or the USA we are raising the club's profile, we get a good commercial return on that and ultimately it then comes back into his pot to buy players. He benefits from it,' adds Thomson. 'The friendly against Yokohama F. Marinos was something we agreed we would do very early on. We had a very good start to that season but came back from that trip and lost to Hearts. We had an agreement with them that as long as six of the travelling squad were regular first-team players, then they were happy. It's good getting out there and letting people see what Celtic are all about. People use this word "family", but that is what we are all about. In Japan, there were a small number of Celtic supporters, but most people at the match had some sort of green-and-white garment on and were there to support Naka.'

Thomson brings an emotional investment to his role as commercial director. He is a lifelong Celtic fan who lived through the lean years of the late 1970s and '80s, which makes him even more determined to ensure the club never returns to the bad old days. 'It's my mother's side of the family who are Celtic daft. They started off in Bellshill and moved to Fife to work in the pits. Then we moved down south, so I spent most of my early years in Coventry. I joined Marks & Spencer as a trainee and worked my way up. I worked for lots of companies, such as HMV, and was also at Leeds United for four years, during which time they had five chairmen. I knew this job was coming up and made sure I was in for it when David McNally [Thomson's predecessor] moved on. I love it. It is twenty-four hours a day, seven days a week. There's always something happening, whether you are talking to someone in the early hours of the morning in Japan or late at night in the States. What really surprised me when I first started, having been a season-ticket holder for years, was that I didn't appreciate the strength of the brand globally. It really is massive, and we are now looking for ways to make sure we make the most of that demand and interact with the fans wherever they are.'

Like Thomson, Lawwell also combines the emotionalism of a supporter with the acumen and hard-headedness of a successful businessman. He has needed every bit of both to succeed. There are easier jobs than being Celtic chief executive. It is a position that is fraught with pitfalls and has claimed many victims over the years. Five years on and Lawwell is still there and flourishing. The general consensus is that he has made a better fist of the job than anyone in the modern era. 'Expect the unexpected' might be the motto of a man in his position.

In a business sense, he thought he had seen and done it all. He thought there were no surprises left. Then he tried to sign Nakamura, a task he describes as 'the most laborious and intricate assignment' he has ever been involved in. And he has been involved in a few. Most deals involve a player, an agent and two clubs. Lawwell soon realised that Nakamura was a one-man industry and that all his negotiation skills and business knowledge would be required to pull the deal off.

'The amount of people involved made it so complicated. When we finalised the deal with Reggina, there was their chairman, four agents and me. Then there were image rights involved. In Italy, clubs hold their own TV rights, in contrast to Scotland, where there is one deal for all the teams. In that sense, Nakamura was a valuable commodity for Reggina, as the club could negotiate their own deals and keep all the profits. So, you have a player from the other end of the world, you've got a posse of advisers and you've got a complicated club in Italy. Then we have to convince him to come to Scotland when the boy has Spain in his eyes. It was quite complicated and intricate, and there was a lot of persuasion required. In terms of the type of football at Reggina, he was defending and playing not to lose, whereas at Celtic we play to win and attack in every game. That suits him, and there was also the profile that appearing in the Champions League would give him.

'It was a real coup for us. We were delighted that we persuaded him and his people that this was the right place for him. Roberto Tsukuda, his agent, has been first class. He's a fantastic mentor for Naka and a fair and reasonable guy to deal with. He's now a Celtic supporter, and I count him as a friend. When he connected with the club and how we went about our business, he enjoyed working with us.'

As of 2008, Nakamura has been at Celtic for three years. He has stayed because he loves it. Celtic have benefited financially because they have a happy, settled player on their books. Once again, the commercial argument returns to the importance of on-field issues. 'He's been such a fabulous footballer for us. His achievements on the pitch and the example he has shown off it in terms of his values and his standards is a model for kids,' adds Lawwell. 'He is a true professional. Like the vast majority of players who come here, he has connected with the club. That is the special difference between Celtic and most teams. Players connect with the club's ethos, how it is run, the values and standards that we have, the traditions, the way we play football and the way they are treated. Naka connects with the supporters. His flair, ingenuity and style excites them. Once you get that two-way connection, people don't want to leave here. You'll see that those who have left recently haven't gone on to find anything better. Brian McClair, Kenny Dalglish and Henrik Larsson are perhaps the only three who have gone on to bigger things.'

Nakamura's image rights were fundamental to Celtic fully capitalising on their capture of one of the most famous Asian sportsmen on the planet. After lengthy negotiations, they eventually secured them for £1.3 million, a sum which was built into the £2.7-million fee that took him from Reggina. This allows the club to use Nakamura's image on a range of products they sell on their Japanese websites and through official club stores and Nike outlets around the world.

Thomson explains that the business relationship between the Nakamura camp, spearheaded by Tsukuda, and Celtic is pivotal to the off-field spin-offs enjoyed by both parties. 'We've got an excellent working relationship with him. We work closely with Nakamura's agent. There are certain things we will approach him on, and he will just say, "No, that's not the kind of thing he is interested in," or else, "No problem." Nakamura has a very close relationship with Roberto, so there is very little that he doesn't know the answer to. With Nakamura, there is just one point of contact. Sometimes people around football players make it quite difficult to get answers, whereas Roberto is very clear on what Nakamura will do, when he will do it and when payments will be made, and he is very honourable and direct. If there is an issue, he will tell you. There are rarely any surprises.'

With Nakamura on board, Celtic's commercial wing clicked into gear. 'There were a number of opportunities that we took advantage of when he signed,' says Thomson. 'We knew that whatever we did, we had to get Celtic on television regularly. We had to have a presence within Japan 52 weeks a year to make sure that we made the most of the commercial aspect of the Nakamura deal. There were deals set up with a couple of television companies in Japan, which we don't directly earn any money from, other than through the central Premier League deal. Every game we play, whether it's against Inverness Caledonian Thistle or Barcelona, is broadcast live in Japan. There's no problem in seeing it. It's on J Sports. In effect, what we are doing is creating value for the Premier League and the rest of Scottish football. With the way the TV money is divvied up, everybody is benefiting from our investment.

'We then did deals with a number of companies to secure broadband rights, and on top of that we have Channel 67. We struck deals with 3G companies so that people could download clips of Nakamura goals. After every game, you can buy five clips of him. We have a number of his sponsors who we do deals with. Oronamin C, one of the drinks companies he endorses, have come and filmed Nakamura at Celtic Park, and we got a fee for allowing that to happen. Again, it is exposure for the club. In terms of profile, it helps us massively. If you've got images of Nakamura in a Celtic shirt at Celtic Park being shown in Japan, that's great for us.

'Likewise, we are doing a Nakamura DVD for the Japanese market at the moment. That venture is between Naka and us, and we will do a revenue share on the DVD. Every deal is slightly different. There's a real willingness from both parties to work together. By doing all of these things, it has heightened the awareness of Nakamura with Celtic across Japan and Asia, which has allowed us to start merchandising, via Nike, throughout Japan.'

Celtic replica strips are de rigueur among Japanese young people, many of whom keep the price tag on as proof of authenticity. Thomson dismisses speculation that the club have sold a quarter of a million shirts in the Far East, but the numbers are in excess of 140,000. Rather than opening official stores, Celtic have used their partnership with Nike to sell their products at 250 outlets throughout Japan. 'I don't think they even had Celtic products in Japan before we took Naka on board,' says Thomson. 'It has gone from that situation to Nike now putting into Japan thousands of training items and shirts with the partners they have out there. It was a case of getting the player established with Celtic and then looking for additional ways to get the Celtic message out there. We have up to half a dozen lines that we have all year round, and they are primarily Nike Celtic products. What we then do is a tailored range of Nakamura products, whether it's T-shirts, caps, mugs, key rings. We liaise with Nike and their Japanese partners to work out what things will and won't sell in Japan. We're not coming at it completely blind.

'It was quoted recently that we had sold a quarter of a million shirts in Japan, but it's nowhere near that figure. However, people do tend to buy the full kits. They love official products, so you will see a lot of stuff with the tags still on. People are proud that they have got official products. Year two on year one in Japan we doubled our sales, and year three is considerably ahead of year two already, so there's good growth out there. On the back of that, we built a Japanese website, which gets 60,000 unique users a week. Most of the content is Nakamura-driven, and through that we have tried to build a relationship with those supporters.

'We also agreed to tour Japan on a yearly basis. If you get a game at one of the biggest stadiums, you can get 60 or 70,000 people to attend. That all raises the awareness and grows the Celtic family.'

Celtic are now the third most popular Scottish brand in Japan, behind whisky and Sean Connery. Their popularity has also led to the creation of a word for 'Scot' – '*Scoto-rando-jin*' – whereas in the past Scots were referred to as being English, in the form of the word '*Igirisu-jin*'.

Nakamura demonstrates other key personality traits that contribute to his commercial success. He may lack the colourful, charismatic persona of Hidetoshi Nakata, but his vigorous work ethic and innate modesty have proved alluring in Japan, where such qualities are at the core of society. As he admits himself, Nakamura might not match David Beckham in the looks department, but he has a pleasant, inoffensive outward personality, which has proved attractive to advertisers and, by extension, a Far East audience. He is also aware of his commercial value. Although he turns down more than he accepts, Nakamura still earns around £1 million in endorsements and add-ons. He is the face of Adidas in the Far East and puts his name to a couple of video games and other products.

Thomson claims that the player is a commercial dream. 'He's got this wholesome image and reputation. He's a real family man, and he's an outstanding footballer.

'Because he doesn't speak directly to the fans, all communication being in his native tongue, there is a little bit of mystery about him. You can see on the pitch that he absolutely loves the club. His first love is Japan and then after that Celtic, but Roberto was telling me that when Scotland were playing Italy recently he supported Scotland. He's got a little lad who I've seen in a Scotland top.

'He's on the front of 90 per cent of the newspaper stands in Japan. He has a team of journalists following him around everywhere. In terms of Nakamura and what he does for the club, the Japanese public want to know how he lives his life, how he eats, how he trains, how he is recovering from his injury. It's not just the football side. They are really into him as an individual and his values. They identify with him.'

If Nakamura was a defensive midfielder, he would not have the same allure. That he is a creative talent makes him more attractive to supporters, particularly the younger generation. His dead-ball expertise is another key area both on and off the field. Nakamura's ability at taking free-kicks has provided many memorable moments at Celtic. 'We sold hundreds of prints of the free-kick against Manchester United at Celtic Park, where he has just struck the ball and it is soaring over the wall,' says Thomson. 'We had limited-edition prints made as well, which he signed, and they just flew out the door. Those goals on those type of occasions just make a huge difference in every way. The supporters are happy, they celebrate and buy more shirts, and they come to more games. The demand now for Champions League games is massive. We didn't have a public sale for the Barcelona game in February 2008. If you weren't a season-ticket holder, you didn't get in. The Champions League, in terms of future sponsorship and exposure for the club, is massive.'

Manchester United are the most popular team in the Far East. Few others have gained a permanent foothold in the region. Nakata generated huge interest in the teams he played for in Italy. Feyenoord cashed in on Shinji Ono and even opened an official store in Tokyo, which was a huge success. When the player moved on, however, the interest immediately vanished, and the club were left with an expensive property on their hands. Celtic's aim is to create a more lasting impression in the Far East. On their Japanese website, there is a facility to download games from previous years. The intention is for Nakamura fans to identify with the club as well as the player. 'What we are sensitive to is that we are not in and out,' says Thomson. 'We don't want to go to Japan, play a game with our reserve team and leave everyone annoyed at us. We're not daft. The Japanese core supporters follow the player and not the club. If Nakamura moved on somewhere else, then his following would go with him. That's the way it is in Japan. But we want to make sure there is some longevity in what we do. That means getting in at grassroots and giving something back to the places we go. We've been to America three times in the last four years, and it is about trying to keep that momentum and relationship going.'

The signing of Koki Mizuno in February 2008 marked another key moment in Celtic's commercial master plan. Once again, football was at the core. The club had scouted the player extensively and were confident that he could make an impact in the Scottish Premier League. At twenty-two, he had already won four caps for his country, and his speed and skill had marked him out as one of Japanese football's emerging talents. Time will tell, of course, but Celtic hope that Mizuno will provide the 'longevity' Thomson speaks about. 'We've had a great experience with Naka, and we want more of it,' adds Lawwell. 'Football-wise, it's been wonderful, and we would like more of the same. Mizuno's 22, and we hope he will be around for many years.'

Nakamura believes Celtic have gained a solid foothold in Japan. 'Most of the supporters are probably my fans,' he says. 'When I was at Reggina, they were wearing Reggina tops, and then when I came to Celtic they bought Celtic shirts. But you can watch the matches on television in Japan, and a lot of people do that. The club is certainly better known in Japan.'

ELEVEN

······················

Lenny, Tommy and
Three in a Row

SHUNSUKE NAKAMURA SAT SILENTLY WITH HIS HEAD bowed. Outside, he could hear the expectant murmur of 60,000 fans. It was 16 April 2008, the penultimate Old Firm game of the season, one of six matches standing between Celtic and a possible third consecutive league title. It was a must-win for the Parkhead side, and the pressure was palpable. In the Celtic dressing-room, his teammates went through their pre-match routines: stretching, sucking down energy drinks, stalking the floor, psyching themselves up. Nakamura preferred a quieter preparation time. So, he sat staring at his bootlaces, centring himself, focusing his mind on the game ahead.

Suddenly, he felt a hand on his shoulder and abruptly snapped out of his reverie. Neil Lennon, the Celtic first-team coach, loomed over him. Nakamura liked Lennon. As a teammate, he had always responded positively to his on-field promptings. As a Celtic coach of less than a fortnight, he had found him to be an inspiring presence. Lennon had bossed his way through dozens of Old Firm games, his bullish, combative style flourishing in the heat of Glasgow's famous derby. Lennon knew what it was all about. He knew the pressure of Old Firm games. More than anything, though, he knew what it took to win them.

Lennon's eyes flashed. He gripped Nakamura by the shoulders and began to shake him. 'This is your day, Shunsuke. We need you. You're a hero.' Nakamura felt the hairs on his neck stand on end and his back straighten. It had been a difficult season, blighted by injury, but maybe Lennon was right . . . maybe his moment was still to come. Maybe tonight was his night. Maybe he was the man to breathe life back into Celtic's ailing title challenge. He stood up. He felt taller. He looked around the dressing-room and sensed a belief among his teammates.

Celtic had lost the previous two Old Firm games of the season, failing to score in either. In fact, they had not taken anything from Rangers since a 2–0 win in September 2006. Walter Smith's resurgent Rangers side currently led them by four points with an additional two games in hand – a mountain to climb – but everything about tonight felt different. Celtic were at home. Fortress Parkhead. A 4–1 thumping of Motherwell three days previously had also raised confidence after a rocky patch. Even the timing of the game was different – a Wednesday evening, the sun shining in the East End. Nakamura felt good. Gordon Strachan had already told him to occupy a more central midfield role, to present Rangers with a different challenge. He had a personal point to prove as well. He had never scored against Rangers. That bugged him.

On the pitch, he glances at the dugout one final time before the referee blows his whistle. Lennon points at him and clenches his fist. Nakamura's back straightens again.

Ten minutes in and he slants a devastating reverse ball in behind the Rangers defence for Jan Vennegoor of Hesselink, but he miscontrols it, and the chance goes a-begging. Nakamura has found his range, though. With 20 minutes on the clock, Gary Caldwell picks up the ball on the right-hand side, just inside his own half. He spots Nakamura in a central midfield position 35 yards out and plays a measured pass to him. His control is instant, cushioning the ball onto his left foot. It sits up invitingly. In an instant, Lennon's words flood back to him. 'This is your day, Shunsuke. We need you. You're a hero.' Instinctively, he knows what to do. Nakamura draws back his left boot and thunders it. The shot leaves his foot like a missile. Allan McGregor shifts to his right, but the ball swerves viciously in the air, moving from left to right, and whistles by the Rangers goalkeeper to nestle in the net – 1–0. Goal of the season. 'He gave me special powers,' Nakamura said later of Lennon. 'He gets his passion about football across.'

As the game progressed, Nakamura was in irresistible form. In the second half, as Celtic pressed for the crucial second goal, the ball came to him inside the frantic, congested penalty area. He sidestepped a desperate tackle and calmly lashed a shot towards the top corner, which defender Carlos Cuéllar handled illegally. The Spaniard was sent off, and Celtic were awarded a penalty, but Scott McDonald missed it. However, the full significance of the sending off only became apparent later in the game. Nacho Novo had equalised for Rangers ten minutes into the second half, but in injury time Caldwell hit a diagonal ball to the left-hand side of the six-yard box, and in Cuéllar's absence the unmarked McDonald headed across to Vennegoor of Hesselink, whose diving header sealed the three points.

Scottish football suddenly had a title race on its hands. 'I would say that was my best Old Firm game, and I really enjoyed it,' Nakamura said. 'It was also really important for me to score my first goal against Rangers. I have been waiting a long time for that.

'I noticed early on that the ball was moving about in the air a lot. So, I decided that I would have a shot from distance the first opportunity I got. As soon as I hit the ball, I thought it had a chance. I hit my shot in a way that would give the ball a lot of movement. These are always difficult for the goalkeeper to save.

'We showed our pride. That was the important thing. We had lost twice to Rangers this season, and it was hard for us all to take.

We couldn't afford to lose again. I didn't even want to think about not beating Rangers. The thought didn't enter my head all game. But when we scored, there was tremendous relief.'

Celtic's victory was built on a commanding midfield performance. Paul Hartley and Barry Robson patrolled the central area with aplomb and, crucially, won the physical battle against their Rangers counterparts. Nakamura highlighted Robson's contribution, in particular. 'He allowed me to get forward a lot more and was finding me with all his passes. He really drove us on and helped the whole team to perform better. His tackling was really good, and that is really important in these games.'

Strachan's decision to replace the impressive Robson with Georgios Samaras after 75 minutes caused many eyebrows to be raised and sparked a lively exchange in the post-match press conference. When one journalist asked the Celtic manager if withdrawing the former Dundee United midfielder had been a difficult decision, Strachan dismissed the query out of hand and took the questioner aside after the press conference. 'Robson wasn't as good as you thought he was. Naka was the man tonight,' insisted the Celtic manager. He was right. The result would mark the turning point in Celtic's defence of their title.

The season thus far had been a difficult one for Nakamura, blighted as it had been by injury and, by his own high standards, a dip in performance levels. His scoring display against Rangers had got him back on track, and he relished his role in Celtic's success. This was not always the case, however. Even in seeming triumph, Nakamura can be brutal on himself.

There is a photograph of the Celtic players seconds after they have secured qualification for the group stages of the Champions League against Spartak Moscow at Celtic Park in late August 2007. Artur Boruc has just saved Maksym Kalynychenko's penalty in the shoot-out, having earlier kept out Egor Titov's. After 120 gruelling minutes and a nerve-shredding shoot-out, Celtic are through. Lined up in a row across the halfway line, they have all started to run towards the Polish goalkeeper to celebrate another historic achievement. It is an image of unbridled joy: Stephen McManus, the newly installed club captain, fist clenched and screaming in ecstasy; a shaven-headed Scott Brown with his mouth wide open in disbelief; Gary Caldwell, arms spread, breaking like an Olympic sprinter from the blocks, closely followed by young Irish defender Darren O'Dea. The joy was mirrored in the stands, which erupted with euphoria after a night of see-sawing fortunes against the classy Russians. Look a little closer, though, and there is one player whose reaction is at odds with the surrounding madness. Standing between Massimo Donati and O'Dea, Nakamura is smiling. Just. His left arm is half-raised in muted celebration. He is not running, though. When his Celtic teammates reached Boruc, there was a mass pile-up of bodies, involving all the players and coaching staff. Well, not quite all of them.

As Celtic's players, coaches and fans celebrated another season of Champions League football and the lucrative financial rewards it brings, Nakamura shook hands with Gordon Strachan, then turned and walked straight off the park with his head bowed. In the dressing-room, he kicked off his boots and shook his head. He was disconsolate. Sure, his team were through to the group stages, but he had let them down. In extra time, he'd had gilt-edged chances to finish the game and fluffed them. Then, in the penalty shoot-out he had struck his spot-kick – the second of Celtic's four – against the underside of the crossbar. He thought that it might have crossed the line, but after checking with the referee realised it hadn't. His failure was a personal one. He had let the side down. Boruc had saved them moments later, but for Nakamura that was not the point. Before the match, the Moscow players had highlighted the Japanese midfielder as the main threat to their chances of progression. Celtic needed him at his best on nights such as these.

It had been an incredible night, one on which two penalties, one for either side, had been missed in normal time and a welter of chances spurned at both ends. Celtic could have been three goals behind after twenty minutes but had weathered the early storm and opened the scoring themselves, through Scott McDonald, after 27 minutes. Roman Pavlyuchenko had then equalised just before half-time, before which Boruc and Lee Naylor had squared up to each other as tempers frayed. As the compelling tie raged into extra time, Spartak's Martin Stranzl was sent off. Cool heads were needed. Nakamura prided himself on being the coolest, the still axis in the revolving wheel. He had the mentality to produce the goods when it mattered most. He had proved that against Manchester United the season before. He knew his time would come. And it did. Twice he was clean through on goalkeeper Stipe Pletikosa and twice he fluffed it. Then he was presented with another great opportunity on his left foot but slashed the half-volley into row Z. Three great chances in extra time, and he had blown them all. Then he had missed a penalty. He had let his teammates down. The majority of other players might have glossed over their individual shortcomings on a night of collective achievement. Not Nakamura.

The concept of group responsibility is huge in Japan. From a young age, Japanese are indoctrinated with the idea that their group, whether it be a corporate organisation, football team or even political party, is of paramount importance. Group responsibility dictates that an individual feels worse about damaging their group and colleagues than they do about the personal impact it will have on them. When it works, it acts as a powerful incentive to good behaviour. Unlike Britain, Japanese politicians and captains of industry regularly resign for things that have occurred at much lower levels in their organisation but which were not directly their fault. In the J. League's early years, a leader of the Yokohama Marinos support group, whose job it was to whip up atmosphere in the stadium, came forward to accept punishment for a fellow crowd member who had thrown a coin at an opposition player. He was banned from the stadium for the rest of the year, even though it had not been his fault.

Not even his colleagues' joy or the achievement itself could console Nakamura. They had got through, but no thanks to him. He had a job to do and had not done it to the best of his ability. Shin Toyofuku recalls his mood that evening. 'He just walked straight to the dressing-room. He was so disappointed, he was almost crying after the game. His performance was very poor. He missed three chances and one penalty. He couldn't be happy. We thought, "This time maybe he won't appear," but to be fair to him he came straight to the press room.'

Afterwards, Nakamura reflected on the pain he felt at his personal shortcomings. 'I did not celebrate with the other players at full-time. I shook hands with the manager and went to sit in the dressing-room on my own. I was really disappointed with myself because I'd missed so many chances during the game. I missed three in as many minutes. I sat and thought about what happened and what I had done. I thought about it for a long time after the game. At the first chance, I only had their keeper to beat and the ball sat up for me to try and lob him. But I thought that is what he expected me to do, so I tried something else, and it didn't work. And at the second chance I should have been quicker to have a shot. I waited too long, and that is what cost me. Then at the third I wanted to hit the ball hard but just had a wild one. I'm always confident at penalties and volunteered to take one. It was almost as if I was in a trance as I walked up because I was so focused – but I missed. I first thought the ball had hit the bar and crossed the line. The referee then told me it hadn't, and I had to walk back to the players knowing I had made a mistake.'

It is just as well that Nakamura is a football obsessive. The extent of his club and country commitments mean that he is never off the pitch or the training field. After his first season at Celtic, in which he played 45 games, he travelled to Germany to play for Japan in the World Cup. On his return to Celtic, he turned in another fifty-three-game season and picked up two Player of the Year awards. After that, he went to represent Japan in the Asian Cup and returned to Celtic for the start of the 2007–08 season having had just one week's holiday. In fact, the Japanese midfielder had arrived in Scotland just 48 hours before Celtic's first league game of the season, against Kilmarnock at home.

Due to his lack of preparation, Strachan left Nakamura on the bench and introduced him after 63 minutes for Donati with the game still goalless. He soon livened up proceedings, bringing zest and penetration to Celtic's attempts to snatch a winner, although he failed to convert two of his free-kick opportunities towards the end of the match. Perhaps he was just finding his range, because the following week against Falkirk he was back to his best. Celtic had gone a goal down inside the first five minutes against John Hughes's impressive side but had restored parity by half-time before Kenny Miller put them in front in the 76th minute. If the result was ever in doubt, Nakamura put the game beyond Falkirk two minutes later. Presented with a free-kick opportunity 25 yards out and in the dead centre of the goal, he sent a sublime curling shot into the top right-hand corner of the net. On the touchline, Strachan, in his 100th game in charge, danced with joy at another display of Nakamura's dead-ball genius. The player himself turned towards the Celtic fans in the away stand, patted the badge on his shirt and raised his arm in salute as he was engulfed by his teammates.

The rigours of his punishing summer schedule seemed to be having no discernible effect on Nakamura, who continued to shine in Celtic's impressive early season outings. A good performance in a 3–1 away victory against Aberdeen was followed by a masterclass in the club's 5–0 caning of Hearts in late August. 'Out-played, out-thought and out-classed,' was the succinct summation of the game, in which Nakamura was rampant, by Hearts head coach Stephen Frail. The first goal, after nine minutes, went down as an own goal by Christophe Berra after Nakamura's shot deflected off the defender and into the net. Celtic continued to slice the Tynecastle side open at will, with Aiden McGeady and Nakamura pulling the strings, and the latter won the penalty for Celtic's fourth goal just after an hour. When the Japanese midfielder impishly nutmegged

Berra, it was more than the beleaguered centre-half could take, and he hauled Nakamura back to concede the spot-kick, which was dispatched by Jan Vennegoor of Hesselink. Nakamura completed the rout with a deft chip over Hearts goalkeeper Steve Banks from ten yards.

The goals continued to flow for the Japanese midfielder, and he claimed his third of the season in mid-September, the third in a 5–0 thrashing of Inverness Caledonian Thistle. He had had a quiet game by his own standards, but in the 55th minute he took a McDonald pass and unleashed an unstoppable swerving shot. Afterwards, the Inverness manager Craig Brewster described the finish as 'world class'.

In Celtic's opening Champions League group game, against the Ukrainian side Shakhtar Donetsk, Nakamura was a peripheral figure, as were the majority of his teammates, who never recovered from the concession of two goals inside the first eight minutes. By that point, the ravages of Nakamura's heavy schedule were starting to take their toll, and a troublesome knee injury kept him out of the three domestic games after Donetsk, two in the league and one in the CIS Insurance Cup. Uncertainty hung over Nakamura's involvement for the visit of AC Milan to Parkhead in their second group game. With Vennegoor of Hesselink ruled out with a hamstring strain, his involvement became all the more important. 'Milan know all about Shunsuke,' said Strachan. 'Everyone knows what Nakamura can do from set-pieces. He makes things happen, as he showed in the Champions League last season with those goals against Manchester United. It is great for everyone in our club to have him back. I never thought Nakamura would have no chance of playing, simply because the doctors felt he had given himself a chance with the way he looks after himself. However, I did devise a team without him, just in case.'

However, Strachan's pre-match comments belied the full extent of Nakamura's injury. The writing was on the wall when he was seen to limp through the reception area at Celtic Park on the day of the game. Remarkably, he was on the bench and made a significant contribution in the game's dramatic denouement. Celtic had opened the scoring just after the hour mark when McManus forced in the opener off Yoann Gourcuff, but six minutes later Kaká's contentiously awarded spot-kick had drawn Milan level. Five minutes remained when Strachan replaced McGeady with the barely half-fit Nakamura, and the substitution reaped almost instant dividends. In the final minute, Nakamura picked the ball up on the right side of the penalty box and expertly made an extra yard for himself with a step-over. He then laid the ball into the path of Brown, who picked out Caldwell on the edge of the box. The defender's controlled shot was palmed out by Dida, and McDonald pounced to ram home the rebound and send Parkhead into paroxysms of delight. The gamble had paid off, in the short term at least.

But Nakamura had a problem, the extent of which was now becoming clear. Inconspicuous performances in the late victory over Gretna and the 3–0 defeat by Rangers led to him being dropped for the away game against Benfica. He managed an assist in the 3–0 victory over Motherwell on 27 October, but the game would mark his last involvement in two and a half months. Originally, the problem was diagnosed as an injury to the ligament on the outside of his left knee sustained by a heavy challenge during the Champions League qualifier against Spartak Moscow. A further MRI scan revealed nerve damage next to the ligament. Towards the end of November, the player expressed his frustration at being sidelined. 'I thought it was going to be over much more quickly,' Nakamura said. 'I was playing with a lot of pain in the first match with Shakhtar, in Donetsk, up to the match with Motherwell. It is frustrating. When I played in Italy, I had one period when I was out, but I am not used to this.'

Nakamura had managed a dozen games before his injury problem sidelined him, a period in which Celtic had won eight games, drawn two and lost two. The enforced sabbatical would lead to him missing the next 13 games. Celtic's record over that period was seven wins, four draws and two defeats. When he departed the scene in October, Celtic were three points clear at the top of the league. When he returned in January, they were a point behind Rangers, who had a game in hand, a strong indication that Celtic were a better team with him in it. It was during Nakamura's injury lay-off that I spoke to Boruc about what the Japanese midfielder brought to the side. He claimed that Celtic's struggles during that period were directly attributable to the absence of Nakamura.

'We are not playing the best football, and the big difference is Naka,' he said. 'When I saw him a few times, at first, I was impressed. We missed him for a few games, but when he came back the training was totally different. Honestly, totally different. It's a different team when he is here. We need players who can pass the ball. We are a young team, and sometimes we don't remember that we need to hold the ball and try to be careful. This is a team sport. Naka knows this. He can keep the ball. He can pass. He is a very good player, a very important player for the team.'

In total, Celtic were deprived of Nakamura's services for 77 days. As Boruc reflected, his absence had been decisive. The team were not playing with anywhere near the fluidity that Strachan hoped for. The Celtic manager was facing the first real challenge to his team's supremacy in the shape of Walter Smith's rejuvenated Rangers side. It was with a palpable sense of relief, then, that he welcomed back Nakamura for their Scottish Cup tie against Stirling Albion. At the press conference the day before the game, Strachan struggled to keep a smile off his face as he waxed lyrical about the return of his Japanese talisman. 'I said to Gary McAllister [the former Scotland captain] the other day, "I hope you don't take offence to this, but in pure football terms Nakamura's the best footballer I've ever worked with,"' said Strachan. 'Gary's lip did go for a wee while, but, in pure footballing terms, in terms of vision and touch and passing, Naka's the best. I've played with better footballers all-round – such as Bryan Robson and Kenny Dalglish – but for pure football he has got it.'

The next day, Nakamura would also show he possessed an impeccable sense of timing. Celtic had huffed and puffed their way to a two-goal advantage against the bottom-placed First Division side, and 15 minutes were left on the clock when Strachan prepared to replace Nakamura with Jim O'Brien. The Japanese midfielder had contributed the occasional creative sparks, but his performance betrayed the rustiness of a player who had been out for ten weeks. Vision might be one of Nakamura's greatest assets, but it was the fourth official's board that Nakamura spotted with quarter of an hour remaining. With O'Brien limbering up, Nakamura sparked to life. The ball dropped on the edge of the area, and he twisted his body to curl an exquisite effort into the far corner of the net. Then he went off. 'It was very exciting, and I was glad to be back. I know that Aiden has been delivering great performances, so if I can do the same on my side, that will make it easier for him,' reflected the player.

'That was good,' Strachan said of the goal. 'It was good to see him back, even if you could see he was rusty. But we had to play him, because there are a lot of games coming up – more important games.'

Afterwards, Nakamura was asked about a story in the Japanese press that reported that Yokohama F. Marinos were seeking talks to bring him home. The midfielder admitted he wanted to finish his career in Japan. 'I will go back to Japan some time in the future,' he said. 'I don't want to finish my career away from my homeland. Marinos is the club I started my career at, so it would be great if I could go back there.' When asked when he was likely to return, he said, 'When Peter [Lawwell] says, "I don't need you any more."'

They say imitation is the sincerest form of flattery, so it was perhaps little surprise, given the huge impact Nakamura had made at Celtic, that they should seek to re-enter the Japanese market. In

January 2008, Celtic were linked with two Japanese players: 26-year-old Le Mans midfielder Daisuke Matsui and Koki Mizuno, the 22-year-old winger from JEF United. It soon became clear that Mizuno was their real target and the deal to bring him to Celtic already well advanced. Mizuno had made his name as a pacy right-winger with his J. League club and had been capped four times by his country. Compared to his countryman, Mizuno's arrival in Scotland for a two-day introductory tour was much more low-key. Nakamura had landed in Scotland 24 hours after Celtic's 5–0 defeat to Artmedia Bratislava in July 2005, a result widely acknowledged as the worst in the club's European history. The fans, the players and the manager needed a lift, and Nakamura's entrance sparked scenes almost comparable to Beatlemania at Glasgow Airport. Just a small group of reporters and photographers were in attendance for Mizuno's arrival. Someone offered him a Celtic scarf, but he declined it. A tour of the club's facilities left him suitably impressed. 'I felt the history of Celtic Park,' Mizuno said after being shown around the stadium and the club's Lennoxtown training centre by Lawwell and Strachan. 'I am really looking forward to playing here. I'm impressed with the stadium. The supporters are very close to the pitch, and that excites me. And I like that the stadium is all covered in green.'

At twenty-two, Mizuno was two years younger than Nakamura was when he arrived in Europe. Strachan made it clear that he would be given ample time to acclimatise. 'We have got to wait a wee bit longer for him, because, unlike Nakamura, who stopped off in Italy before he came to Britain, he came straight from Japan. I can assure him the change of culture will shock him, so he has to get acclimatised on and off the pitch. He is a pure football player, like Naka. Naka took a wee while to get himself beefed up, but since doing that he has been absolutely fantastic.'

When Strachan was asked if they had signed the new Nakamura, he laughed. As if. The Celtic manager knocked back any stylistic comparisons with Nakamura but expressed his confidence in his new acquisition's ability. 'We asked the people who we work with in Japan to keep an eye out for good players, and his name was thrown in. So, we watched the videos and thought, "Yeah, he will do." We had people go to have a look at him live and took their opinion. He's a wee bit different to Naka, maybe a wee bit quicker. He is probably more of a winger than Naka. Mizuno has the potential to be a good footballer, and I think what he's got to do, like Naka, is realise how physical it is. I was asked if he could come straight into the team by the Department of Employment advisory panel. At the moment, I have the Scottish Player of the Year [Nakamura] and potential Scottish Player of the Year [Aiden McGeady], so it's not easy for wide midfield players, but he has the potential to step in for them. The good thing is that as a younger man coming over here there is another Japanese player here, too.'

Mizuno declared himself excited by the challenge. 'When I played alongside Shunsuke for the national team, he gave me lots of advice. I am aiming to be as successful as Shunsuke has been,' he said after signing a three-and-a-half-year deal. 'In terms of style, I don't think I'm similar to Nakamura. But I am quite confident with my crossing and dribbling, so maybe I can do well with that. I was really surprised when I heard about Celtic's interest. But at the same time I was really pleased and happy. Every bit of news about Shunsuke goes back to Japan in the newspapers and on the television. So, even people who don't like football know about Celtic. As soon as I knew about Celtic's interest, I wanted to come here. I didn't have to think about it. My family did not have any worries about me coming to Europe.'

In only his third game back from injury, an away match against Falkirk, Nakamura again displayed his value to the team. His contribution would have come as no surprise to John Hughes, the Falkirk manager, who reflected on the dangers posed by Celtic in his pre-match press conference. 'Celtic are a fantastic team. The way they pass the ball and their movement is fantastic, and in

Aiden McGeady and Shunsuke Nakamura they have a couple of geniuses.'

For the majority of the first half, Celtic were played off the park by Falkirk. They were chasing shadows and didn't look like scoring. Then, on the stroke of half-time, Nakamura picked the ball up on the right wing from McDonald. He made for the by-line and measured to cross the ball with his right foot. As the defender committed himself, he cut the ball back onto his trusty left foot and delivered a superb cross to the edge of the six-yard box, where McDonald stole in front of everyone to glance into the net. It would prove to be the only goal of the game. Nakamura had contributed virtually nothing for the 68 minutes he was on the field but had won the game with one flash of quality.

In the 5–1 destruction of Kilmarnock the following week, Nakamura had a hand in the first two goals. More importantly, there were signs in his general play that he was starting to edge back to full fitness. These were confirmed the following weekend when he opened the scoring in the 5–1 victory over Aberdeen, a day on which McGeady produced one of the best individual performances of recent seasons. The match was also significant for the contribution of Barry Robson, the club's January signing from Dundee United. The 29 year old replaced Nakamura after 73 minutes against Aberdeen and with his first touch of the ball smashed a free-kick into the bottom corner of the net for Celtic's fifth. Nakamura acknowledged that he now had a rival not only for his position but also as the free-kick taker. 'Ever since I came to Celtic, I've not had a trial for my place on the right side of midfield. But now Barry has come here, and he can definitely play out there and cut inside on his left foot, as I have done in the past. It's good to have competition – good for the team and for the individuals involved. I must now fight for my place, although Barry can play in more than one position. He is a strong player physically, and he can play in the centre of midfield or out on the left-hand side as well.'

A 3–0 victory against Hearts on 16 February witnessed another Nakamura assist, this time when he dropped a cross onto the head of McDonald for Celtic's second goal. Celtic had opened the scoring through Vennegoor of Hesselink after fourteen minutes, and Nakamura was unlucky not to break the deadlock with six minutes on the clock when a curling free-kick came off the inside of the post.

Nakamura was rested for the visit to St Mirren the following Sunday, but his presence on the bench would prove significant. It was a day on which Celtic had knocked the ball around for most of the match but failed to breach the home side's rearguard. Strachan introduced Nakamura for Robson after sixty-four minutes, and the Japanese midfielder made his match-winning intervention three minutes from time. The 29 year old picked up possession on the right and cut towards the edge of the box, where he went down under a challenge from Gary Mason. The contact was minimal, and the award was soft. Perhaps the hail of controversy that followed stemmed from the inevitability of what happened next. Nakamura placed the ball 25 yards out and expertly curled it inside the goalkeeper's left-hand post. In doing so, he claimed victory for Celtic and prevented them from falling six points behind Rangers at the top of the league.

'I never touched him, and he just fell over,' protested Mason. Nakamura insisted that he had been fouled. 'Mason came in from behind and tripped me. It was definitely a free-kick. I really wanted to come on and score, and when I saw their goalkeeper covering the right-hand side of his goal, I went to his left.'

Nakamura provided another assist for McDonald in Celtic's 2–1 win over Inverness at the end of February and played his part in the 2–0 victory over Hibs in their next match. The Parkhead side played Barcelona the following Tuesday in the Nou Camp, and Strachan decided to utilise Nakamura in the hole behind Vennegoor of Hesselink. It might have worked had Barcelona not added to their goal tally after four minutes and dominated possession throughout.

Nevertheless, it reflected the Celtic manager's intention to use the Japanese midfielder in a more inventive way.

Celtic's season took a turn for the worse thereafter, and Nakamura struggled to reverse their declining fortunes. They were knocked out of the Scottish Cup in mid-March in a replay against Aberdeen, and their title ambitions were damaged by a defeat to Rangers at Ibrox at the end of the month. It was a game in which Celtic, and Nakamura, played reasonably well but came down to a tale of missed chances and a lack of physical presence. The balance of the Celtic midfield was partly responsible for the problems they encountered. A combination of Nakamura, McGeady and Scott Brown in the midfield left the team without an authoritative physical presence and nullified the creativity at their disposal. There were also signs that the strike pairing of Vennegoor of Hesselink and McDonald had started to struggle with the physical demands of a long, hard season. This also blunted Celtic's creativity in midfield. In the 1–0 defeat by Motherwell at Celtic Park on 5 April, attempts by Nakamura and McGeady to thread balls through to the strikers or pick them out with crosses continually foundered on the front pairing's inability to hold the ball up or direct efforts on target. Motherwell scored, albeit against the run of play, and held on for victory despite playing the last forty minutes with ten men after Bob Malcolm's sending off. At the final whistle, sections of the Celtic support chanted for Strachan's dismissal. Afterwards, the Celtic manager admitted that the result made it 'near impossible' for his side to retain their title. At that point, his team trailed Rangers by six points with six games to play. The Ibrox side also had two games in hand.

An eight-day gap between matches at least allowed Celtic time to regroup, and they returned to action a much stronger unit. A 4–1 destruction of Motherwell, with goals from McManus, McDonald and two from Vennegoor of Hesselink, restored some pride and confidence and ensured that they entered the forthcoming Old Firm game in better fettle. Celtic had to win against their old rivals, and the combination of Nakamura's wonder strike and Vennegoor of Hesselink's last-minute goal made an improbable title challenge seem just about possible. To defend the championship, they needed to win their last five games and hope that Rangers slipped up.

A hard-fought and nervy 1–0 victory over Aberdeen three days after their portentous Old Firm win further strengthened hope. The tentativeness and lack of composure that had held them back for the previous couple of months had started to dissipate, but it was the second Old Firm game in 11 days that really inspired belief that they could defend their title. If the first one was a memorable encounter, the second was a classic. It was a game of unremitting drama from first to last. McDonald's looping shot nestled in the corner of the Rangers net after just four minutes. By the half-hour mark, headers from David Weir and Daniel Cousin had given Rangers the lead, but McDonald restored parity two minutes before the interval. It was gladiatorial combat at its finest, and the outcome was eventually decided with 20 minutes remaining. A clumsy challenge from Kirk Broadfoot floored McDonald inside the box, and Robson stepped up to ram home the penalty. Nakamura, who had an enterprising game, was on the receiving end of a very late challenge from Steven Whittaker at the end of the match, which earned the Rangers player a straight red card. The 3–2 victory took Celtic five points clear of Rangers with three games more played. The title was still in Rangers' hands, but Celtic had struck yet another colossal psychological blow. The Ibrox side's hectic fixture schedule further counted against them in the run-in, and Celtic looked to be the team on the march.

Celtic's 2–1 victory over Motherwell on 3 May marked another pivotal moment in the campaign. Chris Porter had stunned Celtic with the opener after an hour, but the visitors equalised within 90 seconds. Nakamura had been targeted for what Strachan labelled a 'mugging' in the opening stages of the match but responded to the rough treatment and even rougher pitch by providing an exquisite assist for the equaliser. Aiden McGeady drew three players to him on the left flank before slipping a cute ball inside to Hartley. The midfielder shuttled the ball to Nakamura on the right, and his delightfully measured cross was met by McDonald, who levelled the score. Eleven minutes from the end, Robson's corner reached Georgios Samaras, who stooped to head home the winner.

Rangers' goalless draw with Hibs the following day at Easter Road, three days after the disappointment of defeat to Zenit St Petersburg in the UEFA Cup final, further tipped the balance in Celtic's favour. Strachan's side now had the momentum, and a 2–0 victory over Hibs on 11 May in their penultimate league game of the season, with McManus heading home a Nakamura corner and McDonald adding another late in the game, stretched Celtic's lead to four points. Rangers had played two matches fewer than their rivals but had started to feel the effects of a relentless schedule. When they could only manage a 1–1 draw with Motherwell at Fir Park on 17 May and a 3–0 win over St Mirren, the title was effectively in Celtic's hands by virtue of a better goal difference. It set the scene for an exhilarating final day of the season on 22 May. Strachan's side faced Dundee United at Tannadice, while Rangers travelled to Pittodrie to play Aberdeen. Both sides were level on points, but Celtic had a better goal difference of four. Celtic knew that even a 1–0 victory would leave Rangers needing a five-goal winning margin. Events at Tannadice were given another layer of poignancy with the tragic death of Tommy Burns, the club legend and former first-team coach, the week before.

The helicopter charged with transporting the Premier League trophy to the winners sat at Edzell, near Brechin, but it was not until the second half that the championship took a decisive turn. In ten second-half minutes, the title tilted in Celtic's favour. At Pittodrie, Aberdeen's Lee Miller opened the scoring in the 63rd minute to stun the visitors and provoke mayhem at Tannadice, where the news spread like wildfire. The Celtic players were galvanised by the celebrations in the stands and broke the deadlock in their match in the 72nd minute. Paul Hartley's corner was met by Vennegoor of Hesselink, who powered a header into the net for the only goal of the game. The Celtic fans were in ecstasy moments later when word of Darren Mackie's clinching goal for Aberdeen came through. Celtic had won the league. In the space of seven weeks, Strachan's side had completed one of the most impressive Lazarus acts in the history of Scottish football. In doing so, Strachan became the first manager since Jock Stein, and only the third in Celtic's one-hundred-and-twenty-year history, to win three league titles in a row. The evening also began and ended with the same poignant refrain. Burns's name filled the night air in Dundee as a night drenched in high drama and heartfelt emotion finally ended in ecstasy. The Celtic players pulled on T-shirts emblazoned with Burns's face and the message, 'You'll always be with us'.

If the middle period of the campaign had been undermined by injury and indifferent form, then the inspiring late charge had been enough to finish the season on the ultimate high. However, both Nakamura and Celtic face a continued challenge from Rangers to carry on their dominance of Scottish football. It has been the story of the Japanese midfielder's career. Another season, another challenge. He has risen to them all so far. The smart money is on him to do so again. This won't be the final chapter.

Postscript

HOW TO CELEBRATE WITH YOUR PUBLIC

BILLY MCNEILL ONCE SAID THAT WERE HE EVER TO COMPILE a coaching video for young children, he would begin it with footage of Kenny Dalglish celebrating a goal – arms raised, mouth gaping, grinning from ear to ear – an image of unbridled joy, an inspiring and evocative reminder of football's enduring ability to thrill the heart and quicken the pulse. 'When Kenny scores, he shares his joy with everyone,' Brian Clough, the legendary Nottingham Forest manager, once said. Football is not, and never has been, life and death. Football the way Dalglish played it was a joyous, ecstatic distillation of the good things in life. The former Celtic and Liverpool striker's prolific talents in front of goal made it a frequently recurring image. It is no overstatement to say that Dalglish's on-field charisma, that almost indefinable quality, inspired a generation.

Shunsuke Nakamura used to celebrate goals like he had just broken wind in public. A shy and diffident man, he frequently looked embarrassed to have inconvenienced the opposition by scoring against them. That all changed on 21 November 2006. His famous free-kick against Manchester United in the Champions League unleashed a torrent of previously unarticulated emotion. As the ball curls past van der Sar for the second time in three months, Nakamura is off, transported to another world, blowing kisses, grabbing the front of his shirt with both hands as he sprints towards the fans in the north stand. Seconds later, he is engulfed by his teammates.

Nakamura did not appreciate the significance of his historic strike until half an hour after the match. It was only when he was in the gym doing his usual post-match routine that he realised Celtic had reached the last 16. 'Nakamura went straight up to the gym when everyone else was celebrating right after the match,' explains Makoto Kaneko. 'I went with him. We were watching the news on the TV, and it was then that we realised Celtic had got through to the last 16. They had a league table on the screen. Celtic were on top, and they were highlighted in yellow. We said to each other, "We've qualified!"'

The extent of Nakamura's emotional transformation was further evident six months later. It is 22 April 2007, and Celtic are struggling to close out a league campaign in which they have lorded it over their rivals from day one. Nerves are frayed, impatience is rife. Kilmarnock are the opposition, and they are proving obdurate. It is 1–1, and it seems that Celtic's crowning will have to wait for at least another week. Ninety-one minutes have gone. Then they get a free-kick on the edge of the box. Nakamura places the ball and strikes a low, curling free-kick into the bottom corner of the net. Celtic have won the league, and he is off again, only this time the strip comes off and he is twirling it manically round his head as he jumps into the supporters behind the goal. With one flash of his left boot, Nakamura's inhibitions come crashing down, 28 years of Zen-like calm bursting forth in a geyser of raw emotion. It is a cathartic, exhilarating moment.

In a football culture where a meaningless tap-in is often celebrated like the winner in the World Cup final, the significance of Nakamura's celebrations are lost. Japan, however, is a nation where reserve and constraint are celebrated character traits. Nakamura, more than any other national sporting star, embodies those qualities. 'So who was this dervish diving into the crowd?' Nakamura's Japanese fans asked themselves while huddled around their televisions late at night, half a world away. It marked another watershed, a thrilling consummation of Nakamura's relationship with the club he had joined 18 months previously. If his strikes had made their mark on the club's glorious history, then Celtic had left its imprint on him. It had drawn him out of his shell. 'I don't get many chances to celebrate like that, but in Italy I always watched a lot of players act like that when the ball went in the net,' says Nakamura. 'It might have looked a bit aggressive, but I was just happy. I had always wanted to celebrate a goal by jumping into the fans, and when I saw the crowd next to me I got carried away. It was a good feeling. All the boys jumped on top of the crowd as well, but the only bad point was that I got a knock on the nose during the celebrations. It was a bit sore for a while, but I didn't mind.'

Shin Toyofuku shakes his head and laughs at the memory. Not even the journalist who had witnessed Nakamura's every kick of the ball over the previous five years had seen anything like it. 'He has never before celebrated like he did against Manchester United and Kilmarnock. He has always been a very calm man. Against Kilmarnock, it was amazing to see his joy exposed like that. Celtic have made him big, and he is grateful for all they have done for him. It's like Henrik Larsson . . . when he came to Celtic he was a good player, but not a world-class one.'

Scotland's infectious, fanatical passion for football should never be underestimated. Larsson arrived in Scotland in 1997 as the epitome of Scandinavian cool. He initially appeared aloof, an impression which seemed to have its roots in a supreme confidence in his own abilities. It did not take long, however, for Larsson to become a folk hero at Celtic Park. 'Henrik Larsson is the king of kings' sang an adoring public as the Swedish striker steadily built his reputation with plentiful goals. As he did so, and the public adoration grew, so Larsson's inscrutable veneer began to peel away and his charisma shine through. By his second season, his inhibitions now gone, Larsson's trademark was to stick his tongue out and spread his arms in aeroplane fashion when he scored a goal. It was a celebration imitated in playgrounds up and down the country. By the time he left in the summer of 2004, the club had entered his heart. In his last competitive match at Celtic Park, against Dundee United in May 2004, Larsson was overcome with emotion. In an iconic moment, the club's greatest striker of the modern era openly wept as he did one final lap of honour on that sunny May afternoon. When I interviewed him a couple of years later in Barcelona, Larsson was still consumed by his memories of the club where he had spent seven incredible years. Indeed, attempts to turn the conversation around to his current career at Barcelona were greeted with minimal enthusiasm. Not even the daily company of Samuel Eto'o, Ronaldinho and Lionel Messi could distract him from his purpose that afternoon at the Nou Camp. Larsson simply wanted to talk about Celtic and would have done so all day. It was the club that made him, after all.

Brian Laudrup's experience of Rangers was not dissimilar. The Danish striker was already an outstanding and established natural talent when he arrived at Ibrox in 1994, but not even those qualities are a prerequisite for success in the rough and tumble of Scottish football. Laudrup fell in love with Rangers, forming a deep and lasting affinity with the club that continues to this day.

Both Laudrup and Larsson's Scandinavian insouciance had come crashing down around their ears, their true characters shining through in the glare of public devotion. When Glasgow, one of the world's great football cities, decides that you are someone special, someone worthy of adoration, there is no escape. Nakamura's gift of playing the 'Celtic Way' has won the hearts of the fans. They have won his, too. In doing so, history has been made.